Life Writing:
A Writers' &
Artists'
Companion

Writing biography,
autobiography and memoir

Sally Cline and Carole Angier

Bloomsbury Academic
An imprint of Bloomsbury Publishing Plc

B L O O M S B U R Y
LONDON · NEW DELHI · NEW YORK · SYDNEY

Bloomsbury Academic
An imprint of Bloomsbury Publishing Plc

50 Bedford Square	1385 Broadway
London	New York
WC1B 3DP	NY 10018
UK	USA

www.bloomsbury.com

BLOOMSBURY and the Diana logo are trademarks of Bloomsbury Publishing Plc

First published in 2010 as The Arvon Book of Life Writing
by Methuen Drama

This edition published 2013 by Bloomsbury Academic
Reprinted 2013, 2014 (twice)

© Sally Cline and Carole Angier, 2010, 2013

British Library Cataloguing-in-Publication Data
A catalogue record for this book is available from the British Library.

ISBN: PB: 978-1-4725-2706-6
        ePDF: 978-1-4725-2425-6
        ePub: 978-1-4725-3105-6

Library of Congress Cataloging-in-Publication Data
A catalog record for this book is available from the Library of Congress.

Series: Writers' and Artists' Companions

Printed and bound in Great Britain

Sally Cline's previous books

Biographies
Radclyffe Hall: A Woman Called John
Zelda Fitzgerald: Her Voice in Paradise
*Zelda Fitzgerald: The Tragic Meticulously Researched Biography of the
  Jazz Age's High Priestess* (Reissue 2102)
Dashiell Hammett: Man of Mystery (forthcoming)

Literary non-fiction books
Reflecting Men at Twice their Natural Size (with Dale Spender)
Just Desserts: Women and Food
Women, Celibacy and Passion
Lifting the Taboo: Women, Death and Dying
Couples: Scene from the Inside
Writing Literary Non-Fiction: A Writers' and Artists' Companion
  (with Midge Gillies)

Fiction
One of Us is Lying: Selected Short Stories (forthcoming)

Edited books
Memoirs of Emma Courtney (Mary Hays)

Carole Angier's previous books

Biographies
Margaret Hill (Privately commissioned)
Jean Rhys
Jean Rhys: Life and Work
The Double Bond: A Life of Primo Levi

Edited books

Walk Humble My Son by Eric Moss
Tongue Pie by Fred Russell
The Story of My Life: Refugees Writing in Oxford
Lyla and Majnon by Hasan Bamyani
See How I Land: Oxford Poets and Exiled Writers

Series edited books by Carole Angier and Sally Cline

Crime and Thriller Writing: A Writers' and Artists' Companion
   by Michelle Spring and Laurie R. King
Writing Literary Non-Fiction: A Writers' and Artists' Companion
   by Sally Cline and Midge Gillies
Writing Children's Fiction: A Writers' and Artists' Companion
   by Yvonne Coppard and Linda Newbery
Writing Historical Fiction: A Writers' and Artists' Companion
   by Celia Brayfield and Duncan Sprott (forthcoming)

Contents

Foreword

by Michael Holroyd

In *Life Writing: A Writers' and Artists' Companion* you are in the company of two top tutor-writers, and presented with contributions from some thirty distinguished writer-guests as well. It is like attending a writing course and enjoying a literary festival at the same time.

When I began writing I did not have access to such an aid as this, and my development was painfully slow. I worked alone in a public library. But I was not, of course, completely alone – I was surrounded by the work of writers. It was while wandering along the shelves that I eventually chose my first biographical subject – a novelist, essayist, biographer and writer of parodies called Hugh Kingsmill. I learnt to write rather like a skater learns to skate: by falling down, picking myself up and trying again until at last I could whiz along with more confidence. I only wish I could have learnt my narrative skills at the beginning rather than by the end of my book.

I was fortunate in being helped by two writers who had been friends of Kingsmill's: the biographer Hesketh Pearson and the novelist William Gerhardie. I would visit them both, and in a sense they became my tutors. From Pearson, who had been an actor before he took up writing, I learnt how to convey authentic drama in my writing. From Gerhardie I learnt something of the boundaries between fiction and non-fiction – where you may risk crossing these boundaries, and where you may not. But Pearson and Gerhardie did not always agree, and I had to decide, partly by instinct, how to evaluate their differing opinions.

Learning in solitude, as I know, can be an awkward and sometimes frustrating experience. With this book, you are both alone and in company. And though it is primarily addressed to the talented life-writers of the future, good writers of all ages and varieties of experience never cease to learn. We are all, with our compasses and maps, somewhere in the same territory, finding new and challenging directions in which to proceed.

Preface

Life writing is flourishing as never before.

For forty years biography and autobiography have produced some of the most original and admired writing in English, from the literary Lives of Richard Ellmann and Michael Holroyd to the autobiographies of Frank McCourt and Maya Angelou. And now, in the early twenty-first century, memoir is becoming the most exciting genre in both Britain and America – think of Blake Morrison and Alexander Masters, Dave Eggers and Mary Karr.

Our thirst for real lives is insatiable – we can't get enough of TV reality shows, of family history, of political diaries, literary memoirs, 'misery memoirs' . . . and everyone can join in. We record our daily lives on Facebook and Twitter; and some of the best war reporting comes not from special correspondents but from people's blogs, with photographs from their mobile phones.

There are more and more courses where life writers can learn their trade. Fifteen years ago there was not a single life writing course at any English-speaking university (a few pioneers of the 1920s hadn't lasted.) Then, in January 1996, the biographer Jane Ridley offered the first MA in Biography at the University of Buckingham in the UK. The City University of New York, only a few months behind, gallantly conceded that Britain now had 'the first Life Writing course in the cosmos!'

Today over eighty British universities and most colleges, adult education centres and writers' foundations offer courses in biography, autobiography and memoir. It is the same in the USA, Australia and New Zealand.

In the US alone there are many thousands of community writing courses, hundreds of writing camps for young people, and at last count nearly six thousand universities and colleges offering creative writing majors across the US, many of which have at least one life writing component.

Both of us have tutored on university and other writing courses for many years. This taught us that while some genres (the novel, poetry and screen-writing, for example) are well served with both literary analysis and practical guides, others, including Life Writing, are not. Our aim in this new series of *Writers' & Artists' Companions* is to fill that gap. Our *Writers' & Artists' Companions* will combine literary reflection and practical guides; and they will concentrate on the less well covered areas (for example, crime writing, literary non-fiction, short stories), starting with life writing, which is our own genre.

Life Writing: A Writers' & Artists' Companion

The overall plan of this book is the same for all the *Companions* in the series. Each will have two writer-tutors, bringing two complementary voices and experiences to bear on the endlessly varied subject of writing. And each will have a guest section, in which some of the most distinguished writers in each genre will add their voices and experiences to the conversation. For that is what a creative writing course is – a conversation. Writing cannot be taught, beyond its technical rules. It can only be shared, compared and – we hope – made to grow, together.

Our book has a three-part structure (again, like the others.) Part One presents an overview of our genres and their particular excitements and challenges. Part Two is the guest section – the opening out of our conversation. And Part Three is the active, hands-on researching and writing section.

Part One: Life writing

We begin the first part with the challenges. Is life writing art or craft, history or literature, objective or subjective? Can it ever be 'true', adequate to a lived life, even possible at all? Should life writers tell a story, or should they just tell the facts? How much interpretation is allowable, how much speculation, how much fictionalisation? What are the ethical and legal problems of writing about real people – even sometimes members of one's own family? What are the problems of memory, of evidence, of myth-making? What is the role of the life writer?

We then move to the traditions of our genres. We sketch in the classical roots of biography, and sum up its modern history. We then trace the history of autobiography, exploring in particular the historical roots of American autobiography from the seventeenth century, when Europeans first arrived on American shores, and began to record their experiences of their new country.

Next, we look at the rich sub-species of memoir – political, historical, literary, family, sport, travel, adventure, childhood, illness, aging, death – and at the phenomenon of fake memoirs. Finally, we look briefly at the use of autobiographical and biographical writing in other genres, for instance in fiction, creative non-fiction, poetry, journalism and film.

In all this we remember that our readers are writers, not critics – as we are ourselves. We have tried to make this part what good life writing itself should be: scholarly, but down to earth and easy to read.

Part Two: Tips & tales

Part Two, our guest section, contains thirty-two short pieces of reflection or provocation from professional life writers, some of the best and best known in their field. They include literary, political, sport and celebrity biographers, family memoirists and autobiographers from both sides of the Atlantic. Many have written in more than one of the genres; two (Margaret Drabble and Jill Dawson) are novelists, but have sampled biography; and two (Alain de Botton and Geoff Dyer) have invented their own biographical genres. One (Janet Malcolm) is the most famous and trenchant critic of biography in the world.

Our largest group is literary biographers, who bravely agreed to turn their lenses on themselves. Our sports biographer is also a ghost writer, and our celebrity biographer, Andrew Morton, has bagged, among others, the biggest celebrity of all (Princess Di). We have a biographer who is also a literary agent, a first-time biographer, and a student of life writing (who is also a novelist, and an Australian).

Altogether, we have some of the most fascinating talkers about life writing ever found in one book: thirty-two Dr Johnsons captured by two Boswells.

Part Three: Write on

In Part Three we move from talk to action, and offer three mostly participatory chapters of creative exercises and practical advice: one on planning, one on research, and one on writing.

Under planning, we discuss choosing a subject, and the practical issues of starting in life writing – choosing courses, agents and publishers, the type of book to write.

Under research, we talk about archives, internet research, and interviewing, accompanied by several exercises (eg, what do you do with conflicting evidence?) Finally we wrestle with that hardest of all questions: when do you stop researching and start writing?

The writing section includes an exercise for every point. We cover topics such as: how to manage balance (of empathy and detachment, of accuracy and elegance); how to manage time (chronology, pro and con; should you look forward, should you look back?); how to manage narration (the balance of narrative and analysis, the role of narrator in the text); how to manage fictional techniques (eg, drama and suspense, description and dialogue, pace and order, imagery).

Readers can dip into this conversation at any point; each part is free standing. We hope it will offer many new ideas to writers at varying stages of their writing lives.

Nevertheless, it can only hint at the real conversations we have based it on, which are creative writing courses, given by writers, for writers. We hope many emerging writers will try one. Even writers who prefer to work in solitude need friends, and all writers need editors, a fresh eye and a helping hand.

Carole Angier and Sally Cline,
authors and series editors

Introduction

Why do people read life writing?

They read it because, as the actor and writer Anthony Sher says, 'Nothing is more interesting than human lives'. All literature is about human lives, but life writing is the real thing. 'Consider the whole class of fictional Narratives,' Carlyle wrote. 'What are all these but mimic Biographies?'

There are many reasons for the enthusiastic pursuit of the autobiographies and biographies of the famous and infamous, the confessional outpourings or mysteriously withheld secrets of politicians, sports people, writers, or those who have lived through extraordinary times. People read them because they want to know about many real lives, not just their own. Some people read biography because it is a quest narrative, like a detective story or an engaging thriller. Who is this person? Will we ever understand him or her? What is going to happen next? Some read autobiography because they believe it will give them direct access to someone else's genuine experiences and feelings. It is not surprising that in our egocentric age of twitters and blogs, autobiography and memoir in particular – the genres based on the self, on inwardness, revelation and intimacy – are increasingly written and read.

Anyone who has been involved in interviewing, or even gossiping, knows that everybody has a story. And if a writer tells that story well, it is as fascinating as good fiction – or even more. For many years now, readers have turned to life writing because self-doubt has invaded so much literary fiction, denying them the pleasures of a simple story.

These reasons why people read biographies and autobiographies allow their authors a certain freedom in writing them. But still more they impose constraints. Life writers are free to tell a story – but they have a contract with the reader not to invent, to tell as far as possible what actually happened. And they must tell it despite material that is often unknowable or intractable. If they come upon gaps in their stories, if they stop and ponder on a road not taken, if they know a decision was made but not why – then they may begin to have doubts too, much more serious doubts, in fact, about their ability to present a real person. But if they want their readers to keep reading, they must keep their doubts to themselves and stick to the story.

That, at least, is the experience of many life writers. But writing is not market research. Writers do not find out what people want and produce it; they trust to their imaginations and hope readers will follow. And life writing should be no more conservative than any other kind. Nonetheless, the life writer's contract with the reader is to respect reality. This makes readers even less willing to let writers of lives experiment than novelists, who at least own the rights to their fictional worlds. In fact, the greatest biographers and autobiographers *have* also experimented, from Johnson and Strachey on; but though they have won over readers for each great book, they have never succeeded in changing expectations for very long.

Now may be the right moment. Despite this generation's innovation, even in biography – from Michael Holroyd's introduction of irony and artistry to the wilder experiments of Peter Ackroyd's *Dickens* and Edmund Morris's *Dutch* – many readers (and reviewers) still yearn for the classic Victorian tome, confidently authoritative, even, perhaps, reassuringly dull. But this may be changing. For many years pundits have been predicting the end of definitive biography, and a trend towards shorter, 'sleeker' works of art, a move 'away from solidarity and towards biographical imagination', in the words of the political biographer Ben Pimlott. And it seems to be happening at last, as several of this book's guest writers note. Recent biographies, autobiographies and memoirs have been widening their subjects, and drawing on other genres, and altogether opening out not just to imagination but to the rest of literature. We shall see if readers will follow, but the early signs are hopeful. It is an exciting time to arrive.

Part 1:
Life writing

Reflections 1

by Carole Angier

When I arrived as a hopeful writer, Michael Holroyd's *Lytton Strachey* and Richard Holmes's *Shelley* had just come out, and biography was all the rage. I read them, and knew what I wanted to do. Biography was a marvellous genre – and now it even had a chance of being published.

It was the best decision I ever made. There is nothing to compare to the mystery of archives, to the thrill of the chase of an unknown story. There is nothing to compare, in the lonely business of writing, to the contact with other human beings, living and dead – despite the agonies it can also bring. Everything about life writing – both its pleasures and its pains, its special value and its special danger – comes from this direct relation to real people, which fiction writers can escape, or at least keep decently hidden.

Life writing is a wonderful life. But it is also a minefield of challenges, and these are what I want to reflect on. Iris Murdoch's remark applies to all writing: 'No trouble, no story'. So this is mostly an essay on the troubles of life writing. The rewards, however, will insist on shining through.

1. A note

The three sub-genres of life writing blur into each other at the edges – like living things, they wriggle out of our boxes. So group biographies blur into memoirs, quest biographies blur into autobiographies, the line between memoir and autobiography isn't clear. The best we can say is that at one end of the range is the paradigm case of life writing, the research-based biography, at the other the short personal memoir; and somewhere in between lie autobiography and the more historical kinds of memoir. What follows applies most thoroughly to the paradigm case, biography, and most loosely to the personal memoir. But it applies to them all, for better or for worse.

2. Alarums and invasions

First of all, be prepared: life writers have never been first-class citizens in the republic of letters. Since the dawn of Romanticism, creation has been the hallmark of the artist in the West. But life writing is researched, not invented. Life writers, therefore, are accorded only a sort of immigrant status in literature: admired for their 'investigative skills', but only rarely noticed for the quality of their writing.

The truth is that stories are only ever noticed because of the quality of their writing; good research alone is just statistics. But this is a trade secret, and life writers are the closest of all writers to Flaubert's ideal of the invisible artist. That is fine by us, since seeing the artist at work disturbs belief in the portrait. Nonetheless it can be irksome: eg, when reviewers retell your story as though they've discovered it themselves, and never mention your book at all. The biographer 'is a craftsman, not an artist', Virginia Woolf ruled long ago, and biography is not art, 'but something betwixt and between'.[1] Other life writers may be further along this range; but they too remain 'betwixt and between'.

Being a good craftsman is already a high ambition. But there is also something more, as Woolf herself later decided. Because, of course, what life writers unearth is only the facts, not the story. That does not yet exist. It has to be understood, imagined – in fact, created. What life writers cannot invent is the facts. They must invent, or at least construct, the story.

The same is true of history and journalism too, beyond the most basic reporting; it's true even of gossip, if it's good (or bad) enough. Every act of giving meaning is creative. And the more elusive the evidence (and the evidence is always elusive), the more creative the life writer must be. In this way all life writers are like detectives, and the facts they unearth merely their clues. As Kate Summerscale wrote in *The Suspicions of Mr Whicher* (which won the 2008 Samuel Johnson Prize for Biography, and is as much about biography as detection): 'Whicher's job was not just to find things out, but to put them in order. The real business of detection was the invention of a plot'.[2] The plot must fit the facts beyond reasonable doubt; but that is as close to reality as any detective, or any life writer, can get.

There is still a difference between inventing a story and constructing one. Proust's biographer George Painter put it best: 'The artist has creative imagination, the biographer recreative'.[3] Life writers are re-creative artists, living 'betwixt and between' our imaginations and reality, trying to re-create on the page the living and the dead.

This takes us to the heart of the matter – the relation to real people. It's not just that life writers are immigrants into literature. It's that, like immigrants over the ages, we are objects of fear and suspicion to the natives, accused of stealing their jobs and debasing their wages, and bringing disgusting new practices into their country.

The most important natives, in this case, are the subjects of biographies and their families, and those who appear in autobiographies and memoirs – ie, very often, the author's own friends and family. Their main objection is the same as other people's, but more violent, for obvious reasons. It is that life writing is an invasion of privacy and an exploitation. And what for? The answers one can give about fiction – to entertain readers, to expand knowledge and sympathy – won't wash so easily with non-fiction, because real people so clearly suffer. And the answer we often give about famous people – that knowledge of the life helps to understand the work – won't wash so easily either. It might show why someone has done what he or she did (became Prime Minister, wrote about orphans.) But it doesn't tell us anything directly about the political career, or the writing about orphans. 'Read what I wrote,' the writer will say. 'That's all that matters; the rest is gossip.'

This is the doctrine of the autonomy of art, and by extension, of other activities. In a narrow sense it's true: only literary analysis is required to understand a literary phenomenon, only political analysis to understand a political one. But responding to a book or a political event isn't a narrow activity. It's a deep and wide one, which employs all your intuitions and sympathies, and the more you know about everything to do with it, including its author, the richer your response will be.

But even suppose we agree: knowledge of the author's life will only help to understand the author. That is still where life writers come in.

Most people want to understand authors – the famous people who have shaped or are shaping their world, for good or ill. They want to know how *this* person could have written *this* book, or done *that* deed, as the great French critic Ste-Beuve realised at the start of the Romantic era. They want to know about their heroes, and about the villains they fear. And they want to know, simply, what it is like to be someone else. That is not mere curiosity: it is, as Ian McEwen has said, the beginning of morality. (But it is curiosity too.)

So most people want to read about lives; our problem is not with our readers. Our main problem comes from those natives whose territory we invade, our subjects and their – or our – families. And we cannot blame them. We do invade their territory; if our books are successful, we take it over. And we do exploit them, for our books and our readers (though not for money, as they often think: money is rare in our research-intensive trades, which is another problem). If they are public figures we can argue that they are fair game, having stuck their heads over the parapet. If they are not, we have no defence. We just have to make our books as fair as possible, and hope that they are good and true enough to justify the private pain.

The worst subjects of all are the literary ones. They are the ones who accuse us of stealing their jobs and debasing their wages: our books are so much easier, they say, that people stop reading theirs, and just read the biographies instead. Germaine Greer claims this on behalf of Byron, who 'has had more biographies than the sun breeds maggots in a dead dog. All of them sell well, to people who have never read a line Byron wrote'.[4]

If only it were true. There may be a few literary celebrities whom people want to read about without knowing their work, but even in the case of mad bad Byron they will be pitifully few. It's true that people will read something easier in preference to something harder; but the first books to be affected by that are serious literary biographies themselves.

The trouble with having writers attack us is that they are so good at it – like Greer herself, who calls biography 'pre-digested carrion'. George Eliot called biographers 'a disease of English literature'; Dr Arbuthnot, in the eighteenth century, said they 'added a new Terror to Death'. Oscar Wilde said 'Every great man has his disciples, and it is usually Judas who writes the biography'. Betrayal and the exploitation of the dead: these are the recurring themes. They are largely unfair; but they can never be dismissed in a trade that deals in the private lives of real people.

Once again Kate Summerscale's reflections apply. The private detective was especially feared and loathed, she reports, and plants the reason in an image: 'The word "detect" stemmed from the Latin "*de-tegere*" or "unroof", and the original figure of the detective was the lame devil Asmodeus, "the prince of demons", who took the roofs off houses to spy on the lives inside'.[5] Life writers are private detectives who take the roofs off houses to spy on the lives inside. We too, therefore, are outcast and indecent, like devils and spies. People have felt this from the start: about Boswell, following Johnson around like an eavesdropping servant; about Froude a century later, whose biography of Carlyle was actually called 'the unroofing of his home' by a shocked critic.[6] Life writers feel it themselves: 'What we do is morally indefensible', Lyndall Gordon says.[7] Even the most brilliant biographer, the most artistic autobiographer, is tainted with the shade of Asmodeus. As Michael Holroyd says: 'We work in an unweeded garden'.[8]

3. Ethics and legality

Our main problem, then, is moral. What we do is dangerous. The danger is especially acute in memoirs and autobiographies, where we take the lives of our families and friends into our hands. What did you think, for example, of *Iris*, John Bayley's memoir of Iris Murdoch's descent into Alzheimers Disease? There is no doubt that it was a beautifully written book, painfully accurate and sad. Did you think it was worth it – a work of art, about someone who could no longer be hurt by it? Or did you think it was a shameful betrayal? (I thought the first, by the way, and Sally thought the second.)

The tales of families riven by autobiographical writing are legion: 'If you've got a writer in the family', Hanif Kureishi says, 'the family's dead'.[9] Blake Morrison's mother bore his memoir of his father, Arthur (which included Arthur's long affair) in silence, but remarked one day, 'I could've topped myself because of that bloody book'.[10] Kureishi's trouble is his sister, Yasmin. Every time he publishes a book he asks his wife, 'Have we had the letter from Yasmin yet?' The safest thing for a memoir writer is to be an only child, and wait till your parents are dead: like Dominic Carman, for instance, who wrote a swingeing portrait of his father, the celebrated barrister George Carman.

When our subjects are great ones, there are multiple dangers. One is that we will reduce their greatness to mere personality, their achievements (or crimes) to their childhood traumas. Indeed life writing, like all good writing, must take care to avoid reductive explanation. But to leave our heroes and heroines unexamined means falsehood and sentimentality. And so far from offering us models of behaviour, perfect heroes and heroines will only make us give up in despair. So said Dr Johnson, who knew a lot about despair: 'If nothing but the bright side of characters should be shewn, we should sit down in despondency, and think it utterly impossible to imitate them in *any thing*'.[11]

Our subjects – especially when they are writers themselves – want to control what is said about them, and preferably say it all themselves. But that is not a reasonable demand. We all know that others talk about us as soon as we leave the room. Nobody likes it, but only absolute despots make it a crime. And strangely, it is only their own biographies that writers want to ban. Proust, Eliot, Auden, Henry James, the doughtiest foes of biography, all liked reading other people's. When Byron's papers were opened, James exclaimed, 'Disgusting – but wonderfully significant!'[12]

Last but not least, our subjects fear that by revealing their humanity, we will turn their admirers away. This is 'Shakespeare's Second-best Bed' syndrome – the idea that once people know how badly the Bard treated his wife, leaving her this single insulting gift in his will, they won't want to see his plays any more. When Carlyle's and Hardy's even worse treatment of their wives was revealed in their biographies, some readers didn't want to read them again; and similarly in the case of (for instance) Larkin's taste for porn, Koestler's propensity for rape, Eliot's antisemitism.

Most of this depends upon the writing, and if a biography is just a rant against its subject – like Roger Lewis's of Anthony Burgess – it is the author's responsibility if he sows only disillusion. But life writing should be about complexity; and it should be read with complexity as well. It isn't easy. Primo Levi, for example, was shocked to find himself admiring the work of the painter Mario Sironi: 'But he was a Fascist!' he said. Nonetheless, that is what life writing, and life reading, are all about: not making simple judgements, but contemplating the surprising truths of human behaviour.

That is the justification of the warts-and-all life writing that has been the tradition in English literature since Johnson ('If we owe regard to the memory of the dead, there is yet more respect to be paid to knowledge, to virtue, and to truth').[13] It was summed up by Carlyle, in his famous attack on Victorian biography:

 The English biographer has long felt that if . . . he wrote down anything that could by possibility offend any man, he had written wrong. The plain consequence was, that, properly speaking, no biography whatever could be produced.

. . . [O]nce taken up, the rule before all rules is to do it, not to do the ghost of it . . . [The biographer] will of course keep all his charities about him; but all his eyes open.[14]

We owe regard to the dead, and even more to the living, and we must keep all our charities about us. But we also owe regard to the truth, and a book that airbrushes out of the picture anything inconvenient to anyone is of no more use than polite conversation. We are in the awkward area of conflicting values, which is to say, life. Different writers make different decisions. Hilary Spurling was ready to give up a book for which she had done two years' research if it would lead to a possible suicide. But Primo Levi, the gentlest man in the world, used his friends ruthlessly in his portraits, and refused to change a word. Miranda Seymour decided to hide some painful information in a coded hint until the person concerned had died; Michael Holroyd, offered the same compromise for *Lytton Strachey*, turned it down (but so politely that nobody noticed). On the other hand, he showed his typescript to everyone involved – and spent two and a half years going over every word with Lytton's brother. Bernard Crick, by contrast, wouldn't begin his Life of George Orwell until Orwell's widow had signed a contract granting him complete discretion. There is no doubt which arrangement is easier for the writer (if you can get it); we must all decide for ourselves what our conscience will bear.

For myself, I always show my interviewees the part of the story in which they appear – they should at least be warned. And I do change things, or even take them out altogether, if people ask me to. On the other hand, the things I have agreed to take out have never been vital to the story; if anyone ever asks for that, I expect I shall be more like Crick and Levi.

And what about legality? The only certainty is that you can't libel the dead. As for the living, the constitutional right to freedom of speech in America has meant that libel laws have always been weaker in the US than here. And in the last decade UK libel laws have become even stricter, partly because of the right to privacy clause of the Human Rights Act, and partly because of some tough judicial decisions, including two against writers. This has created a boom in 'libel tourism', with American movie stars, international companies et al. bringing libel cases here and winning them, so that London is rapidly becoming known as the libel capital of the world. That is bad news for life writers on both sides of the Atlantic, and it is getting worse. In the last few years the use of 'super-injunctions' has grown – gagging orders so draconian that not only are you stopped from publishing in the first place, you cannot even say you have been stopped. British publishers are running scared, as Andrew Morton describes in Part Two. We can only hope that the campaign against super-injunctions by PEN and the Index on Censorship will succeed, and that the *Daily Mail* is right in its prediction about libel in general: that the law now so clearly favours the rich and famous against investigative writers that people are beginning to take our side.[15]

4. Truth and objectivity

Our next great problem is truth. No one can ask J.K. Rowling, 'Did Harry Potter really do that?' What she says he did, he did; there is no other authority. Consequently, as Flaubert said, 'Everything one invents is true';[16] or more prosaically, neither true nor false apply to fiction. But both apply to life writing, because there is another authority: reality. So people *can* ask 'Is it true?' And they do.

This is where the trouble arises, for if fiction cannot fail the truth test, it is almost impossible for life writing to pass it. No two writers will have the same approach to a subject, especially if they come from different places or times; no two people will even give the same account of a single event – especially if they are members of the same family. So there will be as many stories about any subject as there are writers. But they can't all be true, can they?

No: not in the way that a simple statement of fact is true, for instance that Germany invaded Belgium in 1914. (As Clemenceau remarked, the one thing future historians won't say is that Belgium invaded Germany.[17]) But the accounts of life writers – and historians – aren't simple statements of fact. They are visions and views; they involve the giving of meaning, which as we have seen is a creative act. Beyond their barest factual claims (dates, locations, names), 'Is it true?' is the wrong question to ask of them, as it is the wrong question to ask about our picture of another person, or of a complex event in life (a marriage, a divorce, a war). Fortunately life writing is not a court of law, where we have to choose a single right statement, even though the stakes there are a great deal higher.

A portrait of a person, a family, a whole history, must fit the facts; if not, it is a fiction. But then the right questions to ask are: 'Is it convincing, is it illuminating?' This doesn't protect life writing from judgement, but at least it is the right kind of judgement. And though readers like to think that they are getting the whole truth, the more they read the more they realise that in human affairs this is an infinite pursuit. The answer to 'No single account can be the whole truth' is not to give them all up in despair, but to read, and write, more of them. And the hope of every life writer is not to give the single right account. It is to research (or remember) and reflect so well that one's vision will continue to fit the facts – even new facts – and to be illuminating and as close to human truth as possible, for a long time. It is a high hope, but more than can be achieved with mere facts, however true.

That is the theoretical problem of truth; there are also practical ones. All we can unearth, as we have seen, are clues; and clues can be conflicting, ambiguous, missing. Victoria Glendinning has also compared the life writer to a detective, whose whole case can go wrong because of a missing clue. She describes (or invents) an old man who believed that geraniums lived on bread, because when he sprinkled crumbs on a geranium bed, they always disappeared. 'There was a piece of information, about birds, that he did not seem to have,' she notes. 'Quite often, the biographer, in good faith, must be making the Geranium Mistake.'[18]

Even when we know about birds, we are not safe. Memory is unreliable – both our own and our informants'. It is no more an objective recording machine than we are; it is a living thing that changes with us. Memories decay, are repressed and forgotten. They are replaced by the stories we hear and tell, and the photographs we see. They depend as much on what we know as perception itself, which is equally subjective (I am *not* a camera). Memory, like perception, is a survival mechanism: it interprets our experience in ways that help us to go on living.

Some life writers flee, therefore, into the archives, and put their faith in documents instead. But documents can be equally ambiguous, misleading, or missing. Medical records are closed, birth certificates (eg, Jean Rhys's) disappear in hurricanes and fires, people burn letters, lose them, promise to get them down from the attic but never find the time. People lie to registrars and census takers as well as to us; they write letters and even diaries for all sorts of purposes and in all sorts of moods. There is no such thing as final, foolproof evidence; something else can always turn up.

Once again, however, we shouldn't despair, and stop believing everything on the grounds that nothing can ever be certain. Some things can be more certain than others. A biography or autobiography that is well researched and fairly told is more reliable than one that isn't; and the more accounts of the same person or event there are, the more they begin to converge. Only the most consummate deceivers can cover their traces. Wilkie Collins, the inventor of the fictional detective, agreed. 'Nothing in the world is hidden forever,' he wrote. 'Look where we will, the inevitable law of revelation is one of the laws of nature: the lasting preservation of a secret is a miracle which the world has never yet seen.'[19]

We can never have scientific certainty about human beings, but then neither have many sciences – archaeology and palaeontology, for example, reconstruct whole civilisations from a few pots, and whole animals from a jawbone. For certainty, as for truth, the answer is not to give up reading and writing biography and autobiography, but to read and write them more.

Keeping these qualifications in mind, truth remains our ideal. We need, therefore, the credibility to convey it. When we write of ourselves or our subjects, we must not be too *parti pris*, or we will lose that credibility straight away. We must find the rare, right balance between empathy and detachment, emotion and tranquillity; between imaginative recreation of what it was like to be *me* or *him* or *her*, and the distance to see them, or myself, in the round. And when we write of other real people, alive or dead, we must not presume too much. We cannot, for example, write from inside them, as novelists do, because they are sovereign beings, and we have no right to cross their borders.

Straight away we're in trouble, at least in biography. If we can't enter anyone in the story, we have to speak in our own objective outsider's voice; and a whole book in one objective voice can be wearing. We have to learn to modulate it with Holmesian empathy, Holroydian irony, and a novelist's drama, pace and variety. We cannot employ any of these too much, or the precious suspension of disbelief will be lost. But we can't employ them too little either, or we'll give purchase to the worst expectations of biography: the dull compilation of fact; 'investigative skills' only.

And then there's the question of objectivity itself. We are all post-modern now, and we know it is impossible to be truly objective. However hard we try, we bring to our books our own personal and cultural perspectives, which shape them in ways we are not even aware of. Do we include these reflections in our book – even include ourselves in our book – and make the process of research and writing, in all its subjectivity, part of the story? Or do we stick to the objective way, and keep ourselves out of it? A.J.A. Symons wrote the first famous quest biography, *The Quest for Corvo*, as long ago as 1934; and there have been others since, for example, Ian Hamilton's *In Search of J.D. Salinger*. The aim of honesty, of unmasking the pretension to objectivity, is much admired – but more in principle than in practice, and more by critics than readers. Many people still find the admission of the subjectivity of a story by the story itself hard to bear. The wilder experiments – Peter Ackroyd's *Dickens*, for example, in which Ackroyd chats to Dickens, or Edmund Morris's *Dutch: A Memoir of Ronald Reagan*, in which Morris accompanies Reagan throughout – attracted mostly bewilderment, and in Morris's case opprobrium.

There is no right answer to this question. If you write well enough, like Symons; if you signal from the start that your book is as much about your search as your subject, as Richard Holmes did in *Footsteps;* if you find a delicate balance, as Hermione Lee did in *Virginia Woolf,* bracketing the life with one chapter of self-reflection at each end – if you get all this right, and more, it can work, triumphantly. But it is always a problem, and not only in biography. When John Burnside prefaced his memoir *A Lie About My Father* with the note, 'This book is best treated as a work of fiction', some readers were upset as well.

Things are changing. In Britain today, 'reality TV' dominates popular entertainment, and the most successful works of high literature are the genre-bending books of W.G. Sebald. In other words, at both ends of the market the boundaries between fact and fiction are being blurred. But there will always be limits, especially in biography. Respect will still be due to the living and the dead; and readers will still want to know what they are reading. Sebald transcends all categories, but even *his* publishers must try to identify him – 'Fiction/Travel/History' they say desperately, but accurately, on most of his books. Perhaps we shouldn't need these distinctions. But we do.

5. Art and evidence

Michael Holroyd and Richard Holmes have both come up with the same metaphor for biography: the 'unwanted offspring' of the novel and history (Holroyd),[20] a 'bastard form' resulting from the 'Unholy Alliance' of fiction and fact (Holmes).[21] The result of this awkward marriage is an awkward child. Biographers cannot add episodes to the life to add drama or bring out character, nor subtract episodes from it to avoid shocking or boring readers, hurting participants, or leaving the story in the messy shape it really had. Or if they do so, they should let us know; and if they don't let us know, they must bear the responsibility.

The restriction on invention is greatest in biography, where, if it is allowed at all, it must be made clear, and usually is. Whatever you think of them, Ackroyd's conversations with Dickens cannot be confused with reality. I know of only one biography in modern history that turned out to be largely invention: the first Life of Stephen Crane, published by Thomas Beer in 1923. Beer not only invented much of Crane's life, but seems to have forged the letters he based it on: which shows that you may have to be a bit mad to write biography, but you'd have to be completely mad to invent one.

In the autobiographical genres the restriction is looser, because 'how it seemed to me' is a more legitimate way to tell your own story than someone else's. Writers *do* invent, in memoir and autobiography – and not only elusive figures like J.M. Coetzee, or famous fibbers like Ford Madox Ford. Kind, careful Primo Levi did it too. Some of this was probably unconscious, a product of the natural mythologising that made Levi a writer; but some of it was quite deliberate. When his first love asked him to remove an episode in his account of her, on the grounds that it never happened, he replied that it conveyed her character better than anything that did happen, and refused.

So it is done, and some critics would give *carte blanche* to invention, especially in memoir. But I am sure that we should always hesitate to cheat our readers, and to fasten an untruth on another person. Levi's untruths, and even Ford's, were exaggerations more than outright lies, and they didn't diminish their subjects, but enhanced them. That is what art does; and since life writing is art, perhaps we may also sometimes do it. But with care, and in the service of truth, not ourselves.

If we cannot (lightly) invent, we are left with another problem: the need to speculate. This is perhaps the most symptomatic problem of life writing, and the one with which I shall end.

There are two points at which life writers are reduced to speculation: when there are gaps in the evidence about facts; and when speaking about the inner life of anyone but themselves.

The first case is contingent: the evidence may be found one day, and if you tried harder, you might find it yourself. In this case, therefore, speculation represents a failure. Having to say, 'It is likely that she was already secretly married' or 'He was almost certainly wounded at the battle of Lepanto' not only blocks the flow of your prose and makes it repetitious, since you've had to cover other gaps with similar insertions – 'perhaps', 'must have' and the rest of the ugly tribe. It also signals your failure to your readers, which can be fatal. So she doesn't know, they'll think. If she doesn't know much more than me, why should I go on reading?

If you want to avoid this sort of speculation, there are only two solutions. Either go on researching until you do know; or leave the point out altogether. Unfortunately, neither is usually possible. The identity of Shakespeare's Dark Lady hasn't been proven for four hundred years, and you're not likely to prove it now; and if you simply don't mention her (or him) – or the wound/secret marriage in my examples – that is just as much a failure, and will be just as obvious to your readers.

So in the case of speculation about facts, life writing is stuck with 'perhaps' and the others, at least occasionally. The best you can do is to keep it as occasional as possible, and vary it as elegantly as you can.

In the second case – speaking about the inner life of others – speculation is not contingent, and not the life writer's fault. It marks the limit of our knowledge of other people's minds, which we must hope will never be violable; if it ever is, we will be in Orwell's 1984, or a similar dystopia. Where there is a diary (or letters, or other evidence), 'he thought' and 'she felt' are admissible. Otherwise we are stuck with speculation. But speculation here isn't failing, because you can only fail where you can also succeed. Rather, it marks our respect for the dignity and inviolability of other people, who are, as I have said, sovereign beings. So far from a sign of failure, it is a mark of honour, and should be used without shame.

Two problems remain, however. One is the way the ugly tribe, as I've called them, can make your writing ugly too; they have to be controlled, like guard dogs that protect your property but can turn and bite you. The second is that many readers may find them annoying, not because they mar your perfect prose, but because people don't like to be reminded that there is something they can never know. 'The biography-loving public,' as Janet Malcolm says, 'does not want to hear that biography is a flawed genre':[22] not just sometimes but always, by nature. That is because trying to discover what other people think and feel is flawed by nature; which doesn't make it less important.

Wittgenstein used to clutch his forehead in pain and beg his students not to go into philosophy. That is not what I meant to say about life writing (and perhaps Wittgenstein didn't mean it either).

It is true that life writing is 'morally indefensible', in Lyndall Gordon's words. But it is also morally necessary. It is easier to think that heroes are heroes and villains just villains, but it's neither true nor interesting. And it's a false idea of love. I think readers read biographies of their heroes and heroines out of love, and I know that biographers write them out of love. But that is not inconsistent with wanting to know how those heroes and heroines really were. When you love someone you want to know all about them; everything is precious, even the bad and sad things, because it's *them*. That is what the spirit of life writing should be, not the cutting-down-to-size its critics imagine. And that is what it usually is.

It is also true that real stories cannot be as perfect as fictions. As Robert Louis Stevenson said, 'Of course, [biography is] not really so finished as quite a rotten novel; it always has and always must have the incurable illogicalities of life about it'.[23] But that is not only its failure, it is also its glory. Because fiction has to seem true, it often can't be true; there are improbabilities, coincidences, inconsistencies in life that you couldn't put in a novel, because no one would believe them. Truth is stranger than fiction, as we know; and it is our great freedom that we can tell it, as much as our great limitation that we must.

Notes

1. Virginia Woolf, 'The Art of Biography', from *Death of the Moth*, in *Collected Essays*, Vol. IV, p. 227, Hogarth Press, London, 1925 (1967 edition).
2. Kate Summerscale, *The Suspicions of Mr Whicher*, p. 94, Bloomsbury, London, 2009.
3. Quoted in Jeffrey Meyers, 'George Painter's *Marcel Proust*', in Jeffrey Meyers, ed., *The Biographer's Art*, p. 134, Macmillan, London, 1989.
4. Germaine Greer, 'Real Lives, or Reader's Digest?', *The Times*, 1 February 1986.
5. Summerscale, *op. cit.*, pp. 157–8.
6. Frederic Harrison, *The Choice of Books*, Macmillan, 1886, p. 175, quoted in the Editor's Introduction to *Froude's Life of Carlyle*, ed. John Clubbe, p. 2, John Murray, London, 1979.
7. Lyndall Gordon, 'The Death Mask', in *Lives for Sale*, ed. Mark Bostridge, p. 1, Continuum, London, 2004.
8. Michael Holroyd, 'Smoke With Fire: On the Ethics of Biography', in *Works on Paper*, p. 18, Little Brown, London, 2002.
9. Hanif Kureishi, quoted in Aida Edemariam, *Footnotes*, 'A Family Affair', *The Guardian*, 25 September 2004. Also the second quotation below.
10. Quoted in Claudia FitzHerbert, 'The Bride Stripped Bare', *Daily Telegraph*, 23 November 2002.
11. Samuel Johnson in Boswell's *Life of Johnson*, quoted in Nigel Hamilton, *Biography: A Brief History*, p. 89, Harvard University Press, Cambridge MA, 2007.
12. Lyndall Gordon, 'Biography versus the autonomy of art', lecture delivered at the University of Oxford, 12 February 2002.
13. Samuel Johnson, *The Rambler*, No. 60, 13 October 1750, in Richard Holmes ed., *Johnson on Savage*, p. 115, Harper Perennial, London, 2005.
14. Quoted in John Clubbe, 'Froude's Preface' in *op. cit.* (*Froude's Life of Carlyle*), pp. 79–80.
15. See the articles by Richard O'Hagan and Matthew Hickley in the *Daily Mail*, 9 June 2009.
16. Gustave Flaubert quotes, Thinkexist.com, p. 3. (http://thinkexist.com/quotes/gustave_flaubert/3.html)
17. Quoted in Samuel Brittan, 'Belgium did not invade Germany', *The Spectator*, 12 October 2002.
18. Victoria Glendinning, 'Lies and Silences', in *The Troubled Face of Biography*, ed. Eric Homberger and John Charmley, p. 53, Macmillan, London, 1988.
19. Quoted in Summerscale, *op.cit.*, p. 225.
20. Michael Holroyd, 'The Case Against Biography', in *Works on Paper*, p. 8.

21. Richard Holmes, 'Biography: Inventing the Truth', in John Batchelor, ed., *The Art of Literary Biography*, p. 15, Oxford University Press, Oxford, 1995.

22. Janet Malcolm, *The Silent Woman: Sylvia Plath and Ted Hughes*, p. 10, Picador, London, 1994.

23. Quoted in Miranda Seymour, 'Shaping the Truth', in *Mapping Lives*, ed. Peter France and William St Clair, published for the British Academy by Oxford University Press, Oxford, 2002.

Reflections 2

by Sally Cline

1. Reflections on the role of a life writer

As a life writer three guidelines have become my motivating forces which I have renamed:

1. Acts of empathy
2. More than a life
3. Rescuing lives

Acts of empathy

When I first encountered Carlyle's suggestion that writing about a life should be an act of sympathy, that idea established itself in my work as a rock. My subjects and I leant on it; tested our relationship against its hard surface; knew it would withstand external knocks. But there were problems, rock or not. Often I did not approve of my subjects' actions or behaviour. I was unable to feel sympathy for them. I no longer shared their sorrows nor cherished their joys.

What if I tried to understand my subjects better, get inside their heads, their world? Would that allow an affinity with them? I started with Marguerite Radclyffe Hall, the woman her friends called John. I found I had more in common with her than felt comfortable.

This is how it worked.

The first quirk Hall and I patently shared was list making. I make lists in an attempt to control ever-increasingly shaky surroundings. I live in a cloud of yellow Post-it notes. They adhere to every surface in kitchen, study, bedroom and loo. They tell me what I should do, am about to do, have done, and wish I had done. They tell other people with whom I live the same. They leave me feeling calm but have the power to drive my companions mad. One lover left me because of the constant talcum powder on the bathroom floor and the plethora of sunshine lists throughout the rest of the house. Fortunately for Hall's three significant lovers, she left the bathroom spotless but she did attempt to control them all with her list making. From childhood she had hung on to timetables, sections, categories, and as her belts and braces attitude to survival increasingly showed the characteristic traits of a sexually abused girl, she used lists to try to order her disordered environment.

As an adult she used lists on her lovers as I had done. First on the married lieder singer Mabel Batten, who became Hall's patron when John was a horse-mad tomboy and offered her a life of culture, poetry and art. However, while still in a couple with Mabel, Hall, lists in hand, lust in heart, fought for passionate control of Mabel's young cousin, another married woman, Una Lady Trowbridge. Mabel, discovering John's infidelity, raged, had a stroke and died. Una, with whom John then lived for many years, was too accustomed to power to allow John to control her. So Hall restrained her lists and bided her time until middle-aged Una fell ill. Then John hired as a nurse Eugenia Souline, a young vulnerable white Russian refugee whose weak lungs, poor English, no money and irresistible body meant Hall's list-making again swung into action.

Souline seemed in need of constant care, so as well as love letters, John sent instruction sheets twice daily. A typical list read:

1. No vodka or spirits to be taken.
2. No climbing.
3. A warm wrap always to be taken sunset or evening.
4. A short lying down every day if possible without too much boredom.
5. A sunshade to be taken. Yes.
6. Good wine may be drunk with meals.
7. No drinking on an empty stomach. By order of John.
8. Turn over page.
9. Seven pairs of stout shoes and stockings if the least bit damp.
10. Take your magnificent umbrella every time.
11. Remember always to love John.

This list tells us almost as much about Radclyffe Hall as do her letters and journals. She was compassionate, controlling, protective, believed in galoshes as well as in God, hated injustice, was arrogant but insecure and above all needed affection. Instruction number ten says it plainly, 'Remember always to love John'.

Once I had read that list, though I could see how irritating it would be to receive it, I recognised how many times I had made similar mistakes. The act of empathy between myself and Hall was complete.

Sometimes our choice of subject makes empathy easier. Faulkner felt writers should try to write about people whose spirits are capable of compassion, sacrifice, endurance, courage and honour. Curiously all my chosen subjects had some or all of those qualities. Radclyffe Hall and Zelda Fitzgerald had honour, compassion, endurance, moral and physical courage, Lillian Hellman and Scott Fitzgerald had endurance and were capable of sacrifice. Dashiell Hammett had unflinching physical stoicism and a quirky sense of honour. My acts of empathy were strengthened because my subjects had characteristics I valued.

However, when I gave subjects either insufficient sympathy or too much, I drew unbalanced portraits. Biographer James Mellow,[1] explains how some life writers lose that balance.

I confess that, over the years, I have become less and less sympathetic toward people with major or minor talents in any field who waste their gifts on drugs and drink, egotism and temperamental behaviour.[2]

Mellow points to the cumulative effect on a biographer of Scott Fitzgerald's alcoholism, the wastage of his time and talent, his repeated excuses for failures to meet deadlines or old friends. These tiresome antics were so great an irritant that Mellow confessed he could not be neutral. He never became more sympathetic towards Fitzgerald's profligacy but he was forced to admire Scott's stubbornness in sticking to his dream of becoming one of the most significant writers of his age. Through that annoyed admiration the necessary act of empathy sneaked in.

More than a life

In Millicent Dillon's insightful biography of Jane Bowles, Dillon emphasised ways in which Jane's life was more than itself. Dillon said her life showed, transparently, the world of her time and place and 'another timeless world'.[3]

The question here is whether the life of the person is a window on the times or whether the times are a window into the life of that person? Life writers must ask how much *is* someone a product of their times, their period, the knowledge, scientific, medical, psychoanalytic, literary of that particular society?

The portrait of Radclyffe Hall purposefully illustrated that her life had a value outside itself, yet was specifically rooted in her period. I saw her not only as the melodramatic self-defining iconic and pioneering Lesbian Martyr, nobly bearing unjust persecution against her book *The Well of Loneliness,* but also as a significant twentieth century cultural figurehead. To illustrate both her individual value and the value of the changes made in society because of her stance, I placed her carefully in lesbian social history where I showed how attitudes about same-sex love altered during her lifetime from the romantic view of female friendship to the new medical labelling of homosexual desire as deviant. I also analysed the possible effects on that writer (and by implication on any writer) of becoming a martyr to a cause.

To show that Zelda Fitzgerald's life similarly had a worth above itself, the dynamics of the couple's relationship had to be made starkly clear so that it became not merely a window into a destructive marriage but also a window into an unjust time in history for women who wished to achieve. In demonstrating that the Fitzgeralds' marriage could no longer be regarded as a legendary love story, I suggested both the danger of such deceptive fairy tales and the hazards of a romantic Deep South culture that dramatises a fantasy past to the detriment of the mundane present. A battery of medical research showed that Zelda's 'insanity' labelled schizophrenia (though she met very few of the criteria for the illness) was mistreated with the shockingly barbaric tools of the early twentieth century. Though depression occurred frequently in Zelda's family, her own might have been less a genetic condition than a product of clinical mistreatment by the medical profession and emotional abuse by her husband. If much of Zelda's hospitalisation (like that of Vivienne Eliot) was less for mental illness than for non-compliance with appropriate female conduct, then a wider value can be set on Zelda's life. This more extensive viewpoint allows a biographer to understand the aspects of commonality we have with our fellows as well as the unique separation of the self.

Rescuing lives

An important part of my own role as a biographer has been a rescuer of lives. Biographical rescue work developed from my early semi-autobiographical non-fiction books. In Lifting the Taboo: Women, Death and Dying, the first major study of the sexual politics of death in UK and USA, I rescued mortality from the deathly hush which had muffled it and rescued women's relationship to death and dying from the specific silence surrounding it. In Women Celibacy and Passion I rescued self-chosen celibate women whose lives in our sex-saturated society, were considered valueless, from the pejorative labels 'deviant' or 'invisible'.

Recovering women's lives lost within a male culture has become a strong biographical preoccupation.[4] My rescue attempts included women whose work had been overlooked or whose lives lurked in the shadow of a more dominant or famous person, often men close to them.

Radclyffe Hall had been a writer of eight novels and many short stories but was regarded as a one-book-writer. The bright white spotlight of fame shone on The Well of Loneliness alone. Zelda Fitzgerald was rescued from her obscure position as Scott's mad wife and her work rescued from the one dimensional view of an imitative novelist to that of a multi-talented artist.

In my forthcoming biography of Lillian Hellman and Dashiell Hammett, I highlighted four neglected areas in need of rescue: Hellman and Hammett's conflicting philosophies; the disproportionate critical notice paid to their writings, Hellman's Southern Jewish heritage, and Hammett's lifelong sickness.

In response to similarly disordered childhoods, Hellman became authoritarian, Hammett did not, or not overtly. He controlled himself, she controlled others through money, sex, writing and power. She believed in a world structured by order and meaning and clung to control as if to a raft. Violent arbitrary ordeals within an abusive working class childhood led Hammett along the opposite path. His creed became a stoical silence inside a world he saw ruled by meaningless blind chance. Yet ironically he chose detective fiction, predicated on linear clues and an orderly progression of unearthing 'facts', where Hammett, whose vision was that life is inscrutable, irresponsible and morally ambiguous entered a fictional world that pretends life is ethical, ordered and rational.

A second area of neglect was the unbalanced critical response to their separate literary canons. Hammett's literary achievements rest on five ground-breaking novels, a novella, and sixty short stories.

Hellman's literary successes as a playwright and memoirist reside in thirteen celebrated stage plays, four volumes of published memoirs and two further unpublished memoirs. Hellman unlike Hammett was a consistent continuous writer. Yet Hammett had been seen as a serious novelist whilst Hellman's life had either taken precedence over her literature or had been viewed as merged within it. I tried to redress the balance.

Scant attention had been paid to Hellman's Southern Jewish heritage. I used Richard Holmes' *Footsteps* approach to tread the streets she had trodden, catch trolleys she had caught, track her many homes, talk to surviving friends and enemies, and tap into unused materials in New Orleans, which had and still has a significant Jewish population. By these routes I established ways her Deep Southern and Jewish background (in which Southern rebels romanticised their past, whilst practising Jews were effectively blocked from key positions and ambitions) affected her politics and writings.

Bringing into the light Hammett's denial of his lifelong tuberculosis meant recognising how it had indisputably affected his masculine identity. His status as a sick man occurred during a period when masculinity was defined as hardboiled and healthy by his peers Hemingway and Fitzgerald.

Men could be drunks. Men could be psychiatrically disturbed. Men could be angry and violent. Both Fitzgerald and Hemingway displayed these characteristics. But constant sickness was not part of the masculine brief. Sick men were seen as literally invalid. I'm sure Hammett would be appalled at my attempt to expose the effects of his illness as in his view it would further undermine his shaky masculine ego!

Notes

1. James Mellow wrote an incomparable trilogy about Hemingway, the Fitzgeralds and Gertrude Stein as well as the lives of Nathaniel Hawthorne and Walker Evans.
2. James R. Mellow, *Invented Lives: F. Scott and Zelda Fitzgerald*, pp. xix and xx. Houghton Mifflin, Boston, 1984.
3. Millicent Dillon, *A Little Original Sin: The Life and Work of Jane Bowles*, p. 4, Virago, London, 1981.
4. Claire Tomalin, *The Invisible Woman: The Story of Nelly Ternan and Charles Dickens*. Viking, London, 1990.
   Carole Seymour-Jones, *Painted Shadow: A Life of Vivienne Eliot*. Constable, London, 2001.
   Meryle Secrest, *Between Me and Life: Biography of Romaine Brooks*. Macdonald and Jane's, London, 1976.
   Margot Peters, *May Sarton: A Biography*, Alfred A. Knopf, New York, 1997.
   Jane Dunn, *Antonia White: A Life*. Jonathan Cape, London, 1998.

2. Reflections on myth and memory

The memories of subjects or witnesses can be a tool towards discovering the truth of a life. Memories may be about a single moment, such as a riot in your subject's home town or a long-term event like a war in which your subject's family was killed.

However, memories are tricky, expedient or faulty, so a biographer's reliance on them is a shaky procedure. Memories can be more useful to the memory holder than to the biographer, because they may validate the holder's version of the past. Some people need corroboration of their memories to authorise their interpretations. Challenges occur when a subject's memory is linked to a family, friendship group or community who might have their own agendas or might prefer not to recall events. Sometimes dominant groups subvert memories held by minorities. Life writers might be offered a particular version according to their subject's position in the group. The way a group misremembers events may be passed down until their version becomes the received truth. This subtle weaving into a 'corporate memory' can lead to the invention of a group myth.

Early USA autobiographies show how this happens. Critic Leslie Fiedler in *Cross the Border – Close the Gap*[1] suggested that Americans 'have always been . . . inhabitants of myth rather than history'. Certainly Colonial memoirs often invented mythic versions of the self that served their community's needs rather than producing historical accounts. Although they had roots in factual narratives such as Captain John Smith's *The General History of Virginia, New England and the Summer Isles* or William Bradford's *Of Plymouth Plantation*, motives behind these accounts were to ensure the Puritans' theological goals were shown clearly. So individual life material was shaped into appropriate legends. One myth showed emigrating to America as a spiritual rebirth. Another showed as significant only those lives which had converted from 'sin' and then been selected by God to be offered grace. Those special individuals were seen as mythical models to others in their community: good examples of the New American, the spiritually glowing subjects who would attract worthy Europeans to the New World.

Literary myths have also served the interests of subjects' families and made life hard for biographers. Take the early portrayal of Jane Austen mainly by her family intent on controlling her visual and verbal image. Marilyn Butler wrote acidly that the main qualification to be Austen's biographer for the first century after her death '. . . was to be a relative'.[2] Among the relatives were her brother Henry Austen, her nieces Anna Lefroy and Caroline Austen, her nephew James Edward Austen-Leigh, and her great niece Fanny Lefroy[3] who between them established the legend of the ladylike Christian spinster: Aunt Jane, virtuous, self-effacing and docile. Hardly the sharp-witted, robust professional writer she patently was. The stunning gap between this portrait and Austen's acid novels has of course been contradicted, wept over and passionately refuted by biographers ever since.[4]

Biographers of couples often discover that one of the pair has mismanaged memories to set up myths that will serve only their interests.

I found Lillian Hellman manipulated her memories and rewrote Dashiell Hammett's in order to create a self-serving legend. She invented a thirty-year 'passionate bond' between her two iconic characters 'Lilly' and 'Dash' and airbrushed out everyone else. Hellman's Passion Myth required that Hammett's early love affair with his future wife Jose Dolan, as well as Hellman's lifelong bonds with her playwright husband Arthur Kober, were made invisible.

The remembered 'passion' of Hellman and Hammett was problematic. Although emotionally devoted to each other, sexually Hammett was never faithful. He seduced women, used whores, but liked men. He relaxed in male society, understood male loyalty, saw male betrayal as treachery. He forced Hellman, who dreamed of being faithful to him, to lead a separate sexual life. She had difficulty incorporating those hurtful memories into the legend so what she could not mythologise she removed.

Hellman was helped in her jealous dismissal of Hammett's marriage to Dolan by the scant contrary documentation which existed. But by the time I entered the field a packet of romantic letters between young Dash and Jose had been unearthed which showed clearly theirs was indisputably a love affair.[5]

Hellman similarly played down her committed relationship to Arthur Kober which, despite their amicable divorce and his happy remarriage, never ended. Until his death Kober was Hellman's best friend and not infrequently her lover. But to ensure the supremacy of the Hellman-Hammett legend she had to blot out the Kober-Hellman ménage.

To make this myth foolproof, Hellman also detached herself in public writings from her relationship with the very young novelist Peter Feibleman, who became her lover then companion after Hammett's death.

Hellman attempted to manage other people's memories too. She tried to forbid any biographies of Hammett and heavily censored even Diane Johnson's authorised biography. Publicly she said she did not want her memory of Hammett to be violated. Privately she knew other writers' versions would not concur with hers.

Sometimes memories of certain 'facts' are altered or omitted by subjects or their biographers. Charlotte Bronte's early biographer Elizabeth Gaskell wrote an 'affectionate, venerating biography'[6] which was highly regarded partly because she knew Charlotte personally. Although she approached Bronte with sympathy, she was over-protective in order to defend Bronte from accusations of vulgar immorality which had been levelled at *Jane Eyre*. So Gaskell suppressed Bronte's love letters to the married Heger, creating the myth of the pure sexless Charlotte, stripped of her fierce talent. Further Bronte discussion was hijacked for years by the myth of the victim/saint shadowed by death.

Bronte, who did not consider herself as a Victorian invalid, sensed in her own meetings with Gaskell that Mrs G was at best romanticising her and at worst inventing a new Charlotte Bronte. She wrote to her publisher saying Mrs Gaskell 'seems determined that I shall be a sort of invalid. Why may I not be well like other people?'.

Though protective, Gaskell was nevertheless engaged in that battle for possession often fought over dead literary lives. Gaskell perceived only one side of her subject and turned that side into myth.

When I tackled myths attached to Scott and Zelda Fitzgerald's legendary status as a Jazz Age couple, and Scott's status as a twentieth century literary icon, I confronted two questions.

Firstly, how does being mythologised change or control the lives of biographical subjects involved in the legend? Secondly, if myths can skew the facts, how hard is it for the biographer to achieve a balance in the research?

Zelda, who had several artistic talents, found much of her life controlled by living with Scott lionised for his single literary talent. Because artists who become legends often have intense self-focus (take Scott, Hemingway, Picasso, Ted Hughes) either by definition or as a consequence of mythical status, their artistic partners (Zelda, Martha Gellhorn, Francoise Gilot, Sylvia Plath) often had to leave or mentally retreat to create successfully. Zelda tried to leave several times but failed largely due to her financial dependence. Gellhorn and Gilot succeeded. Plath committed suicide.

Gilot, an established painter and writer who lived with Picasso between 1946 and 1953, says today that she was always her own self. But soon after she had left Picasso she talked about how hard it had been to work alongside the legendary painter. The late Martha Gellhorn, today famed as a novelist and war reporter, had to fight media myth-makers not only during her marriage, but for years afterwards because ignoring her professional writing they always described her as Hemingway's third wife.[7]

If a myth becomes established about only one of two people in a partnership, biographers must ask to what extent does the non-legendary person's life fall within the legend's framework? If legends grow up around both partners is it possible for either one to act in ways that contradict the myth? Or do they constantly reframe their behaviour to match media myths? The Fitzgeralds' actions constantly reinforced the myths. When Zelda, the young bride, jumped fully dressed into the Washington Square fountain, or performed cartwheels in a New York hotel lobby, and when Scott undressed at George White's review *Scandals*, the press headlined their exploits. Journalists turned the Fitzgeralds' bizarre behaviour into legend which encouraged Scott and Zelda to invent further extravagant antics.

The Fitzgeralds' fantasies matched those of the media, who saw their celebrity, followed by their crack-up, as a paradigm of a contemporary Wheel of Fortune. The Roaring Twenties glitter, Scott's successes, their idealised marriage, the birth of baby Scottie, Zelda as Jazz Age High Priestess, was swiftly followed by the thirties wreckage and Scott's descent into alcoholism. Alongside ran Zelda's inaccurate diagnosis of schizophrenia, ten years in and out of mental hospitals, marriage breakdown, conflict over their fiction. Fortunately for legend, these impossible people died impossibly young: Scott at forty four, Zelda eight years later at forty eight.

Posthumous legend saw them as the Golden Couple with Zelda as the Golden Girl of Scott's fiction. Young Scottie, who spent her early years with an alcoholic father and a depressed mother, so internalised the myth that she told journalists she'd had a golden childhood.

Beneath the glitter I discovered three important distortions. First was the way Zelda, as a product of the Deep South, was treated by myth-makers who ignored Southerness as a critical part of her artistic identity. The second was the almost complete omission of Zelda's role as a mother. The third was the way her status as a dancer, writer and painter was selectively dealt with.

Zelda's untamed talents as an experimental writer, a good dancer and a powerful painter, were subsumed under the greater interest of her marriage. Scott's view that Zelda's internationally recognised dancing was an obsession not an artistic commitment allowed him and Zelda's doctors to ban her from ever dancing again and became the standard biographical viewpoint. Her role as a professional writer was seen as secondary to that of Scott's muse and model for his heroines. Legend conceals Scott's plagiarism of Zelda's writings, with and without her knowledge. The myth that Zelda was not a 'serious' painter, was substantiated by the way society rates art higher if painters produce it consistently, continuously, date it, and offer a whole body of art for judgement. Zelda's art is largely undated; lacks the linear development by which one can sometimes date paintings; and the body of work is incomplete.[8] As our culture awards a higher status to artists engaged fulltime on one creative pursuit, the legend distorted Zelda's artistic achievements because her three gifts were seen by the myth as dilettantism. By unpicking these myths in great detail I offered a new account of the Fitzgeralds' lives.

Notes

1. First published in Playboy magazine December 1969, then published as a book by Stein and Day, New York, 1972.
2. Marilyn Butler, 'Simplicity', *London Review of Books*, p. 3, 5 March 1998.
3. Henry Austen, 'Biographical Notice', 1818 edition of *Northanger Abbey* and *Persuasion* (published posthumously).
   Anna Lefroy, *Recollections of Aunt Jane*, 1864.
   Caroline Austen, *My Aunt Jane Austen*, 1867 (not published until 1952).
   James Edward Austen-Leigh, *A Memoir of Jane Austen*, 1870. Fanny Lefroy, *Family History* from the 1880s.
4. The relatives' control extended to pictures. As only one picture of Jane was released for publication, almost every book jacket has the same 1811 watercolour and pen drawing by Cassandra Austen of her sister with caps and curls and peacefully crossed arms.
5. A few biographers did believe Hellman's line that Hammett only married Jose because she was pregnant. One writer foolishly credited Hellman's lie that Mary, Hammett's eldest daughter, was not biologically his despite the lack of any concrete evidence.
6. Hermione Lee, *Biography: A Very Short Introduction*, Oxford University Press, Oxford, 2009.
7. Gellhorn insisted her publicity agents ensured no print or broadcasting journalist ever asked about her private life with Ernest.
8. Though Zelda Fitzgerald produced paintings from 1925 until her death many were lost, destroyed or burnt. The day after Zelda died in a hospital fire, her mother Minnie, who loathed Zelda's art, instructed her other daughter Marjorie to take the paintings stored in the garage and burn them one by one in the yard. Though Zelda left a substantial legacy of over one hundred works it is but a small part of her total production.

3. Reflections on truth

There are certain true events in my past which I am never going to forget.

Take the time when as a stage director I flew to Zurich where I was due to direct a musical show that evening at a small theatre. I was aware that all technicians, electricians, stage hands, and the stage manager were Swiss and might not speak much English. I hoped I would get by with a smattering of French and Spanish. On arrival the chief electrician was ill and I was told I would have to fill in for him. As stage colours are allocated by numbers (a separate number for each colour) I decided I could attempt this. However not one person spoke English, French or even standard German. Many spoke Swiss-Deutsch but most spoke the town's dialect Zuridutsch.

I understood nothing they said. They understood nothing I said. I thought fast. I called a one hour break, escaped to a bookshop, bought a German dictionary with a Swiss-Deutsch appendix and sat in a coffee shop until I felt I had mastered some basic verbs, all the numbers, and several kinds of instructions for moving people about a stage. I managed the lighting effects with my sheet of numbers. The rehearsal was funny, wild and uproarious. We got through. The show was a big success and at the end the stage staff presented me with a bouquet.

I have never forgotten it. I have dined out on the tale for years.

But it wasn't true at all. It never happened, or it certainly didn't happen in the way I have told it.

The 'real' truth', as opposed to this theatrical myth, was that when I suggested we broke so I could go to a bookshop, the hostile technicians rebelled, they wouldn't be paid for a break, they wanted to plough on despite my dilemma. I used my fingers and a chalk board for the numbers, drew pictures on the stage floor to describe actions and locations; they thought, correctly, I was incompetent. I wept twice during the five hours (though offstage), the rehearsal was a fiasco. Despite the fact that the professional stars saved the show, I felt frustrated, humiliated, and a failure. After it was over I crept to the nearest pub and decided to take some language courses!

Yet for years I conveniently 'forgot' the truth, and patently believed the self-serving story I told everyone. What a moral tale for life-writers.

Biographers should try to tell 'the truth' or at least ground their subjects' lives in verifiable concrete details. As biographies and autobiographies are about real people, the writer has a responsibility to tell the truth about what went on.

No experience, however, can be absolutely truthful because memory corrupts it. Hardly surprising that historian John Lukacs believes one cannot write history accurately because what happened in the past cannot be separated from what we think happened. For historical biographers this is especially relevant.

Fitzgerald, who talked about the dangers of falsifying the past, managed to circumvent those risks in his autobiographical fiction, because it is more allowable for novelists than for biographers to recreate the past. Fitzgerald felt strongly that 'biography is the falsest of the arts' and believed 'there never was a good biography of a good novelist. There couldn't be. He is too many people if he is any good'.[1]

Even truth seekers may not know its precise meaning. Dictionaries define truth variously. Collins suggests truth is a 'a proven or verified fact' or 'a faithful reproduction or portrayal'.[2] The Shorter Oxford offers: 'the matter or circumstance as it really is', 'the real thing, as distinguished from representation or imitation' or a 'report or account consistent with fact or reality.'[3]

This poses the question of what is real? Where does truth exist? In the writing? In memory? In a mingling of the two?

Other factors may hamper the search. Information that would help get at the truth may be missing or withheld. What went on may have been hidden by the subjects or by relatives or friends.

If your subject is historical like Cleopatra it may be harder to establish precisely what went on. One idea is to offer a detailed historical background then set your subject within it. Another idea is to establish the class and status of your subject.[4] When the late iconoclastic biographer Diane Middlebrook decided her last biography would be on Ovid, there was no historical record of his life. Everything we know is in his poetry. Middlebrook was forced to rely on the text as her primary source. This challenge had its virtues. When asked why she chose Ovid she said breezily: 'No estates, no psychotherapy, no interviews, no history – I just make it up.'[5] For the authors of this book, who heard Middlebrook read aloud some scenes from her Ovid before she died, it felt as if she knew everything about him.

If your subject is more recent and there are still witnesses alive to whom you can talk, you must be wary for they may be telling purposeful untruths which over the years can gather the weight of approved testimony. These untruths may subsequently be quoted in one biography after another. So life writers need to act like sceptical detectives to spot contradictory statements.

Sometimes truth cannot be established because either the subject or a biographer has misplaced or stolen critical evidence. This happened to me when I was at the Historical Society in Madison, Wisconsin looking through the diaries of Arthur Kober, Lillian Hellman's husband, for the year of her marriage.

I had seen references to these events in a biography, earlier than mine, offering proper endnotes pointing to the Madison archive. When I arrived that particular diary was missing and the archivist said it must be there because it was listed. It *was* listed but it *was* missing. A thorough search of the archives proved fruitless.

Had the previous biographer stolen it? During my research in other areas of the USA I also discovered several significant letters mentioned in that biography were not in their correct library files. 'Gone missing', I was told. I drew my own conclusions.

These gaps in the records meant I couldn't accurately source parts of my biography. I had wanted to tell the whole truth but I was stymied. In some cases, ironically, I even had to fall back on the previous biographer's references.

Another life writer who was prevented from telling the truth was American memoirist Mary Karr. 'What I wanted most of all was to tell the truth,' she said about her best-selling memoir *The Liar's Club*. Her strategy was to tell her childhood friends in advance that they would appear in her book, then send them copies of the manuscript before publication. Only one friend, Meredith, complained. She asked Karr to remove from at least the first edition, while Meredith's mother was still alive, the scene where Meredith cuts herself with a razor. Karr could reinstate that scene when her mother died, suggested Meredith. Or Karr could turn Meredith into a stranger. Karr was not prepared to tell that kind of untruth as a stranger would not carry the same intimacy as a friend. She preferred to omit the whole scene. Then Karr's other friend Stacy, who felt the cutting scene was socially relevant, said she would claim the cutting acts as her own, which could be seen as 'true'. So Karr agreed to tell a different kind of untruth. Later she said, 'This is the only intentional falsehood I've consciously constructed . . . the one time I've let literature rule over fact. And now that Meredith and her mother are both dead, I correct the score'.[6]

When I was researching Radclyffe Hall I found several untruths perpetrated by Hall's second partner, Una Troubridge. As Hall's first biographer, Una was utterly determined that only her version of Hall as a stern lesbian icon should be in the public domain. Una's first fraudulent action was to tamper with a childhood portrait of Marguerite (Hall's given name), a beautiful child with shoulder length golden curls, who wore flowery dresses. The girl clutches at a bouquet of marguerites and sits proudly beneath her ruffled collar. Hall the adult was very proud of the portrait and not remotely uneasy about the curls. She admired her own hair which she kept long until she was forty.

Una, however, hated the portrait. Curls were not in keeping with congenital inversion theories. She waited until Hall's death in 1943 then commissioned artist Clare Tony Atwood to paint out the curls. All subsequent biographies, until mine, showed little Marguerite with a cropped boyish haircut. For seventy years readers believed this was a true image. Then I visited Una's godson, who owned the portrait, amazingly on the day he decided to scrape away the paint. As I watched, he revealed the un-emancipated curly child.

Una's next false move came over the matter of incest in Hall's childhood. I discovered evidence amongst Hall's manuscripts that her stepfather

Alberto Visetti, sexually abused her when she was about eleven. Hall had certainly told Una about the disturbing incidents but in Una's published biography of Hall there is no mention. In the unpublished first draft, however, Una wrote forty pages about the disturbing 'sexual incident' in Marguerite's life at the hands of 'the disgusting old man Albert Visetti'. Later Una removed every incriminating passage.

In her unpublished *Letters to John* which she wrote daily after Hall's death she explains: 'I have deleted the sexual incident with the egregious Visetti lest we have psycho-analytic know-alls saying you (John) would have been a wife and mother but for the experience'.

Una's worst piece of fraudulence did not even have the mask of protection which families assume when they wish to alter evidence for their own purposes. It was done from spite and jealousy. Even when Hall had found Souline, her new young Russian lover, Una hung on, insisting on forming a gruesome trio. On Hall's death, Una as her literary executor suddenly had full possession of the writer with whom she had lived for twenty eight years. Una used this power to expunge Souline from as many records as possible.

Una left instructions that no day book of Hall's was to be published after the date when Souline entered their lives. In Una's hagiography of Hall, Souline who occupied a decade of John's emotional and physical life, is minimised to three pages. Una also burnt Hall's last half-completed novel *The Shoemaker of Merano* because it had contained evidence of John's affections for Souline and hostility towards Una. Una's desire to erase Souline from official documents meant her regard for truth was nil.

A biographer's best way to deal with this is to reveal the duplicities and offer as much evidence as possible for an alternative account to that which has been falsified.

Trying to tell the truth about a subject known as a notorious liar is tricky. I faced this for six years with Lillian Hellman who fought for truth yet consistently told lies. During the Red Scare of the fifties she battled against Joe McCarthy's witch-hunts, told the truth to the House Un-American Activities Committee where with her most famous speech, 'I cannot and will not cut my conscience to fit this year's fashions' she became enshrined as an American cultural heroine. Bankrupted, blacklisted but not broken, she lived by a creed of honesty but died accused of fabrication. Changing careers from playwright to memoirist, her memoirs became instant best sellers but provoked massive controversy. Journalist Martha Gellhorn and critic Samuel McCracken first called them fictional then later lies. Finally, rival novelist Mary McCarthy said publicly on the Dick Cavett TV show that every word Hellman wrote was a lie, including 'and' and 'but'. Hellman sued McCarthy for $2.25 million. Only Hellman's death before the court case saved McCarthy from bankruptcy. Nothing saved Hellman's reputation.

Some contemporary literary biographers are not much concerned with discovering exactly what went on. They use dialogue like a play script, letters as a second fictional frame, and imagination to construct narratives like novels. Some biographers even invent colourful scenes between the literary subject and the subject's own fictional characters. Some insert themselves into the text and interlace what might have happened with musings on the unreliability of their own accounts or the unreliability of their subject's words. Various kinds of experimental examples included Peter Ackroyd's *Dickens* (1990), A.J.A. Symons's *The Quest for Corvo: An Experiment in Biography* (1934), Ian Hamilton's *In Search of J.D. Salinger* (1988).

There are exciting moments in these biographies but the search for 'truth' has been widened to include a search for the imaginative 'truth of a life'.

Miranda Seymour, in these pages, makes the point that integrity, the life writer's most valuable asset, requires a commitment to truth but it is truth as perceived by 'the innately subjective biographer'. Subjectivity does not work against the truth but alongside it. New forms of biographical writing give shapes to life stories that might surprise us. Biographers' responsibility to the life of the subject, by acknowledging the need for accuracy has not wavered but it is being handled in ways we had not dreamt of thirty years ago.

Notes

1. Scott Fitzgerald. *The Notebook of F. Scott Fitzgerald,* ed. Matthew Bruccoli, Harcourt Brace Jovanovitch/Bruccoli Clark, New York and London, 1945.
2. *Collins English Dictionary,* ed. Patrick Hanks, p. 1558, Collins, London, 1979.
3. *The New Shorter Oxford English Dictionary,* Vol 2. Oxford University Press p. 3412, 1973,1993.
4. cf Hilary Spurling on the Life of Ivy Compton Burnett.
5. Cynthia Haven. Obituary of Diane Middlebrook. *Stanford Report.* 15 December 2007.
6. Mary Karr in an interview on *Slate* website, 27 March 2007.

4. Reflections on telling stories, telling facts

Should there always be a gripping story inside a biography or will a record of facts be sufficient?

Richard Holmes suggests:

 There's a kind of fault-line running down between the notion of biography, history, as a kind of fictional retelling and against that the notion that the biographer, the historian must tell the truth, they are committed to the truth, to the facts, to their research.[1]

A lot of Holmes' work runs along that fault line.

Other biographers hold widely different view points. The late Matthew Bruccoli took one view to extremes. He was a passionate believer in the theory that facts alone would make a good biography.

 Facts are the only thing a biographer can trust – and only after they have been verified. Insights are as good as the evidence that supports them. This 2nd edition of Some Sort of Epic Grandeur *provides still more facts.[2]*

Bruccoli admitted he was enraged by fellow biographers who said biography should not be limited by facts. He took against a writer he called 'a one-book biographer' who had dared to declare that too much evidence interferes with the free play of the biographer's insights. 'It [the play] is free', intoned the wrathful Bruccoli, 'because it has not been paid for by research; it may indeed become a form of play or game.'[3]

Bruccoli believed a biographer's first duty was 'to get things right'[4] by assembling details in a usable way, relying heavily on the subject's own words.

Michael Holroyd takes a different view from Bruccoli. Biography, for him is not simply an exercise in information retrieval. It is a form of narrative. The pattern of biographical narrative like the pattern of a story is a matter of seeing which pieces of information work together magically to emphasise or produce a portrait of the person's life. As we tell the story of an individual (or group) we need to think about identity, about what constitutes a self. Facts cannot do that for us.

Both fictional patterns and biographical patterns are works of the imagination. The fiction writer imaginatively invents their story. The life writer imaginatively reinvents their biography. They draw on a past and recreate it using facts but adding interpretations. Biographers should be able to extricate a personality from the facts about that character.

Facts give us the foundation and from that concrete base we build up a picture of how each person became who they became.

The late historian and biographer Ben Pimlott discussed how to shine a light on your subject's spirit: 'However scrupulous the research nobody has access to another's soul, and the character on the page is the author's unique creation.'[5] If facts are dull and prosaic they won't allow readers in. It is interpretation which makes them light up.

In *The Art of Biography* (1939) written by Virginia Woolf, when she was struggling with the life of her artist friend Roger Fry, she suggested that her biographical attempt at 'vision' was hampered by facts but admitted facts were also unstable entities. Her belief that the real life was the inner life meant that factual biography was ill-equipped for the task.

A 'plot' can help. Life writers do not have a plot in precisely the same way as novelists but they have an equivalent. To engage the readers immediately we have to build up a notion of suspense about the central character. What is she or he going to achieve in their life? What are the obstacles in the way? What are their biggest conflicts and challenges? How do they deal with lovers and enemies? Get readers involved in these issues and you have a quasi-plot.

If facts about a person's life won't give us a picture of them, how we select them might. But it will be *our* picture not *the* picture. There is no one picture. There are many versions of reality. If we tell a story of a life even filling it with facts we still tell it slant. Our own colour will shade it. That colour comes from our race, gender, class, culture, education and myriad personal beliefs.

There are other problems too. Biographers leave out or misrepresent many of the facts they come across. Almost all the early biographers of Scott or Zelda Fitzgerald saw Scott's death as the virtual end of Zelda's life. The fact was that she lived eight more years, and those years for her as a painter were her most productive. But as all Scott's biographers' presentation of Zelda was aimed at describing her only in terms of her role as Scott's wife omitting those facts met their agenda.

Facts can certainly lead one astray. Sometimes they are not quite what they seem or may not be facts at all. Question: when is a fact not a fact? Answer: when it is a fake. Every life writer has to be wary of so-called 'facts' because when used by other (possibly envious) life writers they might be inventions.

Take the case of poor A.N. Wilson, the generally smart biographer of poet John Betjeman, who was tricked by his rival biographer Bevis Hillier into publishing what Wilson believed was an authentic love letter from Betjeman to his mistress.

Hillier spent twenty five years completing a three-volume biography of the poet. Wilson who reviewed Hillier's biography in 2002 described it as a 'hopeless mishmash of a book'. When newspapers began to herald Wilson's forthcoming biography of Betjeman as 'the big one', Hillier in a rage concocted a plot. He sent Wilson a letter with a French return address (but a London postmark) purporting to be from someone alleged to be the cousin of Honour Tracy, a real-life friend of Betjeman's. The imaginary cousin, supposedly Betjeman's mistress, was named Eva de Harben, an anagram of 'ever been had'.

A.N. Wilson, who believed every word of the steamy missive, published it in his book. He had not noticed that the letters at the start of each sentence after the opening line of the love letter spelt out: 'A.N. Wilson is a shit'![6]

How much speculation or invention can a life writer use?

For Virginia Woolf, who believed a true understanding of a person's life could only be achieved by empathetic inwardness, one answer was to blur the boundaries between biography and fiction and produce some experimental fictionalised biographies. *Orlando* (1928) was sub-titled *A Biography* but was a subversive comic fiction about a man who changes into a woman, lives through three centuries, and not-so-secretly was a coded love story to her married lover Vita Sackville-West. In 1933 her equally original fictionalised portrait of a spaniel *Flush* told the biographic story of Flush's mistress Elizabeth Barrett Browning.

Since then many fictional techniques – irony, parody, impressionism, playing with time, changing viewpoint, setting scenes, caricature, psychoanalytic characterisation – have been regularly recycled into biography. Even dialogue, which in a conventional biography cannot be invented can be imitated by using brief quotations from diaries or letters. Peter Ackroyd's unconventional *Dickens* invented dialogue from Dickens' characters' own mouths.

Millicent Dillon in her biography of Paul Bowles[7] says she resorted to indirection, imaginative speculation, in achieving a portrait of Bowles.

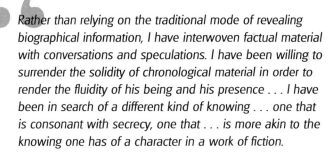

Rather than relying on the traditional mode of revealing biographical information, I have interwoven factual material with conversations and speculations. I have been willing to surrender the solidity of chronological material in order to render the fluidity of his being and his presence . . . I have been in search of a different kind of knowing . . . one that is consonant with secrecy, one that . . . is more akin to the knowing one has of a character in a work of fiction.

Her book becomes as much a meditation on the nature of biography as it is a biography of Paul Bowles. She opens up the hidden elements that usually provide the structure for traditional biography. Thus the portrait of Paul Bowles is a biography turned inside out in which Dillon admits into the narrative her own subjectivity. It is not unlike the upside down biography of the chaotic knife-wielding homeless man *Stuart: A Life Backwards* by Alexander Masters.[8] Masters inserts himself constantly into the text both in conversations with the wildly compelling Stuart and in angry frustrated monologues about his unruly subject. The story is as gripping as a bestselling novel. No amount of solid pedantic facts could have produced either of these books.

Notes

1. Richard Holmes in an interview for the Open University with Derek Neale, published in Sara Haslam & Derek Neale, *Life Writing* p. 144, Routledge, London & New York, 2009.
2. Matthew Broccoli, *Some Sort of Epic Grandeur: The Life of F. Scott Fitzgerald,* Cardinal, Harcourt Brace Jovanovitch, New York, 1981.
3. Ibid.
4. Ibid.
5. Quoted by Barbara Schwepcke in a talk to the Biographers' Club London, 31 March 2005.
6. The fake love letter story can be found at http://www.cbc.ca/arts/story/2006/09/03/love-letter-betjeman-hillier.html
7. Millicent Dillon, *You Are Not I: A Portrait of Paul Bowles*, pp. x, xi, University of California Press, Berkeley, 1998.
8. Alexander Masters, *Stuart: A Life Backwards*. Fourth Estate, London, 2005.

Tradition

Biography by Carole Angier

> *Biography is in fact the oldest profession – forget the other one.*
>
> Victoria Glendinning[1]

This is not so much a history as a biography of biography. It doesn't only order the facts, but traces what Henry James called 'the pattern in the carpet'. This pattern was first picked out by Harold Nicolson in 1927, in *The Development of English Biography* (though he drew on Edmund Gosse's entry on 'Biography' in the famous eleventh edition of the *Encyclopedia Britannica*.) It has shaped accounts of biography ever since.

No systematic new history was written for the next eighty years. But recently two have appeared: Nigel Hamilton's *Biography: A Brief History* in 2007, and Hermione Lee's *Biography: A Very Short Introduction* in 2009. Hamilton follows the standard pattern (that is, Nicolson's). Lee argues that it is misleading in the neatness of its divisions, and in its model of progress – thus echoing a general criticism of biography, whose occupational hazard is hindsight. She is right, of course. Nonetheless, she too agrees that 'these lines can, to an extent, be drawn'; and minus the progressive model, her history of biography has the same overall shape as Nicolson's. So does my short biography below.

Beginnings

The oldest biographical stories are the founding myths of societies and religions: the stories of the Old Testament and ancient Greece, of the lives of Buddha, Jesus and Mohammed, Romulus and Remus, Beowulf and Cuchulainn. The oldest of all, perhaps, the Epic of Gilgamesh, tells the tragic life of Gilgamesh, king of Uruk in Assyria in around 2600 BC

But the roots of biography proper – accounts of real people, based on evidence – lie in the Classical world of Greece and Rome, like so much else in Western culture. There are biographies of Socrates and Aristotle, for example, and Aristotle's successor as head of the Lyceum, Theophrastus, wrote an important set of portraits called *Characters*. The Roman historian Tacitus wrote a biography of his father-in-law, *Agricola*, and his contemporary Suetonius wrote *The Lives of the Caesars*, as well as *De viris Illustribus, Of Famous Men*, the first literary lives.

But the most important early biographer was Plutarch, who lived from 46 to 120 AD. Plutarch was the first to divide biography clearly from history, saying in his *Life of Alexander*, 'It is not Histories I am writing, but Lives'.[2] His *Lives of the Most Noble Greeks and Romanes* was translated into English in 1579, and from then on was an important influence not just on English biography but on English literature in general. All Shakespeare's Roman plays were based on Plutarch's *Lives: Anthony and Cleopatra*, for example, on the *Life of Anthony*.

Plutarch's *Lives* are often called the *Parallel Lives*, because they are constructed on the compare-and-contrast principle. Their aim is the analysis of public achievement, and their point is to celebrate success, not understand failure. Plutarch's *Lives* look back to the *encomium*, the eulogising funeral oration, with its intent to elevate and ennoble; they deal exclusively with the powerful and celebrated, and almost exclusively with men.

All this makes Plutarch the father of a main biographical lineage: the ethical tradition, which sees the proper study of biography as public life, and its proper aim as moral and political instruction. He is the major source, for the Renaissance and the modern world, of Greco-Roman standards of conduct: courage, temperance, public service. It is these standards that are his real subject; his aim is to portray not individuals, but the ideal Roman citizen, for the edification of readers and the instruction of their leaders.

Plutarch is our father: but we know what children do to fathers, and his civic and didactic conception is one from which modern biography has been a long process of breaking away. However, as Hermione Lee argues, things are rarely so simple. Perhaps despite himself, Plutarch was what Harold Nicolson called a natural biographer: interested in character, and in telling a good story. His writing is vivid and spiced with anecdotes; he kept neither murder nor tender love stories out of his *Lives*; and he tests the evidence much more than the orators of *encomia* before him, or the biographers of saints after him, both of whom were allowed to make up more or less anything, so long as it was ennobling. Plutarch is the father of ethical biography in particular; but in these ways he is the father of us all.

Middle Ages

With the fall of the Roman Empire comes the end of the first Golden Age of biography, in Nicolson's schema. His Dark Ages cover the fifth through to the fifteenth centuries, as Gosse had argued before him ('Biography hardly begins to exist in England until the close of the reign of Henry VIII'[3] – that is, until the middle of the sixteenth century.)

It is in this long period that we find some of the mythic forebears that opened this short biography: Beowulf in the eighth century, eg, and the Norse Eddas, composed between the eighth and the thirteenth. But the main ancestral genre throughout it – indeed the main literary genre in general – was hagiography, the lives of saints I have just mentioned. Some stand out, such as Bede's *Life of St Cuthbert* from the eighth century, which Nicolson admired for its more personal tone and for its vivid images, such as that of a sparrow fluttering through a great hall. Most interesting of all are Aelfric's *Lives of the Saints*, from the tenth century. These were written for the first time in the vernacular, rather than Latin; many of them were about quite ordinary people; and all of them were dramatic and well-constructed stories. Nonetheless, from start to finish hagiography remained firmly in the idealising mode. So much so that one of its earliest critics, the seventeenth century biographer Thomas Fuller, said plainly that the lives of the saints were 'forgeries';[4] and 'hagiography' today is no longer used to mean 'the lives of saints', but 'fawning whitewash'.

From about the ninth to the twelfth century is also the period of chronicles and annals – that is, accounts of secular rulers instead of saints, the most famous of which are the *Anglo-Saxon Chronicles*, initiated by King Alfred in the ninth century. There are also some good individual lives: everyone agrees on Eadmer's *Life of Anselm* in the twelfth century, for example. But then, from the fourteenth to the fifteenth centuries we are in the biographical Slough of Despond, in Nicolson's words. There were popular collections of saints' lives, such as the fourteenth century *Legenda aurea*, the source for Piero della Francesca's famous frescoes in Arezzo. But the genre did not advance, and after the fifteenth century it faded.

The Renaissance

The renewal of biography began, like the Renaissance itself, in Italy, with Giorgio Vasari's *Lives of the Artists* of 1550. These are one hundred and sixty-odd short biographies, from sketches to full-length portraits, culminating in Vasari's hero, Michelangelo, who gets one hundred and twenty pages. Vasari's *Lives* are very much in the Plutarchian tradition of types and public achievement, short on personal detail, and focused on deriving lessons for the reader. But the subjects are ordinary gifted men, not saints or kings; the lessons are for the conduct of professional life, not the saving of empires or souls; and the *Lives* are dramatic wholes, striking enough to provide Robert Browning with stories ('Fra Lippo Lippi', 'Andrea del Sarto'), as Plutarch had done for Shakespeare. Above all, Vasari was the first to relate an artist's work to his life, inaugurating an analytic tradition that comes down through the nineteenth century French critic Ste-Beuve to literary and artistic biography today.

In Britain, the late 1500s laid down the foundations for biography as a major genre. In 1577 came Holinshed's *Chronicles of England, Scotland and Ireland*, descendant of the *Anglo-Saxon Chronicles*. (Holinshed's *Chronicles* gave even more stories to English literature than Plutarch, being the source for probably a dozen of Shakespeare's plays.) In the 1590s Theophrastus's Greek was translated into Latin, the lingua franca of Renaissance scholars; and before and after it came translations into

English of other key classical texts – in 1579 Plutarch, in 1591 Tacitus's *Agricola*, and in 1606 Suetonius. And in the late sixteenth century the first English biographies of neither saints nor kings began to be written: Nicolson picked out William Roper's *Sir Thomas More* and *Cardinal Wolsey* by George Cavendish. Before these, in 1517, was More's own *Life of Richard III* – dubiously reliable, but well crafted and influential. Later scholars – including Hamilton, Lee and the *Encyclopedia Britannica* – have agreed about all three. And it's not only scholars who agree: Shakespeare used *Wolsey* for his *Henry VII*; and in 2009 Hilary Mantel used it for her Booker-winning novel *Wolf Hall*, saying that it is 'startlingly modern' – accurate and gripping, full of drama and dialogue.[5]

The seventeenth century

Nicolson's story of modern biography now begins to take its final form. The humanism of the Renaissance provided the first strand – the opening out of interest from saints and legendary leaders to ordinary (though still important) people, and from public events to private life and the engagingness of art. With the sixteenth century, however, came the Reformation, and in England the growth of Puritanism, and of religious and political strife. In the first half of the seventeenth century, therefore – Nicolson argued – English creative genius fled into drama and poetry, where disguise is possible, and away from biography, where it is not. And it certainly seems true that, in the first fifty or sixty years of the seventeenth century, biography was dominated by featureless panegyric: for instance in Fulke Greville's *Life of Sir Philip Sidney*, written in 1610–12, and published in 1652; or in Thomas Sprat's *Cowley*, published in 1668, in which, as the *Encyclopedia Britannica* says, 'Although he referred to the charm and interest of Cowley's letters, he considered it an impropriety to publish them'.[6] Hermione Lee too moves from More, Cavendish and Roper to the later seventeenth century without naming any work of equal interest.

Nicolson attributes this becalming of biography partly to the recent arrival of Plutarch and Theophrastus, with their powerful didactic model, but even more to Puritanism and the Civil War. Religion in general, he argues, and Puritanism in particular, are inimical to the art of biography, because they discourage love of this world in favour of the next, and because they are suspicious of art. And, he suggests, peace and tolerance are more necessary to biography than to other forms of literature, because of its connection to the real. We must, I think, agree. It is easier to contemplate different, even opposing, ways of life in the safety of our imaginations than in reality – especially in the reality of conflict, such as the English Civil War.

Thus all the strands of Nicolson's story came together. Modern biography, in this story, depends upon several conditions: a value for all kinds and classes of people, ie, democracy; and an interest in character, without the schematising of a moral, political or religious ideology, ie, empiricism. That is why biography is a classically Anglo-Saxon art: the product of an irreligious, empiricist tradition, and a long history of civic peace. And that is why, every time an ideology dominates in British history – as a religious one did now, and as a moral and political one would from the mid-nineteenth century to the First World War – biography goes into decline, to flourish again only when greater freedom returns. This is the Nicolsonian pattern in the carpet. It is a value judgement, preferring art and truth to edification, and an ordering, organising story. But it fits the facts, and it is the best story we have so far.

But there are always exceptions, and now there was a major one: Izaak Walton's *Lives* – of Donne, Wotton, Hooker and Herbert – the first of which, the *Life of Donne*, appeared in 1640. Walton is generally recognised to be a bridge between classical 'ethical' biography and modern biography in Nicolson's sense, which begins in earnest with Johnson and Boswell a hundred years later. Walton's *Lives* are traditional eulogies of their subjects; but he aimed at accuracy, and his portraits are full of vivid detail and warm feeling (Donne and Wotton were both friends.) He made use of anecdotes and letters, and even included imaginary conversations – there is nothing new in biography, as we shall regularly see. And last but not least, Walton's *Lives* are literary masterpieces, in Nicolson's words; 'eloquently written' and 'carefully structured' in Lee's.[7]

Art, accuracy, personality: the main points of modern biography are already here.

Then in the 1660s came the end of Puritan rule, and soon after, the scientific revolution. This new burgeoning of empirical, secular knowledge was all biography needed. Now comes the Golden Age of autobiographies and diaries, such as those of Evelyn and Pepys (though they weren't published until the early nineteenth century). Now too come more lively and accurate private lives, such as Margaret Cavendish's life of her husband, the Duke of Newcastle (1667). But the most important arrival in this period was that of John Aubrey, the first modern biographer entirely outside the Plutarchian tradition.

Aubrey's *Brief Lives*, collected for a biographical dictionary between 1669 and 1696, are famously indiscreet, anecdotal and personal. They are wholly secular, about the poets, scholars, statesmen and scientists of his age, and they include among their more than five hundred original portraits a good half dozen of women. (Some of these are only a line or two long, but many men receive no more.) Aubrey knew many of his subjects personally, so the *Brief Lives* are full of original research, or at any rate of quirky first-hand information. They are leavened with a new and very modern element, humour; and inspired, in Nicolson's proud words, by no graver motive than 'sheer native prying'. All this made Aubrey's own biographer, the novelist Anthony Powell, call him 'the first English biographer',[8] which suggests that he too saw Aubrey's vivid, gossipy style as the first step in a new English tradition.

The early eighteenth century

Though Aubrey was writing in the late seventeenth century, the *Brief Lives* were not published until 1813 (at much the same time as the *Diaries* of Pepys and Evelyn), and it took biography some time to catch him up.

What happened first, in the early eighteenth century, was an explosion of interest in the opposite of exemplary lives – in outcasts and criminals: for example, in Captain Alexander Smith's *History of the Lives of the Most Noted Highwaymen, Footpads, Etc.*, published in 1714. This happened equally in the early novel. Thus we get, for example, Daniel Defoe's

Robinson Crusoe (1719) and *Moll Flanders* (1722) – and also his biographical studies of the house-breaker Jack Sheppard (1724) and the corrupt thief-catcher Jonathan Wild (1725). There was also a burgeoning of the new 'Grub Street' school of journalism, with hundreds of True Histories produced by such as Edmund Curll, the inspirer of Dr Arbuthnot's epigram about the new Terror added to Death; and the sensational *Newgate Calendar*, purporting to describe the crimes and punishments of the inmates of the infamous Newgate Prison.

All this, however, is relatively minor. The only major biographical achievement of the early eighteenth century is generally agreed to be Roger North's *Lives* of his three eminent brothers, written between 1715 and the 1730s and published in the 1740s. They are firmly in the Aubrey mode – candid and truthful, lively and humorous – but unlike 'magotie-headed' Aubrey's miniatures, these are full-length portraits, integrating a mass of materials (letters, memoranda) into their narratives.

In the Preface to *Lord Keeper North*, Roger North also provided the first British reflections on biography after Dryden's, in the Preface to a new translation of Plutarch in 1683. Like Dryden, North emphasised the importance of private life, which reveals more about character than public performance; and he added ideas about the interest of ordinary lives, and the value of truth and candour, which anticipated those of Johnson thirty-five and more years later. Thus, as Hermione Lee says, the pattern is not one of linear progress. Biography moves more in a spiral than a straight line.

The eighteenth century: the arrival of modern biography

The great waves of secularising, empiricising and democratising ideas have succeeded each other in Europe, and modern biography is ready to appear. Our first sighting comes in 1744, with the publication of Johnson's *Life of Savage*, the first great literary biography in English.

The *Life of Savage*, as Robert Gittings said, stands the traditional biography of praise on its head. It is about Richard Savage, bastard and outcast, poet and murderer. It deploys the drama of the courtroom, and the themes of myth and fairytale – the Rejected Son, the Despised Genius;

at the same time it invents critical biography, including acute interpretations of Savage's poetry.[9] It is far from impartial, indeed much of it is special pleading; and Johnson simply accepted all the dubious accounts of Savage, starting with his own, without checking them, which is the first duty of the biographer. It is also an indirect portrait of Johnson's troubled psyche, as much as Savage's: almost a 'displaced autobiography', in Richard Holmes' words. As a result, *The Life of Savage* is a great work of literature, but not at all reliable. It dramatises the gap between biography, history and art. But just for that reason it stands as the great precursor of modern biography, with all its ambiguities brilliantly exposed.*

What happens next, of course, is Boswell. We see it coming in Savage; but modern biography begins, Richard Holmes says, on 16 May 1791, with the publication of Boswell's *Life of Johnson*.[10]

Boswell set out his plan in the *Life*: to let Johnson speak for himself, wherever possible, through his letters, and above all through his conversation, collected by Boswell over twenty years; and not to suppress any truth, but to present Johnson in all his great but fallible humanity: 'for I profess to write not his panegyrick, which must be all praise, but his Life'.[11] All this he did – and encountered praise and abuse in equal measure from the start. The foundation of modern biography is also the foundation of the attack on biography, split between praise for its portrayal of real, fallible human beings, and fear and revulsion at the same thing.

The Life of Johnson is a prodigious work. It is the most famous biography of all time, and yet it is inimitable, and as far as I know has never been imitated. No one has stalked his biographical prey as Boswell stalked Johnson, and no biography since has captured so much, so memorably, of its subject. Despite great works of scholarship revealing other Johnsons (the young Johnson, Hester Thrale's Johnson) Boswell's Great Cham has

---

* There is, of course, more to Johnson in the history of biography (not to speak of the histories of lexicography and literature). After Dryden's and North's anticipations, his *Rambler* No. 60 and *Idler* No. 84 are the ur-texts of biographical criticism in English, laying down the principles of truth, impartiality, and the importance of private and inner life. And like Walton before him, he looks both backwards and forwards in this history. His style was thoroughly Plutarchian – formal and Latinate, built on balance and contrast. And by the time he wrote his other great biographies, the *Lives of the Poets* (1779–81), his aims were thoroughly Plutarchian as well: the drawing of moral lessons from the lives and works of the great writers.

never been replaced in our imagination. There is no popular canon of biography (though Richard Holmes has proposed one[12]): Boswell's *Life of Johnson* is it.

The late eighteenth to the mid-nineteenth century was the Romantic age, and not surprisingly the age of autobiography, with bold self-revelations such as De Quincey's *Confessions of an Opium Eater* (1822), Hazlitt's *Liber Amoris* (1823) and Harriette Wilson's *Memoirs* (1825). It also produced some excellent biographies: William Godwin's memoir of his wife, Mary Wollstonecraft (1798), for example, and John Gibson Lockhart's *Life of Scott* (1837–38). But things were about to change.

Victorian blight

Victorian propriety was a brief aberration in a much more robust tradition, but it made such a powerful myth that it has dominated ideas of English character ever since. And it dominated biography at the time. From about 1840 up to the First World War – from Dean Stanley's *Life of Thomas Arnold* (1844) through Samuel Smiles' *Self Help* (1859) to Morley's *Gladstone* (1903), we are firmly back in the Plutarchian tradition of didactic, exemplary lives.

Such Lives were hardly Lives at all, but as H.G. Wells said of *Gladstone*, 'embalmed remains'; or as Gladstone said himself (of John Cross's biography of his wife, George Eliot), 'a Reticence in three volumes'.[13] Now, therefore, we get Carlyle's lament for poor mealy-mouthed English biography, and Virginia Woolf's for its subjects, like 'effigies that have only a smooth superficial resemblance to the body in the coffin'.[14] 'Who does not know them?' Lytton Strachey cried, those fat volumes, with 'their tone of tedious panegyric, their lamentable lack of selection, of detachment, of design? They are as familiar as the cortège of the undertaker, and wear the same air of slow, funereal barbarism.'[15]

Strachey exaggerated, of course, and as always there were exceptions to the rule: for example, Mrs Gaskell's *Life of Charlotte Bronte* (1857), or J.A. Froude's *Life of Carlyle* (1882–84), which was reviled at the time, but is prized as the greatest Victorian biography now. Nor did hagiography end tidily in 1918 (one classic example, Trevelyan's *Life of Grey*, appeared in

1937.) Nonetheless, the pattern remains. The Victorian period was the peak of high-mindedness, and also therefore of hypocrisy in England; and in English biography too.

The early twentieth century

Then came the reaction – the decadence of the 1890s and the first stirrings of Modernism in the 1900s; and 'in or about December 1910', as Virginia Woolf famously said, 'human character changed'. She should have said that Victorian character changed, or started changing – a good example of how a phrase crafted to last a hundred years is likely to simplify the facts. But in biography at least it was more or less true. In 1907 English biography changed, with Edmund Gosse's *Father and Son*.

Once again, Gosse was a fulcrum, a Janus figure looking both ways. In his theory he was still a Victorian. But *Father and Son* has all the hallmarks of modern biography: the focus on private life; the drama and artistry of a novel; and an openness to failure and weakness, since the father is wrong about everything, and the son is just a child. There is no historical background, just the portrait of a small, eccentric family of Plymouth Brethren in obscure parts of London and Devon. But there is no more unforgettable account of the great crises in the late Victorian world – the clash between religion and science, and between the old unquestioned dominance of the paterfamilias, backed by the churches, and the will to freedom of the new secular generations.

After *Father and Son* came the turning point of the twentieth century in Europe: the First World War. After that, most of the remaining sons lost faith in their fathers, and the nation-building glorifications of the Victorian age were no longer possible. The time was ripe for revolution; and biography got it, in the shape of Lytton Strachey's *Eminent Victorians*.

After Aubrey in the seventeenth century, and Johnson and Boswell in the eighteenth, Strachey is the next great father of modern biography. He stands especially for four key modern features: candour; irony and satire; borrowing the techniques of fiction and Freudian psychology; and beauty of language and design, ie, literary art.

The only modern feature Strachey doesn't stand for is original research: he always worked from published sources. The combination of this with his bold expansion of biographical method made him 'the favourite whipping boy of sober historians' from the start, one scholar of biography said in 1962[16] – and it's still true today. Strachey is accused of simplification, and even invention, for effect: of saying, for example, that Thomas Arnold had short legs, as a (cruel) image of his character, though it wasn't true. According to Michael Holroyd, Strachey's biographer, his speculations are always signalled by a 'perhaps', if you look closely. And his critics have to admit that his insights have mostly proved sound, even where he went beyond his sources. That is the great hope of every biographer, since new facts will always appear: that if we have studied our material well enough, we'll get it right, and further evidence will only confirm what we have intuited.

Between the wars

After Strachey there was a great flowering of experimental biography: for example, in Geoffrey Scott's *Portrait of Zelide* (1925), Virginia Woolf's *Orlando* (1928) and A.J.A. Symons' *The Quest for Corvo* (1934) in Britain, and the biographies of Catherine Drinker Bowen in America.

All these are the ancestors of the post-modern biography of our own day: biography which is self-conscious and experimental, which knows that an 'objective' biographer is an illusion, and which dares to use the techniques of drama and fiction – as Strachey did, and Boswell and Johnson, and indeed Plutarch himself, when his guard slipped. Once again there is very little that is new in biography (any more than there is in fiction, where there have never been more experimental works than *Don Quixote* or *Tristram Shandy*). But again our more sober critics remain stuck in the Victorian era, that period of power and certainty that no Englishman wants to leave. The great modernist artists – Joyce, Eliot and the rest – have long been part of the most conservative canon; but Strachey and his heirs are still outlaws, and the battle for 'experimental' biography has to be fought anew in every generation.

The post-war period

The period of Stracheyan experiment was ended by the Second World War. That was a very different war from the first, at least for Britain and America: one which was felt to be just and bravely won. After that, Robert Skidelsky has pointed out,[17] Stracheyan satire was out and hero-worship was back in. By then, however, Freudian psychology had entered the general culture, and as Skidelsky says, the hero-worship was of a new, post-Stracheyan and post-Freudian kind. We now neither celebrated success nor debunked it, but looked for its roots. Biography became 'warts-and-all' – a celebration of the whole human, in which the greatest heroes and heroines are not flawless, as the Victorians pretended, but have overcome their flaws, or explored them in their art.

That is where English biography had arrived by the 1950s, which was its next great peak. By now 'English' meant at least half American: the classic mid-century biographies are Leon Edel's *Henry James* (1953–72), Richard Ellmann's *James Joyce* (1959) and George Painter's *Marcel Proust* (1959–65) – and Painter was British, Edel American, and Ellmann an American who spent fifteen years at Oxford. These great literary biographers retained Strachey's psychological insight and artistic vision, but expanded his scholarship – and, it must be said, his length.

From that mid-century high point, this time there has been no retreat: perhaps because there has been (roughly speaking) civil peace in Britain and America; and imperialism, religion and other forces for conformity have faded in Britain, and in the US stopped short of the academy, from which American biographical writing springs. Instead, in 1967 the most important British biographer of the second half of the century arrived: Michael Holroyd, with *Lytton Strachey*, and since then *Augustus John*, *Bernard Shaw* and a trio of Edwardian theatrical lives. Holroyd's biographies are in the Ellmann tradition – both artistic and scholarly, both lively and long. To this tradition he has added sexual candour, and his own particular note of ironic humour. He has single-handedly made literary biography an admired and even popular genre in Britain – though still not a respectable one. He would reject with horror any such accusation.

Holroyd is the last father of modern biography so far. The question is, What now? Will there be a new Boswell or a new Strachey? Will someone make biography still longer and more protean, or give it another short sharp shock – or both, or neither? For the answer that a change is coming – or has already arrived – I refer you to Part Two: to the literary editor and critic Boyd Tonkin, to Richard Holmes and Alexander Masters, both of whom have experimented brilliantly themselves.

I am agnostic. Experiments have come regularly in the history of modern biography, which itself began with two experiments, Johnson's *Life of Savage* and Boswell's *Life of Johnson*. They will come again. They have already come, with group biographies, quest biographies, and experimental biographies of every kind, from Ackroyd's *Dickens* and Morris's *Dutch* to – for example – Diane Johnson's *Lesser Lives* and Phyllis Rose's *Parallel Lives* in America; and Richard Holmes' *Footsteps*, Geoff Dyer's *Out of Sheer Rage*, Julia Blackburn's *Old Man Goya*, Alexander Masters' *Stuart: A Life Backwards*, and the winners of the Samuel Johnson Prize for the last two years, The *Suspicions of Mr Whicher* and *Leviathan*, in Britain. Several of these are masterpieces; some have been critical successes, some reviled. Conservative critics and publishers tend to resist experiment, as I have said, and we must fight again and again to keep it alive. But readers also remain faithful to the single, straightforward Life, told with insight and sympathy.

As I write, the book pages of magazines and newspapers still start with biography. Paula Byrne's group life of the Lygon family (Evelyn Waugh's models for *Brideshead Revisited*) is on all of them, and John Carey's biography of William Golding is Book of the Week on Radio Four. Lyndall Gordon's new biography of Emily Dickinson is due out in 2010, Hilary Spurling has just finished a part-life of Pearl Buck, and Hermione Lee has embarked on Penelope Fitzgerald. In biography's house there are many mansions. As long as there are books, there will be room for us all.

Notes

1. Victoria Glendinning, in a discussion on 'Biography and Creative Writing', colloquium on biography organised by the British Council in Paris in November 1997, in *Franco-British Studies*, Nos 24–25, Autumn 1997/Spring 1998, p. 114.

2. Plutarch, *Life of Alexander*, quoted in Sergei Averintsev, 'From Biography to Hagiography', in Peter France and William St Clair eds., *Mapping Lives: the Uses of Biography*, p. 25, Oxford University Press, Oxford, 2002.
3. See Online 1911 *Encyclopedia Britannica*, 'Biography', in the 4th paragraph.
4. Quoted in Hermione Lee, *A Very Short Introduction to Biography*, p. 28, Oxford University Press, Oxford, 2009.
5. Hilary Mantel, 'The Other King', *The Guardian*, 25 April 2009.
6. Thomas Sprat, *Encyclopedia Britannica Online*, introductory paragraph. Retrieved 15 November 2009. http://www.britannica.com/EBchecked/topic/561205/Thomas-Sprat
7. Lee, *op. cit.*, p. 36.
8. Anthony Powell, Introduction to *Brief Lives and Other Selected Writings by John Aubrey*, p. x, The Cresset Press, London, 1949.
9. This analysis of the *Life of Savage*, and 'displaced autobiography' below, from Richard Holmes, 'Biography: Inventing the Truth' in John Batchelor ed., *The Art of Literary Biography*, Oxford University Press, Oxford, 1995.
10. Holmes, 'Boswell's Bicentenary', in *Sidetracks*, p. 371, HarperCollins, London, 2000.
11. Boswell, Preface to *The Life of Johnson*, quoted in *ibid.*, p. 372.
12. In 'The Proper Study?', in Peter France and William St Clair eds., *Mapping Lives*, pp. 13–14.
13. Quoted in Hermione Lee, *op. cit.*, p. 63.
14. Virginia Woolf, 'The Art of Biography', in *Collected Essays*, p. 222, Vol IV, Hogarth Press, London, 1967.
15. Lytton Strachey, Preface to *Eminent Victorians*, p. 6, Oxford World's Classics, 2003.
16. James L Clifford, Introduction to *Biography as an Art: Selected Criticism, 1560–1960*, p. xv, Oxford University Press, Oxford, 1962.
17. Robert Skidelsky, 'Only Connect', in *The Troubled Face of Biography*, ed. Eric Homberger and John Charmley, pp. 5 and 8, Macmillan, 1988.

Biography in fiction by Carole Angier

Biography is hidden in thousands of *romans à clef* and *sans clef*, in lyrical and confessional poems, in works of political satire. But it enters fiction openly in two main ways.

First, it has always appeared in the background of historical fiction, and often in the foreground, from Shakespeare's plays – for example, the *Henrys, Julius Caesar, Antony and Cleopatra* – to historical novels. Robert

Graves' *I, Claudius*, Marguerite Yourcenar's *Memoirs of Hadrian* and Mary Renault's *The King Must Die* are merely three of the many classic biographical-historical novels.

As these examples show, the traditional subjects for biographical fiction were the same as for biography: emperors and kings, national and super-national heroes and heroines. Jesus, Cleopatra, Joan of Arc, Napoleon, Elizabeth I – all have been done over and over again on the page, and even more often on stage and screen. This still continues today, especially on screen, to the point of satire (eg, *Life of Brian*, *Blackadder*.) Royals in particular are undying favourites, from Garbo's *Queen Christina* in the thirties to Judi Dench's *Mrs Brown* (the story of Queen Victoria and her servant John Brown) and most recently Helen Mirren's *The Queen*.

Like biography, however, biographical fiction has been steadily democratised. The heroes and heroines of biographical novels, plays and films of the modern age are artists, scientists, spies, sporting heroes and heroines, even animals. Somerset Maugham's *The Moon and Sixpence* and *Cakes and Ale* were based on Gauguin and Hardy respectively (though admittedly with their names changed); Penelope Fitzgerald's *The Blue Flower* was about Novalis; Stoppard's *Travesties* starred Lenin, Joyce and Tristan Tzara; Alan Bennett's *A Question of Attribution* was about Anthony Blunt (and again the Queen, played this time by Prunella Scales). Michael Frayn's *Copenhagen* was about Niels Bohr and Werner Heisenberg, and Stoppard wrote the screen plays for *Shakespeare in Love* and *The Invention of Love*, about A.E. Houseman.

In novels today, the list is endless. It should begin with Julian Barnes, whose *Flaubert's Parrot* is not only a satire of biography, and a biography of Flaubert, but a novel – like Virginia Woolf's *Orlando* of fifty years before, which was also a satire of biography, a biography of Vita Sackville West, and a novel. More recently Barnes has written *The Porcupine*, based on the Bulgarian dictator Todor Zhivkov, and *Arthur and George*, about Sir Arthur Conan Doyle. In the 1990s and 2000s we have also had Tracy Chevalier's best-selling *The Girl with a Pearl Earring*, starring Vermeer, Beryl Bainbridge's *According to Queeney*, about Dr Johnson and Hester Thrale, and two simultaneous novels about Henry James, David Lodge's *Author!*

Author! and Colm Toibin's *The Master*. And that is only in Britain. Over the years there have been Peter Carey's book about Ned Kelly, *True History of the Kelly Gang*, in Australia, C.K. Stead's *Mansfield* in New Zealand, and in the US Bruce Duffy's *The World As I Found It*, about Wittgenstein, and Evelyn Toynton's *Modern Art*, about Jackson Pollock and Lee Krasner.

On the popular front the Romans still fascinate, as in Robert Harris's thrillers *Pompeii, Imperium, Lustrum* and *Conspirata* – not to speak of Jesus and *The Da Vinci Code*. And in films we get the romantic heroes and heroines, the sports stars, the politicians, the animals. For example (a tiny selection): *Lawrence of Arabia* with Peter O'Toole; boxer movies, from *Somebody Up There Likes Me* in 1956 to *Raging Bull* in 1980 and *Ali* in 2001; musical movies like *Amadeus, Shine* and *The Pianist*; writers' movies like *Iris, Capote* and *The Hours*; ordinary hero movies, like *The Elephant Man, The Diving Bell and the Butterfly* and *A Beautiful Mind* (about the mathematician John Nash); political movies like *Gandhi, JFK, W, Frost/Nixon, Milk, Downfall*; animal movies like *Born Free, Shergar, Sea Biscuit* . . .

The enduring appeal of biographical subjects is both simple and mysterious. To writers the appeal is simple: biographical stories look like *objets trouvés* – they just need to be put between covers and the job is done. Of course this isn't true, as we've seen. Nonetheless the wealth of detail that reality offers is invaluable. Only Shakespeare could imagine a Hamlet, a Malvolio, a Lear. But any good writer can describe one.

The appeal to the audience is more mysterious; and the first person to feel that appeal is the writer. It is the appeal of the real, and we will come across it again in this book. There is a difference in your joy if a child is born in reality or in fiction, and a difference in your sorrow if one dies. However strong the effect of catharsis from an invented story, it is even stronger (*pace* Aristotle) if the story is not invented, but real. If the events are happening now, then it is no longer just a story, and the catharsis will have to wait until it is over. If it is a real story, but one – like a biography – that happened in another place or time, then that is the best kind of story to release emotion in tranquillity, to enlarge empathy and understanding.

The second way biography can enter fiction is rarer: by the use of the biographer as a character, and the biographical quest as a plot or theme.

The classic example here is Henry James, who wrote several dark stories about biographers, most famously *The Aspern Papers* (which is almost a biographical novel as well, since it is based on the real case of a scholar in pursuit of some Shelley papers). *Flaubert's Parrot* is once again a modern classic of the genre, since it is told by the obsessive Flaubert scholar Geoffrey Braithwaite; a few others are Bernard Malamud's *Dubin's Lives,* Vladimir Nabokov's *The Real Life of Sebastian Knight,* Alison Lurie's *The Truth About Lorin Jones,* and A.S. Byatt's Booker Prize-winning *Possession.* In few of these does the biographer come off well; with the exception of the last two, and of *Flaubert's Parrot,* all of which show a complex sympathy for the pursuit of the dead. But all of them prove that the biographical quest is a rich theme: an archetype of the pursuit of love, the preservation of memory and the invasion of privacy. Indeed the biographical quest is an archetype of literature itself: the attempt to imagine, even become someone else. That is why it is so well worth studying and writing biography.

Autobiography by Sally Cline

What is autobiography?

Facebook, texting and twitter alone show us that telling the world minute trivia about ourselves has become the new autobiographical mode. But autobiography is not new at all.

The word was first used by poet Robert Southey in 1809[1] but has a form that goes back to antiquity where 'autobiographies' were typically entitled 'apologia', implying as much self-justification as self-documentation. St Augustine (354–430) applied the title *Confessions* to what is probably the first autobiography in Western Europe, in which he tried to explain significant life events. In the eighteenth century Jean-Jacques Rousseau used the same title *Confessions,* initiating a chain of revelatory works sometimes known as confessional literature. Usually written in the first person, they are distinguished by intimate often hidden details of the author's life.

Contemporary confessions are written by and about people caught up in emotionally fraught or morally charged situations. With the advent of the magazine *True Stories* in 1919 a flurry of romantic confessional fiction overtook the autobiographical non-fiction. Their formula has been characterised as sin-suffer-repent which has something in common with the 'misery memoir' where the formula is besinned-against-suffer-dreadfully-tell.

But what *is* autobiography? The word's three Latin roots: autos, bios and graphe meaning self, life and writing give us writing of and by the self. Curiously the identity of the 'self' is that of author, narrator and protagonist who all share the same name. But does 'self' mean personality, identity, or the I persona? Is self female, male, child, adult? Does 'life' mean religious, sexual or entire life history? What about 'writing'? Is the writer meant to confess through writing, to rediscover a self through writing, or invent a new self through writing?

Another difficulty in defining autobiography is that it is defined not by form but by content. Indeed some autobiographers use several forms of life writing inside one book. Paul John Eakin suggests that the 'self' expressed in autobiography is a fictive construct. A fictional protagonist articulated in a quasi-fiction. Yet he also sees as autobiography's defining assumption that the story of the self refers to biographical and historical fact. One of autobiography's fascinating contradictions.

Autobiography relies on a tricky pact between writer and reader that the book is a true account. This notion of an autobiographical pact is not a contract to preserve historical exactitude about the author's life events. It is a contract between reader and author that autobiographers will commit themselves to an honest effort to understand and come to terms with their lives.

'Telling the truth about the self, constituting the self as complete subject – it is a fantasy,' says Philip Lejeune. 'In spite of the fact that autobiography is impossible, this in no way prevents it from existing.'[2] Lejeune concedes the fictive nature of the self but accepts that it goes on functioning as experiential fact. Thus the nature of autobiographical truth is in some sense a special sort of fiction: the self and truth are not factual realities which the autobiographer can rediscover but are being created by the autobiographer.[3]

If the pact which has as its supposed basis biographical truth is so hard to practice why don't we collapse 'autobiography' into other literatures under the heading 'fiction'? We don't because readers can spot autobiographers' intentions not to turn their lives into novels but to base their life stories on recollected facts and emotions.

There are real differences between autobiographers and novelists: fiction writers juggle plots, characters, context, take real settings, turn them upside down, camouflage them, make them dramatic, tell the truth backwards. To a greater extent autobiographers decide to stay within three limitations: truth as they remember it, using memory as accurately as possible, and offering facts as they were.

Obviously truth is a subjective matter. Five friends go to a party. On return each writes their version of that party. Five different stories. But there *is* the truth of authenticity. The autobiographers' pact is to be true to their authentic experience.[4] Autobiography is generally judged by dual standards: those of truth and falsity and those of artistic success.

As with biography the autobiographer must select, sift and shape. The difference is not only how much the writer remembers about the past but which particular things do they wish or not wish to recall? What we learn from an autobiography is not what actually happened but what the author remembers.

Important differences exist between autobiography and biography. Whereas biographers try to strike a balance between historical perspective and personal involvement, autobiographers tip that balance towards personal involvement. Historical background becomes roots or context. Autobiographers want a sense of intimacy with the past. Biographers choose detachment.

Distinctions between fiction and non-fiction which still hold good for biography have recently become more blurred in autobiography as authors discover that writing about themselves may not be entirely or necessarily a non-fiction adventure.

The working definition that I as an auto/biographical writer use is that of a narrative account in non-fiction prose usually written by one person that purports to depict that person's life, character and personality, especially the inner life, with immediacy and authenticity, told retrospectively.

To write autobiography we need curiosity to unravel patterns in our lives. We also need courage, as choosing to write about ourselves means that we have to come to terms with our own feelings of vulnerability and responsibility. Telling 'how it is for you' won't work unless it appears to be based on essential psychological truth. But that has to be balanced against a sense of responsibility to other people. Other lives are entwined in ours, their feelings may be hurt by our version of events.

I often wonder what Mrs Winterson, Jeanette Winterson's adoptive mother, thought about Jeanette's vividly extreme presentation of childhood events in her autobiographical novel *Oranges Are Not the Only Fruit*. Was she angry? Sad? Disappointed? Disbelieving?

Why do people write autobiographies?

Some autobiographers write from a desire to impose order and structure on random experiences. Others because autobiography is based on what the writer knows best. Disclosure can be powerful and many writers say autobiography is like therapy. But for some autobiographers omitting painful details is more important than confessing them. Eudora Welty in *One Writer's Beginnings* is silent about several distressing events in her life. She omits her pain at her ugliness, her mother's possessiveness, her constant death wish, and her enforced sad return to the South during the Depression.

Some autobiographers write from a conviction that they can tell a good story and that their life, job, or social circle makes it a story worth telling. However, some writers who *do* have good stories, feel uncomfortable when they turn the spotlight on themselves. Alexandra Kollontai, the Russian political activist, shows this discomfort in *The Autobiography of a Sexually Emancipated Communist Woman*.[5]

> *Nothing is more difficult than writing an autobiography. What should be emphasised? . . . It is advisable, above all, to write honestly . . . For if one is called upon to tell about one's life so as to make the events that made it what it became useful to the general public, it can mean only that one must have already wrought something positive in life,* accomplished a task that people recognise. *Accordingly it is a matter of forgetting that one is writing about oneself . . . so as to give an account, as objectively as possible . . . this autobiography poses a problem for me. For by looking back while prying, simultaneously, into the future, I will also be presenting to myself the most crucial turning points of my being and accomplishments. . . .* I may succeed in setting into bold relief that which concerns the women's liberation struggle . . . [6]

Because Kollontai wrote as a Communist Revolutionary as well as a Soviet diplomat and one of the earliest female ambassadors, in a country where most women amongst the Marxist revolutionaries came from the upper class, her autobiography centres around social and political changes in Russian society. She married a young military school student against parental opposition, had a baby, then separated because despite being in love she felt trapped and detached from domesticity by the revolutionary uprisings. Her story is one of politics and as a writer she notices and assesses the split between her political self and her personal self.

Where to start

Many writers start with childhood experiences. One writer who uses childhood effectively is the African-American writer and poet Maya Angelou in *I Know Why the Caged Bird Sings.*[7]

This coming-of-age story about Angelou's early years illustrates how strength of character and love of literature can help fight racism and trauma. The protagonist, Maya, has been called a symbolic character for every black girl growing up in America. The book explores women's lives in a white male dominated society characterised by abuse, confused identity and low level literacy.

The book starts in the 1930s when Maya, three, and her older brother are sent to Stamps, Arkansas to live with their grandmother. It ends when Maya becomes a mother herself aged only seventeen. The scene where at eight Maya is raped by her mother's lover overwhelms the book and rape is used throughout the text as a metaphor for the suffering of her race.

The protagonist starts as a deeply-scarred victim of racism who transforms herself into a self-confident young woman. She successfully seized the power of words in her quest for independence and dignity.

Angelou starts by recalling the emotions she had during her early years. It is a childhood church scene.

> 'What are you looking at me for?
> I didn't come to stay . . .'
> I hadn't so much forgot as I couldn't bring myself to
> remember. Other things were more important.
>   'What are you looking at me for?
> I didn't come to stay . . .'
> Whether I could remember the rest of the poem or not was
> immaterial. . . .
> The children's section of the Colored Methodist Episcopal
> Church was wiggling and giggling over my well-known
> forgetfulness.[8]

The emotions Angelou conjures up in this scene include humiliation, anger, frustration and above all a feeling of not belonging to that community. Later in the chapter Angelou sums up those feelings:

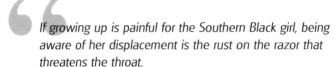

If growing up is painful for the Southern Black girl, being aware of her displacement is the rust on the razor that threatens the throat.
It is an unnecessary insult.   *(p. 6.)*

Reviewers sometimes categorise *Caged Bird* as autobiographical fiction but the prevailing critical view sees it as autobiography, a genre Angelou attempts to critique and expand.

History and development of contemporary autobiographies

The explosion of modern autobiographies in the UK came as a result of the growth of three movements: the sixties; the Confessionalist Literature Movement, The Women's Movement (seventies/eighties) which with its tenet of 'The Personal Is Political' focused on exploration of suppressed female selves and voices; and the Gay Movement (seventies/eighties) which gradually revealed its cloistered sexual selves. These intense hidden experiences led to outpourings about incest, violence against women, and homophobic abuse.

Confessionalist literature in the sixties was a literary movement in which the dominant feature was the use of the writers' most extreme life experiences as literary material. This grew out of the confluence of the Beats (Burroughs, Corso, Ginsberg, Kerouac) on the West Coast of USA, and Robert Lowell, Elizabeth Bishop, Randall Jarrell and John Berryman, who represented the East Coast poetry establishment.

Autobiographies in the UK, once the testimonies of straight white male middleclass authors, now include many fine feminist black and gay autobiographies. Autobiographical theory was similarly discriminatory until Julia Swindell's research team began to redress the balance in a pioneering study, *The Uses of Autobiography* in 1995.[9]

Autobiography in USA has developed from a non-literary form of record keeping to its current literary form characterised by a mixture of fiction and non-fiction.

In the Colonial period, autobiographers invented myths often to validate specific religious or nationalistic goals. Puritan spiritual autobiographies abounded. Highly characteristic in terms of illustrating conversion from sin was the early Puritan autobiography *My Birth and Life* of Thomas Shepard. Like Puritan autobiographies, Quaker versions, such as the *Journal of John Woolman,* which focused on living a Quaker life in New England rather than on conversion, influenced later autobiographies. Benjamin Franklin's *Autobiography* which borrowed from both traditions though secular allowed him to narrate his personal life within the metaphor of the life of America.

From spiritual autobiographies came the slave narrative and the Indian captivity narrative. Slave accounts such as *Narrative of the Life of Frederick Douglass, an American Slave, Written by Himself* and Harriet Jacobs' *Incidents in the Life of a Slave Girl, Written by Herself* show successful escapes from American slavery and were originally intended as propaganda by abolitionists.

Indian captivity narratives often showed white settlers having wild adventures, but who when captured by 'savages' showed their spiritually superiority.

Taking their lead from spiritual autobiographies, both Indian captivity accounts and slave narratives focused on life before and after spiritual conversion. So popular were slave and Indian captivity narratives that fictional versions soon appeared. James Fenimore Cooper's *The Last of the Mohicans* developed from captivity accounts which in turn led to Westerns where exotic Indians capture and torture the whites. Slave narratives were used in conjunction with the sentimental novel in such fictionalised versions as Harriet Beecher Stowe's *Uncle Tom's Cabin.*

Critic Timothy Dow Adams points to several twentieth century black autobiographies, influenced by captivity and slave accounts, which emulate the same basic structure: the physical and mental torture of slavery then escape to the North, followed by spiritual conversion and finally rebirth as an individual. In *The Autobiography of Malcolm X* where he tells his story to Alex Haley, the relationship between the two men shows the slave narrative's typical ambiguity about authorship.

Classical and contemporary American autobiographies have in common the ideal of the autobiographer telling their tale as an example of the value of the individual life in a democracy.

Are all autobiographies written by their subjects?

No. Some autobiographies are based on interviews with a professional writer either when subjects are alive or even after death. *The Autobiography of Malcolm X* was published 1965 after the black Muslim activist had been assassinated. His collaborator, journalist Alex Haley, based the book on Haley's taped interviews during the years 1963–65.

Angel on My Shoulder (2000) and two other autobiographies by singer Natalie Cole were co-written with literary critic Digby Diehl.

There are interesting generic problems in Gertrude Stein's *The Autobiography of Alice B. Toklas* where Stein projects her autobiographical persona through the supposed writing by her lifetime companion Alice Toklas. Here Stein's game with the readers is to write her own life story by pretending to write that of Alice. There is a double layer of fun as Toklas's decision appears to be to write a biography of Gertrude rather than a story about herself.

Many autobiographies of celebrities are written by ghost writers.[10] Some ghosts, as their name suggests, remain invisible. Others, many well-established authors, have recently become highly visible. Two of the best known are Hunter Davies, biographer of The Beatles and Rebecca Farnworth the 'voice' of Katie Price. Davies, whose six ghostly successes include autobiographies of footballers Dwight Yorke – *Born to score*, Paul Gascoigne – *Gazza: My Story*, and *Wayne Rooney: My Story So Far*, as well as John Prescott's 2008 *Prezza: My Story: Pulling No Punches*, said he felt like a ventriloquist trying to capture the person's character. Davies doesn't necessarily use the person's exact words but concentrates on ensuring the phrases and style to accord with their received image.

Rebecca Farnworth who ghosted Katie Price's bestselling *Being Jordan*, *Angel*, and *Angel Uncovered* said she had to create a direct unflinchingly honest authentic voice for Price. She says she has to think herself into Price's head, put her own ego onto the back burner and 'go into empathy overdrive'.[11]

Few ghosts crave their names on covers. Pepsy Dening who ghosted Fern Britton's autobiography, *Fern: My Story* and Sharon Osbourne's *Extreme: My Autobiography* said she never thinks of her ghosted books as her own. She sees her role as that of a midwife bringing into the world something that already exists. She pointed to the problem that occurs in both biographies and autobiographies where people who have long been in the public eye prefer to recycle tired anecdotes than think up fresh words. Pepsy removes her subjects from their comfort zone cutting though easy laughs or PR veneer and persuades them to delve into what made them who they are.[12]

Notes

1. *The Quarterly Review.*
2. Philip Lejeune, 'The Autobiographical Pact [bis]' in *On Autobiography*, pp. 131–32, ed. Paul John Eakin, University of Minnesota Minneapolis, 1981.
3. Some post-structuralists similarly argue that autobiography is neither non-fiction nor referential but is a type of writing that uses a constructed self's life as a narrative.
4. Timothy Dow Adams in *The Continuum Encyclopaedia of American Literature*, p. 62, ed. Steven R. Serafin, Continuum, New York, 2003.
5. Alexandra Kollontai, *The Autobiography of a Sexually Emancipated Communist Woman*, 1926, translated by Salvator Attansio, Herder and Herder, New York, 1971.
6. Kollontai, p. 3 in 1973 ed. The sentences in italics were crossed out in galley proofs and left out in her time. They were later reinstated.
7. Maya Angelou, *I Know Why the Caged Bird Sings*, Random House, USA 1969 Vol. 1 of 6 of autobiography.
8. Virago ed, 2007, p. 3.
9. Julia Swindells (ed), *The Uses of Autobiography*, Taylor and Francis, London, 1995.
10. Several esteemed politicians, military experts and lawyers have enlisted help from ghosts. Barr McClellan, ex-presidential attorney, and father of the former White House Press Secretary Scott McClellan, wrote his autobiography *Blood, Money and Power*, with expert ghostly guidance. Frank Camper, veteran military intelligence operative, himself an author, worked alongside a ghost to produce *The Mk/Ultra Secret.*
11. www.guardian.co.uk/books/2008/ghostwriters-celebrity-jordan
12. The cost of getting your book ghosted varies depending on the book's proposed length, the number of months agreed for completion and the reputation of the ghost writer. One of New York's most reputable agencies provides a three hundred page manuscript completed in three to six months at a starting fee of $15,500. Auto/biographies that require financial or business knowledge cost between $35,000 and $50,000. On the web ghosting services for autobiographies and memoirs cost around $50 or £30 per double spaced page.

Autobiographical writing in other genres by Sally Cline

Changes

Autobiographical material has catapulted into novels, stories, poems, non-fiction, even fictional 'autobiographies'. By the end of the twentieth century differences between autobiography and autobiographical novels were becoming hard to distinguish as fiction writers drew extensively on their life experiences.

James Weldon Johnson's novel *The Autobiography of an Ex-Colored Man* is a famous early example. In 1912 Johnson anonymously published his only novel purporting to be the autobiography of the pale skinned illegitimate son of an African-American mother and a white father. When the school principal publicly called the boy 'colored' he reacted to the instant discrimination by embracing his black mother's identity and becoming a famous black musician. Later, having become uneasy with his choice, he travelled South, witnessed a lynching then changed his name, abandoned his mother's race, married a white woman, had two children and submerged himself into the white kingdom. When Knopf republished the book under the author's name in 1927 reviewers and readers so often mistook it for autobiography that in 1933 Johnson felt forced to write a non-fiction life story called *Along This Way.*[1]

Autobiographical novels

Graham Greene offered a useful hint to new autobiographical novelists: make use of your experiences, write autobiographically but always change one thing. That starts the transition from pure autobiography to fiction. One small alteration will move to another.

A useful distinction is between autobiographical novels based strictly on the life of the author, with a plot line that mirrors events in the author's life and semi autobiographical novels, only loosely based on the author's life. Motives behind semi-autobiographical novels may be to protect the privacy of friends, family, colleagues or to achieve emotional distance from the subject. It also avoids inventing complex plot lines. Neither semi- nor fully autobiographical fiction pretends to be exact truth as names and places are changed, events recreated to increase drama; and unlike autobiography there is no requirement to fulfil the autobiographical pact.

Thomas Wolfe's first novel *Look Homeward, Angel* (1929) is considered autobiographical. Hero Eugene Gant is believed to be Wolfe; the setting, Altamont, Catawba, a fictional town and state, mirrors precisely Wolfe's hometown Asheville, North Carolina. The stone statue of an angel looking East found in Hendersonville NC was part of the book's inspiration. Wolfe's descriptions of family and Ashville community are so thinly veiled that the novel's success resulted in Wolfe's estrangement from many in his hometown.

Siri Hustvedt's radically postmodern *The Sorrows of an American* (2008), also semi-autobiographical, deals with the troubles of a Norwegian American family in which psychiatrist Erik Davidsen has a sudden identity crisis.[2] Underlying themes focus on loss and grief, art and madness, mind and spirit, and the construction of the self. Hustvedt's autobiographical blending of fiction and non-fiction gives coherence to a life. The author, of Norwegian descent though born and raised in Minnesota, uses passages from her own deceased father's actual journal about the Depression in America and his experiences as a soldier in World War Two in the fictional memoir attributed to psychiatrist Erik's father. One question which constantly occupies Hustvedt: 'Why do we become who we are?' is a significant one for all autobiographers.

Paul Auster and Philip Roth are novelists obsessed with the construction of reality and how barriers break down between what is lived and what is written and read.

Auster, enmeshed in material about how identity is constructed through the medium of stories, believes like J.G. Ballard that 'we live inside an enormous novel.'[3] He is always present in his fiction, through which he filters his own life. Authors are his constant characters; the significance of writing a repetitive theme. Sometimes Auster uses his own name or that of Siri, his wife; often he uses autobiographical locations. Auster lives in a Brooklyn brownstone, so does Sidney Orr in *Oracle Night* (2004). In *City of*

Glass (1985), *The New York Trilogy's* first story where a crime novelist assumes disguises, the protagonist Quinn pretends to be a private detective called Paul Auster who has a wife called Siri. Quinn (or Auster?) appears again as a detective in *The Locked Room* (1986), *The New York Trilogy's* third story, a tale of a biographer who assumes the identity of his missing subject's life.

In his political novel *Leviathan* (1992) the wife's name is Iris a rearrangement of the letters of Siri. On the back jacket of *Leviathan* the protagonist is deliberately misnamed Paul (after Auster) though inside 'Paul' is called Peter.

In Auster's landscape, a menacing metaphysical territory of puzzles and games, characters explore Hammett's idea that people can disappear from one life to reinvent themselves in another.

Philip Roth, a brilliant political satirist, with a violent phallocentric world view, is a novelist who purposefully blurs the edges between fiction and autobiography. He famously claimed that 'making fake biography, false history, concocting a half-imaginary existence out of the actual drama of my life is my life'.[4] He steadfastly views his life as a Jew and an American as an integral part of his fiction. His Jewish background in Newark, New Jersey with his parents Herman and Bessie Roth feature controversially in his fiction, his mother as the overbearing Sophie in *Portnoy's Complaint* (1969) and his elderly father as the inspiration for *Patrimony* (1991).

In his breakthrough third novel *Portnoy's Complaint*, which sold 400,000 hardback copies and made Roth a literary star, the protagonist masturbates so persistently that fellow novelist Jacqueline Susann famously remarked: 'I'd like to meet him, but I wouldn't want to shake his hand'. Subsequent works go further than simple autobiography in exploring the relationship between character and creator as well as issues such as family, community, Communism, the McCarthy witch hunts, Judaism, male sexual desire, ageing, and death.

Roth's 1974 mock-autobiography *My Life as a Man*, in two sections, features in part one Roth's surrogate protagonist (who appears as character/narrator in many Roth novels) randy Jewish novelist Nathan Zuckerman. Like Roth, Zuckerman shot to fame with a scandalous sexually explicit bestseller with a mightily similar plot to Portnoy. Zuckerman allows Roth to write about his own emotions and intellectual life without using precise autobiography. When asked about his literary alter egos Roth said: 'Am I Roth or Zuckerman? It's all me . . . Nothing is me'.[5]

Part two of this fake autobiography focuses on fictional author Peter Tarnopol who in an autobiographical narrative *My True Story* says he is the inventor of Nathan Zuckerman. Roth's 1987 novel *The Counterlife* validates this misleading statement by stating that Zuckerman is a literary character invented by writer Peter Tarnopol. Confusion is added in *The Counterlife* when Zuckerman appears to die of a heart attack only to be reincarnated in subsequent books.

Peter Tarnopol's wife and nemesis Maureen Tarnopol is based on Roth's first wife, Margaret Martinson, whom Roth said had tricked him into marriage and who died in a car crash in 1968. In 1990 Roth married the British actress Clare Bloom who had been his companion since the seventies. Five years later the couple split up so acrimoniously that Bloom wrote a memoir *Leaving A Doll's House* (1996) in which she describes a terrifying marriage in which Roth is a controlling misogynist monster who forced Bloom's eighteen year old daughter out of the house because her conversation bored him. Roth, unable to sit down quietly under criticism, retaliated with *I Married A Communist* (1998). Here the Bloom character becomes actress Eve Frame who ruins her husband's life by writing a confessional autobiography.

Roth himself appears both as protagonist and narrator in several novels. In *The Plot Against America* (2004) Roth the character suffers as a Jew in this alternate history where pilot Charles Lindberg is thirty third President of a Fascist USA.

Roth devotes four books (*The Facts*, 1988; *Deception*, 1990; *Patrimony*, 1991; and *Operation Shylock*, 1993) to exploring the relationship between the lived and written worlds, or 'fact' and 'fiction'. In all four his protagonist, the character 'Philip Roth', questions the genres of autobiography and fiction, and mischievously invites readers to become entangled in his literary game. He labels *Deception* a novel, calls *The Facts* autobiography, decides *Patrimony* is memoir or 'true story', and delineates *Operation*

Shylock as a confession. According to *Shylock*, the real Roth had a mental breakdown in the eighties, in the book the fictional Roth meets a doppelganger The Other Philip Roth who claims to be the author.

The Facts purports to be an unconventional autobiography of a writer who reshapes the idea of fiction revealing the constant interplay between life and art. Roth wished to explore boundaries between life and craft and create 'serious mischief' with this 'novelist's autobiography'. With another sleight of hand he gives readers a unique slant on autobiography by topping and tailing this invented 'factual account' with a letter to the fictional Nathan Zuckerman asking for Zuckerman's take on Roth's work at the start and Zuckerman's reply at the end.

Roth writes to Zuckerman: 'Memories of the past are not memories of facts but memories of your imaginings of the facts. There is something naïve about a novelist like myself talking about presenting himself "undisguised" and depicting "a life without the fiction".' Searching through his past may have been a 'kind of therapy'. He believes that 'you search out your past to discover which events have led you to asking those specific questions. It isn't that you subordinate your ideas to the force of facts in autobiography but that you construct a sequence of stories to bind up the facts with a persuasive hypothesis that unravels your history's meaning'.

Zuckerman's reply Roth is candid: 'I've read your manuscript twice . . . Don't publish . . . you are far better off writing about me than "accurately" reporting your own life'. Zuckerman feels that Roth is still as much in need of him as he is of Roth. 'That I need you is indisputable . . . I am your permission, your indiscretion, the key to disclosure . . . In the fiction you can be so much more truthful without worrying all the time about causing direct pain.'[6]

Autobiography in creative non-fiction

Many imaginative non-fiction writers scatter autobiographical passages through their work. To my surprise I discovered I did it all the time. Having said firmly there was no way I would write an autobiography, I now realise that if some patient soul unpicked every confessional passage from my ten books they would have the bones of just such a work. I appear to have constant themes: food, feminism, loss, the writing process, versions of reality, solitude and death. My mother's death wound its way into a book about solitude and celibacy. My poetry-writing childhood inserted itself into a book about women's relationship to dying. A Passover trauma in my Jewish adolescence lurks in a book about women and food. The love of my life infiltrates the novel I am currently writing. I have even managed to insert myself into all my 'detached' biographies. The only person this has surprised is me. Evidence leads me to suggest that if you are at heart an autobiographer nothing will stop you from telling part of your own story.

Autobiographical poetry

Several twentieth century confessional poets in the 50s and 60s wrote autobiographical poetry which revealed intensely personal often painful emotions. They trafficked in intimate or lewd details of their sexuality, illnesses, depressions, and death wishes. Poets included Sylvia Plath (*Ariel*) and Anne Sexton (*To Bedlam and Part Way Back, All My Pretty Ones,* and *The Death Notebooks*) who had both taken several of Robert Lowell's Harvard poetry classes. *The Birthday Letters* by Plath's husband Ted Hughes is similarly autobiographical in tone and similarly coded.

The term 'confessional' was used in 1959 by reviewer M.L. Rosenthal in a critique of Lowell's *Life Studies* subtitled 'Poetry as Confession'. Rosenthal suggested that earlier poets had shown tendencies towards extremes of autobiography but always behind a mask. Lowell removed that mask. It was hard not to think of *Life Studies* except as a series of . . . some critics said shameful . . . private confidences.

Other confessional poets, who lived at the edge and wrote about their experiences, included Theodore Roethke, Allen Ginsberg, Jack Kerouac, William Burroughs, William Snodgrass, and John Berryman. Of this intense group three committed suicide: Sylvia Plath in 1963, Anne Sexton in 1971, and John Berryman in 1972.

What defines hyper-autobiographical poetry is not the subject but how poets' personal lives are explored. Confessional poetry eschews modesty and discretion.

As Ginsberg wrote in his 1955 poem *Howl* '[To] stand before you speechless and intelligent and shaking with shame, rejected yet confessing out the soul to conform to the rhythm of thought in his naked and endless head . . .' Had Samuel Taylor Coleridge looked into the future and heard Ginsberg he might have been amused – in February 1797 Coleridge wrote to Thomas Poole: 'I could inform the dullest author how he might write an interesting book – let him relate the events of his own life with honesty – not disguising the feelings that accompanied them.'[7]

Exploitation

Confessional material, in poetry or prose, can lead to exploitation. Writers often say that this is due to 'the splinter of ice' in every writer's soul.

There is a revealing interchange of letters about this problem between Lowell and Elizabeth Bishop.[8]

Lowell, who had been married to writer Elizabeth Hardwick since 1949, left her in 1970 for the British author Lady Caroline Blackwood. Hardwick wrote anguished letters to him during his absence in London with Caroline. Three years later Lowell used those letters in his Pulitzer prize-winning poetry collection *The Dolphin*. Lowell mixed fact and fiction, changed some letters to suit his purposes and exploited his relationship with Hardwick. His poet friend Bishop, despite conceding *The Dolphin* was 'magnificent' poetry, was so appalled by his actions that she wrote to him quoting a line from Thomas Hardy about the way in which mixing fact and fiction can cause 'infinite mischief'.[9] Bishop wrote, 'It is not being "gentle" to use personal, tragic, anguished letters that way – it's cruel'. She points out 'Lizzie is not dead' . . . and 'you have *changed* her letters. That is "infinite mischief" . . . One can use one's life as material . . . but these letters, aren't you violating a trust? . . . *art just isn't worth that much*'.[10]

This was not the first problem concerning autobiographical exploitation between Lowell and Bishop. An earlier incident had Bishop as the victim. In 1953 she published a highly autobiographical story, 'In the Village', in

The New Yorker. In 1962 she received a typescript of Lowell's new book of poems *For the Union Dead* which included a poem called 'The Scream'. That poem used and misused Bishop's entire autobiographical story. Lowell went ahead and published it in 1964.

A surprisingly mature and dispassionate view of what might have been seen as exploitation has been taken by Dame Joan Bakewell about the clandestine affair she had with Harold Pinter for seven years between 1962 and 1969 (during his turbulent marriage to actress Vivien Merchant and hers to the BBC's then Head of Plays Michael Bakewell) which was suddenly and dramatically made public by Pinter. After their affair had ended, Pinter wrote a stage play *Betrayal* in which their sexual relationship was only thinly disguised. When Bakewell was interviewed on 15 August 2009 by Kirsty Young on BBC Radio 4's *Desert Island Discs* she said that though at the time it had been a 'great shock' she felt immediately that she should 'get over my shock and live with it'. Earlier in *The New Statesman* in 2003 she wrote that seeing the play had been two experiences: 'pleasure at a brilliant and amusing play and heartache at the retelling of events from my own life'.

Because Bakewell's affair with Pinter had developed from a long friendship which continued for years after their romance was over she felt their friendship was more important than his dramatic betrayal. She said Pinter wanted her so much to understand his play, talk about his play, love his play, that finally she tried to do just that. All these years later she looks back on the affair and even on the incident with a great deal of pleasure. 'I smile when I think about it.' I smiled when I read her brilliant memoir.[11]

Notes
1. Da Cappo Press/Viking Penguin, 1933.
2. Siri Hustvedt, *The Sorrows of an American.* Henry Holt, New York, 2008.
3. J.G. Ballard, Introduction to his novel *Crash.*
4. Stephen Amidon, The Times on Line, From *The Sunday Times,* 23 September 2007.
5. Ibid.
6. Quotes taken from Vern Wiessner's review of *The Facts: A Novelist's Autobiography.* On Bookreporter.com
7. The Complete Works of Samuel Taylor Coleridge, Volume iii, 1854, p. 601.

8. Thomas Travisano & Saskia Hamilton, eds, *Words in Air: The Complete Correspondence Between Elizabeth Bishop and Robert Lowell 2008.*
9. Thomas Hardy letter, 1911.
10. Elizabeth Bishop, *One Art: Letters,* pp. 561–62, selected & edited by Robert Giroux, Farrar Straus Giroux, New York, 1994.
11. Joan Bakewell, *The Centre of the Bed,* Hodder and Stoughton, London, 2003.

Memoir 1 by Carole Angier

It is a perennial problem in life writing of all kinds that the easiest books to sell, to both public and publishers, are about (or by) famous people. Life writers have regularly regretted this and tried to change it, but without much success (with the exception of Alexander Masters: see his piece on this subject in Part Two). We have campus novels, and novels set in trains, offices, hotels (plenty of those). But can we imagine the memoir of a lecturer, a commuter, a hotel-worker? Only if it is about much more than lecturing or commuting or hotel-working; only, in fact, if it is as interesting as a novel. And of course there are memoirs as interesting as novels, for example, Orwell's *Down and Out in Paris and London,* partly set in a hotel kitchen; or (sticking to kitchens) Anthony Bourdain's *Kitchen Confidential.*

But the point about *Kitchen Confidential* – or *How I Lived On Just a Pound a Day,* in which Kath Kelly does just that, or *A Round-Heeled Woman: My Late-life Adventures in Sex and Romance,* in which Jane Juska has as much sex as she can in her late sixties – is that they may be about ordinary people, but they are not about ordinary experiences. And that is true of most memoirs. If they are not about famous people, they are about people who are special in some other way – because they work in a high-pressure environment and take drugs, or have masses of sex when they're old; or because they've sailed around the world, passed for white (or black), been a spy, a hostage, a trader who lost millions of pounds.

There is one exception: an ordinary life lived in a distant time or place. There was, for example, *The Country Diary of an Edwardian Lady,* a publishing phenomenon of the late 1970s and early 80s: unremarkable in itself, it became a best-seller for years, because it had (as it said on the cover) 'the nostalgic charm of a vanished world'. Or take, for example, the famous *Diary of Samuel Pepys*. That is remarkable in itself. But what makes it precious is the way it speaks to us across time: the way it makes us feel that someone so long dead was truly, tangibly alive.

Edmund White captures the reason for the specialness of memoirs in Part Two. Fictional characters, he says, are always to some extent representative: because they are not real, they can stand for more than themselves. Whereas, just because the characters in memoirs are real, they cannot stand for anything other than themselves; they are stubbornly, irreducibly individual.

Thus, apart from bad reasons (the lust for celebrity, for example), there is also a good reason why memoirs of ordinary, non-famous people are hard to sell. The ordinary is too stubbornly real to be used for art. Only when it is removed from every-day reality, so that people can see it as representative, evocative – only then is it art. So Duchamp's toilet is art, but my toilet is just a toilet; so Adrian Mole's Diary is a book, but mine is just a diary.

Our taste for celebrity and sensation, then, is not the only reason why most biographies and autobiographies are of famous people, and most memoirs of special, even extreme experiences – abused children, extreme sports, wars, massacres and genocides. There is a good reason too, or at any rate an objective one. Memoirs avoid ordinary reality because it is not easy to use for art; it is not easy to see its significance beyond itself. That is why the typical memoir recreates an extra-ordinary person or place, a special time, event or experience.

Travel and adventure

Travellers' tales have been popular ever since Marco Polo's *Il milione* appeared in 1298. And travel writing has always been supreme in English, from Sir Richard Burton in the nineteenth century and Freya Stark in the early twentieth, through Robert Byron and Bruce Chatwin to contemporaries like Jonathan Raban and Paul Theroux. Travel produces the sense of newness so important for writing; and movement alone, it seems, is friendly to ideas. Wordsworth never went on one of his gargantuan walks without his notebook. In Part Two, Alain de Botton notes that 'Journeys are the midwives of books', and that the best writing place for him is on a train. For me, it's walking downhill. Not uphill, which is hard work; but on the way down, thoughts flow.

Travel books are a species of memoir, because they are non-fiction accounts of personal experience. But in bookshops and encyclopedias travel writing mostly appears as a genre on its own, like thrillers or science fiction. And that is right too. For of all memoirs, travel writing is the closest to other kinds. War memoirs stick to wars, childhood memoirs to childhood; but travellers' tales can tell anything about anyone, provided only that it happens away from home. Other types of memoir are quite often by people who haven't written before, like Anthony Bourdain or Jane Juska. Whereas dozens of great novelists wrote travel books – Fielding and Smollett, Dickens and Trollope, D.H. Lawrence and Henry James, among others. The point of literary travel writing is not the travel but the writing.

Travel has always been intimately connected to literature, for example in the *Odyssey*, in Dante's travels through *Inferno* and *Paradiso*, in *Pilgrim's Progress*; and in the central trope of myth and fairy tale, the journey of the hero to seek his fortune or goal. The earliest picaresque novels are journeys, and so are many other classics, such as *Robinson Crusoe*, *Gulliver's Travels* or *Pickwick Papers*. The journey is our most common metaphor for all stories, and since Dante, for life itself; when Carlyle asked if all fictional narratives were not disguised biographies, he might just as aptly have said 'disguised journeys'.

The novelist is a traveller in his own land, and the only difference between a novel and a traveller's tale is that the latter is meant to be true. But in fact we all know that travellers' tales, like those of fishermen, are likely to involve dramatisations at least, and we don't mind. Travel writing is not fiction; and especially if it has a political aim, like Rebecca West's *Black Lamb and Grey Falcon* about Yugoslavia, it must be careful not to distort. Nonetheless, of all life writing, memoir is closest to the freedom of fiction, and travel writing is the closest of all. That is probably why travel writing is the most popular genre after fiction, and the most fun to write. If you ever feel blocked in your writing, take a trip somewhere; or at least go for long walks (as much as possible, downhill!)

Travel is often testing, but that is not usually the point of the story. And then there are 'idyll memoirs', like Peter Mayle's popular books on Provence, or more complex dreams of peace such as Laurens van der Post's *Lost World of the Kalahari* or Sara Maitland's recent *Book of Silence*. When we turn, however, to adventure memoirs, the idylls disappear, and we are firmly in the heartland of memoir: the trying and testing experience.

Taste comes into all reading, and I must admit to being bored to death by accounts of sailing around the world (or still worse, rowing). Even polar exploration is not my thing, though Apsley Cherry-Garrard's *The Worst Journey in the World* – the story of Scott's expedition to the Antarctic – is one of greatest adventure stories ever written. The only extreme adventure that interests me is mountaineering; but it will stand, I hope, for the rest.

The most famous Victorian mountaineer was Edward Whymper, whose *Scrambles Amongst the Alps* (1871) perfectly captures the amateur atmosphere of those early times. Today mountaineering is professionalised, the latest technology replacing Whymper's hemp ropes and leather boots. But the challenges remain the same. They are partly technical, and one of the pleasures of reading *Scrambles Amongst the Alps*, or a modern equivalent like Joe Simpson's *Touching the Void* (1988), is to be thrown into a new language – pitons and crampons, couloirs, cornices and flutings. There are also the heart-stopping dramas – the inching over icefields and balancing over thousand-foot drops, with only one thin rope between life and death, victory and oblivion. But these are not the point of mountain memoirs, or of the other kinds of adventure either. The point is partly spiritual: a reminder of the glory of the natural world, which we forget as easily as the fragility of life in the concrete convenience of cities. But even more, the point is moral. The key event in both Whymper's book and Simpson's, a hundred years later, is the same – the moment when one or more climbers slip, and the others have to decide what to do: to try, impossibly, to save their companions, or to cut the rope and save themselves.

In *Scrambles Amongst the Alps*, four people fell and three survived, including Whymper; his account has the rope snapping naturally, but the suspicion that it was cut hung over him ever after. In *Touching the Void* it is Simpson himself who slips, but who against all the odds survives to tell the tale – not only of his own miraculous escape, but of the battle of fellow-climber Simon Yates with his conscience, when he finally cut the rope, and lived for days with the belief that Joe had died.

At their heart, these mountain memoirs are like the memoirs of war to which we are about to turn: they are about the dilemma of ordinary morality in extraordinary circumstances, and whether we can ask of human beings in such circumstances that they continue to obey its rules. We know we can't, but feel we must; and so do they. This conflict will never be resolved, but will give birth to books forever. Some will border on sensationalism (accounts of cannibalism among the survivors of air crashes, for example); but many will be good or even great books, like Whymper's and Simpson's, and all will be worth reading and writing. The most important questions are the ones to which there is no final answer.

War and Holocaust

Ever since World War One, war memoirs have had one aim, to tell the truth: the pity, not the glory, of war. The model is no longer Horace's *Dulce et decorum est pro patria mori*, but *Goodbye to All That*, Robert Graves' famous memoir of the Great War.

One memoir of World War Two took the cause of truth a step further: to tell what really happens in war not to men, but to women. This was a step too far. *A Woman in Berlin*, an account of the mass rape of the city's women by Soviet troops in April and May 1945, was not published until 1954 in English, and in the original German only five years later. In Germany it was met with hostility and denial, and disappeared. It was finally republished nearly fifty years later, in 2003: only after the death of its author, and still, according to her wish, anonymously.

A Woman in Berlin is mercilessly honest. We see how people get used to anything, how they adapt and survive. After the first horror, the women quickly realise that if they accept one 'protector', they will be saved from the rest. They share their shame, they talk about it openly, even their language changes. Only their men cannot change, and the women feel sorry for them. 'Among the many defeats at the end of this war,' the author writes, ' is the defeat of the male sex.' No wonder her book was hated for fifty years. Honesty is the best policy in memoir-writing, but also the costliest.

Many Holocaust memoirs are masterpieces: masterpieces of childhood memory, like Aharon Appelfeld's *The Story of a Life* and Elie Wiesel's *Night*; of story, like Imre Kertész's *Fatelessness* and Béla Zsolt's *Nine Suitcases*; of savage honesty, like Tadeusz Borowski's *This Way for the Gas, Ladies and Gentlemen*; of reflection, like Primo Levi's *If This Is a Man*. To me the most important is Levi's, because it confronts the question of all such memoirs directly, as its title shows. The question is: What do these terrible events reveal about the nature of man? Is our true nature exposed in Auschwitz, is morality a sham? And Levi's answer is: No. Though it is weak, and cannot survive in such extreme conditions, our true nature is moral. Seeing men reduced to beasts reveals precisely that that is not what they are. Dante was right: *You were not made to live like beasts/ But to pursue virtue and knowledge*. This is what Levi salvages from the horror of Auschwitz, and why his book is both unsparing and uplifting at the same time. It is also a literary masterpiece, full of unforgettable characters and scenes, carefully crafted to explore his great question. Some people and scenes that didn't fit this purpose he kept back, and put into the stories called *Moments of Reprieve*: which shows (if it still needs showing) that even when every word of a book is true, it can still conform to an artistic vision.

Frauds, fakes and fiction

The most famous fraud of recent years is James Frey's addiction memoir, *A Million Little Pieces*, first published in 2003. Interestingly, no one ever suggested that Frey was not an addict, or that his treatment was not as he described. Two main charges have been made against him: first, that he makes himself out to have been a tough guy with a police record, when really he was just a college boy with a habit; and second that he makes a helpless drama out of his girlfriend's suicide, when in fact he was not in jail at the time, as he claimed, and so could have rushed to her side. The (almost certainly) fake episode that caused the most outrage of all was one in which he has to have root-canal treatment without anaesthetic, because his drug-ravaged body won't tolerate it.

The suicide story, with its false claim that he was in jail when it happened, is a clear case of false representation, and Frey's exploitation of the death for drama and sympathy is distasteful. But the other inventions, or exaggerations, are less central to the story; in the case of the root-canal operation, not central at all. So do they really matter? Should they have made the disastrous difference they did to Frey's reputation, and the reputation of his book?

I think they should. The key relationship between writer and reader is trust; and if trust is broken in any part of a book, it is broken for all of it. It may even be broken for all books of the same kind: so that Frey may have damaged not only his own reputation, but (at least for a time) that of memoirs in general. Oprah Winfrey apologised for angrily exposing him on television; but I am not sure the right person apologised.

In the last twenty-five years there have been at least three fake Lives: Julian Barnes' classic *Flaubert's Parrot* (1984), Alain de Botton's *Kiss and Tell* (1995) and William Boyd's *Nat Tate* (1998). *Flaubert's Parrot* and *Kiss and Tell* wore their falseness on their sleeves, and their readers laughed at biography together with their writers. *Nat Tate* went further: fooling its readers as well, and including readers' belief in its satire.

Or rather, it half fooled its readers, or half tried to. The book included dozens of pictures, and testimonies from David Bowie, Gore Vidal, and Picasso's biographer John Richardson; all Tate's fellow-artists were real members of the New York School of the 50s and 60s; and Bowie, Vidal and Richardson all attended the launch, talking of the artist and his work. On the other hand, there were plenty of clues. The artist's name was a compendium of the *National* and *Tate* Galleries. The launch party was held on April Fool's Day. And the source of most of Boyd's information was an obscure writer called Logan Mountstuart, whose journals Boyd said he was editing, and would publish in 1999. As it turned out, they weren't published until three years later, but at that point the game would have been up anyway (in fact it was rumbled straight away, by *The Independent*):

Logan Mountstuart was a fictional character, and his 'journals' were Boyd's 2002 novel, *Any Human Heart*.

I hope Boyd enjoyed the joke. He took care to make it harmless, and it is useful to us. A portrait may never be one hundred per cent accurate; but *Nat Tate* shows that if it is zero per cent accurate – if it corresponds to nothing at all – it isn't a portrait. So, if someone says that a book is a portrait, and as a result we believe its subject exists, we are not being foolish, or insufficiently postmodern; we just understand English.

Where, finally, does the work of W.G. Sebald fit? Not so much his last book, *Austerlitz*, which was declaratively a novel; or *Vertigo* and *The Rings of Saturn*, which mix literary, historical and personal reflections. I am thinking mostly of his first book to astonish us, in 1996: *The Emigrants*, with its four portraits of exiles from Germany. These are neither fakes nor frauds, since they make no standard biographical claims to be real. They are just stories; and only their rich detail, and their inclusion of documents and photographs, stop us from thinking *'fiction'* from the start. But more and more they do stop us, and soon we are really not sure. But then quite quickly I was sure again. It was not just the exquisite patina of the writing, though it was also that: it would almost be wrong for a work of history to be so beautifully written. It was especially one feature of the writing that gave the game away. All four portraits were linked by the image of butterfly-hunting, which is an image of art; and in particular by the image of Vladimir Nabokov, the great artist and butterfly-hunter. And I thought: four completely separate real stories could not all include Nabokov. They are fiction.

Alas, this shows the opposite of my thesis that non-fiction can be art. The most sublime beauty is closed to us: that requires invention, and steals attention away from its only proper centre in non-fiction, which is the subject. Life writing can be art; but modest art.

Memoir 2 by Sally Cline

What distinguishes memoir from autobiography?

All memoirs include some autobiographical information whilst every autobiography is in some sense a memoir. Though usually in book form, memoirs may also be found in speeches, poems, or journals.

Whereas autobiographies focus on a writer's life usually up to the time of writing, generally in chronological order, usually told in the first person; memoirs are rarely an entire life or told chronologically. The scope of the memoir is determined by the book's context. The form offers room for creativity and interpretation. It is a first person account of one aspect, experience, place or period in someone's life. Whereas the autobiographer focuses on the self, the memoirist focuses on others.

Memoirs may relate to recent events or recollections from years ago. Many memoirists try to distinguish what they actually felt yesterday from what they feel today when recalling what they believe they *should* have felt. Memoirists who are selective, see the past as divisible. Remembered events have already shaped themselves in writers' minds; the new question is how to reshape them for memoir.

Contemporary memoirists have found the intervention of the person writing in the present, is pertinent to the work. When authors intervene they become more attentive to the interplay of the narrative.

Types of memoirs

They can be theme or subject focused, may include romantic or sexual issues, emotional bonds, places of sentiment, professions, careers, pursuits, geographical or psychological journeys, and lost or found political or religious beliefs. They can be based around childhood, old age, sickness or death, and can allude to periods of happiness or misery. But whether it is subject or theme that defines the memoir begs the question of what actually happens as we write and remember. Whatever it is that happens becomes the memoir's narrative.

Misreading of memoirs can occur when we fail to recognise that the nature of memoir is prioritising what is recalled over an historical account.

A famous example of wild misreading occurred when novelist Mary McCarthy and memoirist Lillian Hellman collided. McCarthy accused Hellman of filling her four memoirs with lies. Hellman responded with a lawsuit and with the evidence that *An Unfinished Woman*, *Pentimento*, *Scoundrel Time* and *Maybe* are all related by the common theme that increasing unreliability of memory may not produce (and are not meant to produce) 'accurate' records of the past. Ironically McCarthy's own *Memories of a Catholic Girlhood* is stuffed with revelations of how she fictionalised the past. Inability to tell 'the truth', because there is no one truth, shines as a metaphor for both women's separate selves.

Family and childhood memoirs

Writers' families and their wondrous or wicked interactions bring out an avalanche of material. Novelist Julia Blackburn wrote a startling turbulent account of her startling turbulent family, the alcoholic poet father Thomas Blackburn and the eccentric sexually-fixated mother, painter Rosalie de Meric. In *The Three of Us* (2008) Blackburn's father's whims include a one night stand with Francis Bacon, her mother's fancies include lodgers whom she sensually and openly deprives of sleep. It is an exhausting book brilliantly written with some moving moments towards the end when Blackburn's mother is dying of cancer.

The agonies of tense and difficult mother–daughter relationships, is further explored in the elegant and philosophical classic *Memoirs of a Dutiful Daughter* by Simone de Beauvoir (1959) and years later in the compassionate, and in parts hilarious *Memoirs of a Not So Dutiful Daughter* by Jenni Murray (2008).

De Beauvoir admitted there were times when she loathed her mother. Murray anguished at the constant put-downs of Win, *her* mother, who did not pay her one 'unconditional compliment' until Murray was fifty six. Finally, Win told Jenni she was beautiful and loved when Murray visited her in hospital where Win was fighting to stay alive. That same year Murray was diagnosed with breast cancer, had a mastectomy and would see both her parents die. Murray's fearless examination of her early abandonment when her parents went abroad for months without her, and her subsequent determination to shut down pain and avoid emotion is achieved with similar scalpel precision that De Beauvoir uses to deal with her mother's death.

Amongst many excellent childhood memoirs, two stand out in my mind: *In the Blood* (2007) by poet Andrew Motion and *This Is Not About Me* (2008) by novelist Janice Galloway. Both meticulous narratives move fast. Motion's exactitude about the antics of the English rural upper classes is matched by Galloway's scrupulous detailing of the cosy horrors of council house life on Scotland's west coast. Motion's childhood suddenly ended at sixteen when after a hunting accident, his mother fell into a coma from which she never recovered. Carole Angier reviewing the book noted that all Motion's fine writing is a form of mourning for his mother and this memoir shows readers why. Galloway's dazzling down-to-earth prose takes the first twelve years of her life which began badly when her ill-tempered mother mistook her pregnancy for the menopause. Galloway's subsequent life was threaded through with her mother's refrain: 'If I'd known you were coming . . . if I'd found out. Things would have been different'.[1]

They become different and worse when Janice 's elder sister Cora, glamorous, manipulative and mad, leaves her own child and husband and storms back into the tiny family home to wreak further damage. Emerging memoirists should notice how both books are free of self-pity, and how both avoid the confessional critical tone of some memoirs and the journalistic investigation of others.

Misery memoirs

This term coined by *The Bookseller* magazine describes a genre concerned with the protagonist's triumph over abuse or trauma usually during childhood.

Jung Chang's *Wild Swans* 1992 and Frank McCourt's *Angela's Ashes* (1996) are regarded as seminal but it was Dave Peltzer's 1995 memoir *A Child Called 'It'* which started the genre's extraordinary popularity.

Pelzer detailed the dreadful abuse he said he suffered at the hands of his alcoholic mother. His recovery narratives continued for two further books all of which remained for 448 weeks on the *New York Times* non-fiction paperback bestseller list. They created wild controversy including doubts as to the veracity of Pelzer's claims.

In the last three years, 'miseries', described as 'the book world's biggest boom sector',[3] have contributed over eleven of the top one hundred best selling English paperbacks. Readership is estimated at between eighty and ninety per cent female.

'Recovery' is a trademark of this genre which some publishers refer to as 'inspi-lit' (inspirational literature). Today the Waterstone's chain labels their misery memoir shelves Painful Lives, while Borders followed with Real Lives and W.H. Smith's with Tragic Life Stories.

Many misery authors say they write to come to terms with traumatic memories and help readers do the same, but the most common criticism of the genre is that of prurience and voyeurism. *Her Last Death* by the acid, well-connected Susanna Sonnenberg is a typically brutal account. It describes the treacherous glamorised Manhattan society in which she grew up amidst poor parenting from a brilliant self-focused father and an unpredictable pill-and-alcohol-addicted mother. Her apparently traumatic childhood in which her mother 'Daphne' tells her about orgasms when she is eight, offers her *Penthouse* at ten, cocaine at twelve, and pretends to seduce a boy in the child's circle at fourteen, has an endless list of maternal horrors. The author paints her mother like the monster *Mommie Dearest*.[2]

The memoir has become dangerous territory since James Frey's *A Million Little Pieces*, where Frey tells readers, 'Remember the truth' then proceeds to lie throughout. Sonnenberg confesses that living with a mother she describes as a pathological liar left her, the memoirist, often unable to distinguish truth from fiction. She then reveals she has created 'occasional composites' rather than individual characters based on real people. She further admits that members of her family 'may remember shared experiences differently'. Here as in many misery memoirs veracity is at stake. Some of what the sassy savage Sonnenberg wrote may be devastating but true. Some of what she wrote may be due to a calculated mixture of intense imagination and shrewd understanding of how the misery memoir market works.

What the memoirist may not be aware of is the unbearable harm her gripping little read might have done to an already badly damaged woman who happened to be her mother. A situation unfortunate for them both. Sonnenberg (and aspiring memoirists) might recall that the capable, sane Katharine Whitehorn sensibly called *her* memoir *Selective Memory;* whilst the cautious title of Sonnenberg's own grandfather's memoir was *It Ain't Necessarily So.*[4] The syndrome of uncertain memory might just run in Sonnenberg's family. It certainly runs in the breed of misery memoirists.

Emerging memoirists learn one thing: tread carefully when you evoke 'traumatic memories'. Yours may be only one version of reality that might fit more appropriately inside a novel.

Illness

Severe sickness has produced an abundance of memoirs, some poignant inside perfect prose, others cheap essays in voyeurism. Suffering torment bravely or badly is not sufficient reason to share that pain with a world that may not be waiting for it.

I have read dozens of illness memoirs, from David Paul Schreber's 1903 account of his nervous illness while a patient in a psychiatric asylum to the 1998 narrative by the courageous thirty three year old journalist Ruth Picardie of her last months living with breast cancer. I have engaged with memoirists who detail life after colostomy, living with Churg-Strauss syndrome,[5] coping with strokes, rectal cancer, and temporary blindness from optic neuritis. One glaring fact stands out: many sufferers can endure troubles but cannot write. Unsurprisingly the striking contemporary illness-memoirs come from already recognised authors or editors. *Elle* editor Jean-Dominique Bauby's faultless *The Diving-Bell and the Butterfly* is one. Edmund White thought it wonderful because it helped readers 'fall back in love with life'. A unique book written by a man who in his early forties in 1995 had 'locked-in-syndrome', a rare stroke which left him conscious but physically paralysed, unable to communicate except by blinking his left eye. He laboriously dictated the whole book by blinking his left eyelid at particular letters of the alphabet as they were shown to him. It took him two hundred thousand blinks, four hours a day for ten months. Its beauty is that the words seem effortless. Poignantly, he died of pneumonia two days after the French publication.

Broadcaster/columnist John Diamond's *C: Because Cowards Get Cancer Too* (1998) is another exceptional illness memoir. In 1997 Diamond had unknowingly lived with cancer for a year when he went for tests on the lump on his neck believing he would soon be writing a column about his near-brush with death. Shockingly after losing four stone and most of his tongue until finally he could no longer eat or speak Diamond did indeed write a regular column savagely detailing what it is like suffer one of the worst kinds of cancers and to know that he would shortly die. The columns became a book in which with powerful perception and terrible rage Diamond discards any attempt at heroism and shows how an ordinary coward deals with treatment, pain, work and the appalling consequences on his family, his second wife Nigella Lawson and their two children. The memoir is vicious, funny, full of warmth but not easy to read.

Memoirs about ageing have become fashionable thanks to the efforts among others of Joan Bakewell, Katharine Whitehorn, and Diana Athill. Bakewell in her witty inspiring memoir *The View from Here* recalls that the Big O gave a public label to something she did not feel: being old . . . a view with which many over seventies would concur. In that spirit she began her newspaper column *Just Seventy* whose effect on her was a renewed sense of purpose about life.

Once you have read ninety-two year old Diana Athill's candid and uninhibited *Somewhere Towards the End* you will see seventy plus years as spring-kittenish. According to Athill, former editor at André Deutsch, there are robust things to look forward to even as she meditates on her notorious affairs, her ménages a trios, her romantic partnership with Jamaican playwright Barry Reckord, and the not entirely sad ebbing away of sexual desire. There is no sorrow over ageing, no misery, masses of information, sound sense and above all exhilaration at life.

Some interesting memoirs are written in the form of letters. *Dear Girl: Diaries and Letters of Two Working Women 1897–1917* evokes a period as well as a special friendship between two young London women who had no social position, money nor notorious deaths to mark them out as did Emily Davison and Sylvia Pankhurst but whose stories through these letters are remarkable. As they adventure into women's suffrage and socialism, fields previously unknown to girls of their age and class, they take their readers on breathless trips to the unknown.

Dirk Bogarde at the height of his film fame began a correspondence with an unknown American woman which he turned in to a fascinating memoir: *A Particular Friendship* (1989). The letters begin in 1967 when Mrs X writes to him until 1972 when she dies of cancer. Mrs X (Dorothy Gordon) who had lived in Bogarde's house, Adam's Farm, before the war was curious to know how it had fared. A librarian at Yale University she was neither a fan nor interested in his fame. An intellectual and keen postal conversationalist she instigated discussions about his house, garden, English politics, the state of the arts. Recognising intuitively that she was mortally ill, he wrote to stimulate her. She in turn realised he needed sharp editing if he was ever to succeed as a writer. Five years later, with her advice, he wrote the first of his fifteen books. They never meet but their correspondence runs to nearly one thousand letters. Sadly only Bogarde's letters were published (edited and revised).

Though Bogarde's memoir contained more letters than that of another amazing memoir *84 Charing Cross Road* (1971), by Helene Hanff, the latter are more riveting because they are a dialogue. This, my favourite memoir, indeed my favourite book, the one I would take (along with Virginia Woolf's *Letters*) to a desert island, was made into a stage play, film, and TV drama. The memoir is based on the twenty year correspondence between American author Hanff and Frank Doel, chief buyer for Marks and Co, the British antiquarian booksellers in Charing Cross Road. In search of out-of-print British literature, Hanff notices an advert in a literary journal and contacts the shop in 1949. She and Frank begin to correspond as he deals with her purchases. She sends Christmas packages, birthday gifts and food parcels to the bookstore's staff in war-deprived Britain. Regularly she promises to fly to England and visit them. But New York life intervenes.

Hanff calls the book a love affair between her and a bookstore. But it is also a postal love affair between her and the man she never meets, for in 1968 Frank dies unexpectedly from peritonitis. When Hanff eventually reaches Britain in 1971 the bookshop is closed, empty but still standing. She ends her memoir with the words: 'If you happen to pass by 84 Charing Cross Road, kiss it for me! I owe it so much' (p. 91). The memoir is about loss and literature, grief and fun. I cannot pin down why it is so eminently re-readable but it is the mark of a compelling memoir that it be so.

Death does not need adjectives. We cannot describe death. We cannot come back from death. Words, the usual, the familiar, the suspect, the overblown, will not do. And Joan Didion, who had been forced to live through the deaths of the two people closest to her, the writer who works with the most powerful words, does not use adjectives in her memoir about death.

There is not a lame sentence, not a wasted verb, not a meaningless modifier, in her shocking book *The Year of Magical Thinking* (2005). It is shocking because of its ruthless restraint. It is shocking because it dwells scene by scene, sentence by sentence, on the unbelievable. It is also shocking because the writing belies the tragic material – the language is exhilarating and the reader embarks with awe yet with a strange kind of warmth on the journey Didion takes.

Grief, Didion reports, makes one crazy. Her craziness started just before Christmas 2003 when Quintana, the only daughter of Didion and her husband, writer John Gregory Dunne, fell ill with what seemed at first flu, then pneumonia, then complete septic shock. Quintana was put into an induced coma and placed on a life support machine. The night before New Year's Eve Joan and John sat down to dinner, after visiting the hospital, when Dunne suddenly suffered a massive fateful coronary. In one second their forty year partnership was over. 'Life changes fast. Life changes in the instant' (p. 3).

The memoir was Didion's attempt to make sense of insanity. There are two voices in the book: the internal voice of magical thinking that denies desperation, believes there are signs that will restore loss. If she doesn't give away Dunne's shoes they will be there for when he returns. If she doesn't delete an unfinished e-mail, he can close it when he comes back. Then there is the outer voice, the deadpan discussion of external details, hospital technologies, funeral rites, domestic trivia. There is Quintana to care for as initially she pulls through, then relapses, undergoes six hours of massive brain surgery.

Quintana is surviving as Didion completes her last sentence. Then suddenly in a New York hospital Quintana dies. Will you change the ending, publishers and journalists ask. 'It's finished', Didion says.

Notes
1. Janice Galloway *This Is Not About Me*, p.5, Granta, London, 2008.
2. *The Independent*, 3 April 2007, Anthony Barnes. Figures are for 2006.
3. The book and film of Joan Crawford's abuse of her adopted daughter.
4. Katharine Whitehorn, *Selective Memory*, Virago, London, 2007. Larry Adler, *It Ain't Necessarily So*, Fontana Collins, London, 1984, 1985.
5. Complex rare form of asthma.

Diaries, blogs, twitters by Carole Angier

Diaries are a precious source of contemporary and (often) spontaneous information, not only for biographers, autobiographers and memoirists but also for historians (think of Pepys' and Evelyn's *Diaries* in the seventeenth century, or Anne Frank's in the twentieth). However wary we must be for signs of a distorting purpose (public consumption, for example), still the discovery of a diary is a researcher's dream.

The point about a diary is that it is private, and its privacy is what underwrites its honesty. In today's internet world privacy is extinct. Web diaries – web logs, or blogs – are posted to be read; comments on Facebook, messages on Twitter, videos on YouTube, are all there to be shared. A private tweet is a contradiction in terms. And yet the ideas of honesty and spontaneity still attach to blogging and tweeting. New generations tell each other what previous generations would have kept to themselves, and repression may really be dead.

We have to look out for manipulation of more sinister kinds than in a traditional diary (except for a politician's), for example disinformation. But the main problem with blogs and tweets is different. It is familiar from e-mail, which has been around for a couple of decades longer: how do we keep them? For diaries and letters there was at least the attic. Website providers and the Twitterverse are ephemeral or non-existent, and governments storing our every exchange (as they threaten to do) would be too high a price to pay. Failing such dystopian solutions, it looks as though the job of biographers and autobiographers will get harder every year.

The other problem with Facebook, blogs and Twitter is that they are not only records, as diaries were. Because they speak to vast numbers of people, they can do what Marx desired – not just understand the world, but change it. And that means that they are hot property for mere writers. Twitter users flashed information around the world faster than any news agency in the Iranian elections of 2009; during the Virginia Tech shootings in 2007, Facebook had more accurate information than the emergency services; and from 2003 on bloggers have produced the best accounts from Iraq. All this has revolutionised the way news is gathered, with TV, radio and the press all inviting people to text them reports (and photos: a Twitpic of US Airways Flight 1549 ditching in the Hudson River, for example). It has also revolutionised the way people share information among themselves during such events, and in general.

The internet is living up to its promise to democratise the power of knowledge, not only through Google and Gutenberg, but now through Facebook and Twitter as well. All still have undreamed-of potential, inevitably not only for good. The unlimited access to information has already reduced people's habit of thinking for themselves; text-messaging reduces the habit of writing whole sentences; and now Twitter is reducing the habitual thought-bite to one hundred and forty characters. Penguin has just published *Twitterature*, in which over sixty great works of literature are reduced to tweets. *Oedipus Rex*, for example, becomes: 'PARTY IN THEBES!!! Nobody cares I killed that old dude, plus this woman is all over me. Total MILF'. It's witty, and *The Reduced Shakespeare Company* has done it all before. But where, writers may ask, will it end?

Part 2:
Tips and tales

Guest contributions

Diana Athill

Diana Athill was editorial director of André Deutsch Limited for nearly fifty years. She published three books of her own during the sixties, and went back to writing when she retired at the age of seventy-six. Since then she has published three memoirs: *Stet*, about her life in publishing, *Yesterday Morning*, about her childhood, and *Somewhere Towards the End*, about ageing, which won the Costa prize for biography in 2008.

I have been lucky in that I never pursued writing, it came to me; and did so twice. Because I was a publisher's editor, all my working life I was concerned with other people's writing, and that must have taught me much about using words, but I never employed them myself except to write blurbs (and letters, which I loved doing).

Then, when I was forty, to my astonishment and delight a small incident triggered a story, which was soon followed by eight more, one of which won a prize. They revealed to me that writing was a source of a unique kind of satisfaction, but when the ninth story fizzled out after three pages it was over a year before it occurred to me to try for more of that satisfaction, and fish those pages out of a drawer in order to see if I could make something out of that story after all. I sat down at my typewriter, and what happened then was that my autobiographical book *Instead of a Letter* began to come out, and continued at a tremendous rate without a single moment of planning until it reached its end. I know that sounds improbable, but it is exactly how it was, and at the time, although it was wonderfully exciting, it didn't seem at all surprising.

'Therapeutic' writing has a bad reputation, not as a remedial activity but as art. That book was miraculously therapeutic in that it freed me absolutely from a sense of failure due to a painful experience in my early twenties.

The writing uncovered and probed that experience, thereby giving me quite literally a new life. And surprisingly, its reception showed that in spite of being so useful to me it also worked from the readers' point of view; and in the next few years I was to write two more books that 'sorted out' disagreeable experiences, yet also worked reasonably well. When no more traumatic events entered my life, no more books happened, so naturally I concluded that since it was sad things that made me produce books, now that my life had turned kind I must say goodbye to writing: part loss and part gain.

My second delightful surprise came when I was eighty. I had retired from publishing when I was seventy-five, and since then several people had said that I ought to write about my experience of the trade and 'meeting all those interesting people'. Each time I said, 'No, not my kind of book'. But on the other hand, a good many funny or fond memories did float about in my mind, and some of them I did scribble down for my own amusement – the 'portrait' memories in more detail than the others. Eventually someone mentioned one of these to Ian Jack who at that time was editing the magazine *Granta* and running Granta Books as well, and he said that if ever my bits and pieces amounted to a book he would like to see it. More digging about in drawers, and I saw that with a little more work there really might be a book there – perhaps it was worth doing that little work. I set about it, found that I enjoyed it, and *Stet* came into being and proved to be a success – which I enjoyed even more. It was such an unexpected thing to happen to someone of my age. Indeed it was so invigorating to discover that now no 'cures' were needed I could still write for the very different reason that doing it was interesting and amusing, that I went on to produce two more books, *Yesterday Morning*, about my childhood, and *Somewhere Towards the End*, about being old. To be granted such an Indian summer. . . Well, the pleasure of it is delicious. I think I must be an amateur, but when I hear more serious writers speak of the blood, sweat, toil and tears they go through in the course of finishing a book, I creep away to have a secret gloat at my own good luck.

Alan Bennett

Alan Bennett is one of Britain's best-known playwrights. He has also written short fiction, including *The Uncommon Reader*, and two memoirs, *Writing Home* and *Untold Stories*.

All I can say about biography, autobiography or indeed fiction is: don't start at the beginning. Write about the period that interests you, then go back – gradually pick up the rest.

Alain de Botton

Alain de Botton is the author of nine books of non-fiction, including *Essays in Love*, *The Art of Travel*, *The Architecture of Happiness*, and an essay on the purpose of literature, *How Proust Can Change Your Life*.

A young student once wrote to the French novelist André Gide to ask him whether he should try to become a writer. 'Only if you have to,' answered Gide, neatly summing up the best advice any writer can give a prospective recruit. The job clearly makes no sense from any practical point of view. It only intermittently satisfies ordinary longings for security and status. Trying to tie writing talent to a mortgage is akin to connecting a bicycle to the national power grid. So if one's to become a writer, it clearly has to be from a motive other than the search for money or status. It has to because of the deep fulfilment that some people feel in arranging thoughts on experiences on the page.

I wrote my first book at the age of eight. It was the diary of my summer holiday, spent in the Normandy seaside resort of Houlgate with my parents, dog and sister. 'Yestday nothing much happend. Today the wether is lovely. We went swiming for the hole day. We had salad for lunch. We had a trout for diner. After diner we saw a film about a man that found gold in Peru,' reads a typical entry headed Wendsay 23 of August, 1978 (not dyslexia, just learning English). If the book is unreadable, it's because, despite the best intentions and neat handwriting, the author is unable to capture much of what is actually happening. There is a list of facts, the trout and a weather report, but life has slipped out of the picture. It's like watching a home video, in which you're shown only the feet or the clouds, and wonder, bemused, what might be going on at head-level.

The desire to record experience never left me, but as I matured, my technical skills slowly improved. I learnt that wanting to say something very badly doesn't always mean that one has managed to do so. Writing is about capturing experience. For me, the finest books are those where an author has put his or her finger on emotions which we recognise as our own, but which we could not have formulated on our own. We have a feeling that the author knows us – perhaps better than we know ourselves. I aspire to write books that offer a feeling of recognition, and ultimately, of friendship.

As for where I write, it seems that my work is always best done in places where it isn't supposed to happen. At a desk, in front of a computer, my mind goes blank, but as soon as I take off (to the supermarket, to Australia), inspiration strikes. Journeys are the midwives of books. Few places are more conducive to the internal conversation that is writing than a moving plane, ship or train. Best of all is a train. The views move fast enough for me not to get exasperated but slowly enough to allow me to identify objects. They offer me brief, inspiring glimpses into private domains, letting me see a woman at the moment when she takes a cup from a shelf in her kitchen, before carrying me on to a patio where a man is sleeping and then to a park where a child is catching a ball thrown by a figure I can't see. Out of such fine filaments, books are born.

Hotel rooms offer a similar opportunity to escape my habits of mind. Lying in bed in a hotel, the room quiet except for the occasional swooshing of an elevator in the innards of the building, I can reflect on, and write about, things from a height I could not have reached in the midst of everyday business – subtly assisted in this by the unfamiliar world around me: by the small wrapped soaps on the edge of the basin, by the gallery of miniature bottles in the mini-bar, by the room-service menu with its promises of all-night dining and the view onto an unknown city stirring silently twenty-five floors below us.

Hotel note-pads can be the recipients of unexpectedly intense, revelatory thoughts, taken down in the early hours while the breakfast menu ('to be hung outside before 3AM') lies unattended on the floor.

I began my last book in a Sydney hotel room on a jet-lagged night in May 2009. I'm hoping that the Muse won't desert me.

Jill Dawson

Jill Dawson is a poet, the editor of six anthologies and author of six novels, including *Fred and Edie*, which was short-listed for the Orange Prize and the Whitbread Novel award, and *Watch Me Disappear*, which was long-listed for the Orange. Her latest book, *The Great Lover*, is a biographical novel about the poet Rupert Brooke.

What did his living voice sound like? What did he smell like? How did it feel to wrap one's arms around him? Was he a good man? These are the questions I asked myself about the poet Rupert Brooke when I started my novel about him, *The Great Lover*. I wove them into the text by having Brooke's putative daughter ask them directly of a woman she believes knew Brooke well: my fictional character Nell Golightly.

These are subjective, emotive, relative questions that fiction – especially fiction written in the first person, which never claims to be objective but only human – is well placed to answer. In *Orlando* Virginia Woolf writes: 'A biography is considered complete if it merely accounts for six or seven selves, whereas a person may well have as many as a thousand'. That concept went into *The Great Lover* too, spoken by Tatamaata, Brooke's Tahitian girlfriend, who declares we have as many selves as there are clams on a beach.

Do you change facts, if they don't suit the plot? I was asked, at a book event, on a panel discussion. I was shocked when the other writer on the panel, writing her own family's story, agreed at once that she did, if it improved the storyline. I felt like a fraud then. Surely hers is the proper reply for a novelist, surely our job is to *fictionalise*, to make things up? I immediately understood my own compulsion better: not making up, entirely, but a belief in fiction, or the logic of imagination as a means of finding out.

I think of it as *applying* fiction to facts like a poultice; to draw something out . . . My 'novels based on true stories' evolved because of the eleven years of psychoanalysis I underwent in my twenties, and my interest in poetry. I wanted psychological truths, not representational social realism. I opened my first novel, *Trick of the Light* with a dream, something young novelists are told never to do. 'Tell a dream, lose a reader,' Henry James said. Excellent advice, which I've ignored in every novel since.

I don't see dreams as secondary or decorative in my fiction. Anais Nin, in her essay on the poetic novel, says: 'What the psychoanalysts stress, the relation between dream and our conscious acts, is what poets already know. The poets walk this bridge with ease, from conscious to unconscious, physical reality to psychological reality'.

When I have a 'fact' about a character I'm writing about, I want to investigate it, the way a therapist might. Tell me about your mother, I might ask Rupert Brooke. Tell me about this fact that she lost a child, a daughter, who was one year old, before you were born. Then I will go over this detail: the accounts, the references by other biographers; the letters; possible references in his poetry; the phrases Brooke used to describe this one small 'fact'. It's as if I have my client (Brooke) on the couch and can get him to tell me, over and over, until the truth, or, I admit, *what feels like the truth to me*, emerges, in certain words, the perfect words, which briefly feel not to be mine, but coming directly from somewhere else.

Millicent Dillon

Millicent Dillon is a fiction writer and biographer. Her biographies include *A Little Original Sin*, a biography of Jane Bowles, *You Are Not I*, a portrait of Paul Bowles, and a duo biography of Isadora Duncan and Mary Cassatt. Her novels include *Harry Gold*, nominated for the Pen Faulkner Award, and *A Version of Love*, among others. She is a five-time recipient of the O. Henry Award for the short story. She

has recently completed a memoir of the years 1944–48, when she worked on a nuclear project and then for the anti-nuclear Einstein Emergency Committee.

To be a biographer is to enter into a profound relation with the other.

When I began my biography of the writer Jane Bowles, she seemed likely to be familiar to me in many ways. Like myself she was born in New York, of Jewish heritage. Her mother's first name and my mother's first name were the same, her grandfather's first name was the same as my grandfather's, we lived in the same building in New York, though at different times, she broke her right leg in 1931, as did I. She was small and dark, as was I. There was even, some informants said, a physical resemblance between us. But it was precisely these too easy points of identification that I had to struggle against in writing her biography. For, in profound ways, as I came to discover, she was indeed the other, in her life story and in her work.

My next two subjects, the dancer Isadora Duncan and the painter Mary Cassatt, were each from the moment I began their biographies – both in the same book – 'the other.' Born in the nineteenth century, practitioners of an art not the same as mine, with family lives and backgrounds totally different from mine, they seemed at the outset totally unfamiliar to me, even as their lives were radically different from each other's. Curiously, in the course of writing the book, yet another figure seemed to emerge, a third being, another 'other' entirely, arising out of the juxtaposition of their two lives.

My third biography was of Jane Bowles's husband Paul Bowles. As he had been the primary informant for my biography of her, I had met with him a number of times in Tangier. In life he was charismatic, brilliant, often devious, fifteen years older than I, a composer as well as a writer, with a mysterious and compelling life history. My struggle in that book was to reconcile the one I had come to know in 'real' life with the 'other' he had to become in my biographical portrait of him.

As for my recently completed memoir, dealing with my life from 1944–48, I came to discover that there was the 'other' even in memoir.

That other, the one I was in my early years, did many things and thought many thoughts often mysterious to the one I am now.

> And yet she was I and I was she.
> We were the same and yet not the same.

Margaret Drabble

Margaret Drabble was born in Sheffield in 1939 and educated at Newnham College, Cambridge, where she studied English Literature. She has published seventeen novels, most recently *The Sea Lady* (2006). She has also published biographies of Arnold Bennett (1974) and Angus Wilson (1995) and a memoir, *The Pattern in the Carpet* (2009). She is married to the biographer Michael Holroyd and lives in London and Somerset.

Memoirs lie, and fiction tells the truth. I attribute that aphorism to Philip Roth, though I don't think he put it as bluntly. I know what I think he meant by it.

It's the first person that's the problem. I was never able to keep a diary for any length of time, because I didn't know why or for whom I was keeping it, so my rare efforts became bedevilled by self-justification and posturing. I could not tell the simple truth, because truth was not simple. I realise now I could have confined myself to one well-defined area of reportage – nature notes, people met, events visited, even books read or money spent – and that would over time have built up a valuable documentary and descriptive record, as did the journals of Dorothy Wordsworth, Francis Kilvert, and Arnold Bennett. But I didn't.

Memoir presents worse problems than diaries and journals. My most recent publication began as a short history of the jigsaw puzzle, but wandered off into memories of my aunt. The difficulty here was that these memories belong equally to many other living people, who have an equal right to them, and who might well object to my appropriating what they regard as theirs. Some writers of memoir and autobiography are evasive about the ethical issues involved here, and others are either brutal or sentimental about friends and family. It's very hard to tell the truth, and to get the tone right. Life writing is a very dangerous genre.

Fiction evades some of these dangers, and allows the writer to speak obliquely, and thus more bravely and freely. Novels embody many true life stories, which biographers in turn may come to analyse. I now think that biography is the most honourable branch of overt life writing. It is time-consuming and immensely demanding, requiring the highest standards of research, imagination and discipline. It is in many ways (not least financially) unrewarding. Britain has produced some remarkable biographies over the past half century, and while judging the biography section of what was then the Whitbread (now the Costa) Prize I was deeply impressed by the scholarship and the narrative powers of many of the entries. Hilary Spurling's superb life of Matisse, which won, was one of at least a dozen books which would have been worthy winners, and which I am very glad to have read. I don't think I would have felt the same about the entries for a fiction prize. So I salute the art of biography, and admire those who undertake this most serious and taxing of literary forms.

Geoff Dyer

Geoff Dyer's many books include *The Ongoing Moment*, *But Beautiful*, *Yoga For People Who Can't Be Bothered To Do It*, *Out of Sheer Rage* and, most recently, *Jeff in Venice, Death in Varanasi*.

I seem to have snuck in to these pages under someone's coat-tails. Whose? Mine, I suppose. I'm guessing that I'm here on the basis of my crazy little book about D.H. Lawrence, *Out of Sheer Rage*. Somehow, over the years, the idea has got around that this is an account of how I tried and failed to write a biography of Lawrence. Which is not true at all. It's an account of how I tried and failed to write 'a sober, academic study of D.H. Lawrence', even though that claim that I wanted to write a sober, academic study was never more than a conceit or pretext because, from the beginning, I intended writing a completely deranged book.

I got the idea from Lawrence himself who, in July 1914, signed a contract to write 'a little book' on Thomas Hardy for the series 'Writers of the Day'. The success of any series depends on each individual volume conforming to a broadly agreed format or template but, for one reason or another, Lawrence made no progress on this commission until, on 5 September, he announced, 'Out of sheer rage I've begun my book about Thomas Hardy. It will be about anything but Thomas Hardy I am afraid queer stuff but not bad'. Writing a book about D.H. Lawrence that was about anything but D.H. Lawrence or that was, at least, about a lot of things besides Lawrence therefore seemed a completely appropriate and faithful undertaking.

The weirdness of that book should not be taken as any indication of impatience with traditional biographies. On the contrary. In the late 1990s I spent a couple of months at the Center for Documentary Studies in North Carolina, writing about the photographer William Gedney whose archive had ended up at Duke University. There was no biography of Gedney. Just working out roughly when he went where and did whatever he did took a lot of time and effort. I realised then how thoroughly we take biographies for granted, how much we rely on biographers to do the donkey work for us. Books like mine depend on the existence of straight-ahead biographies. Just to provide the basic chronological outline to 'give us all the facts', as Auden put it, is valuable in itself, but of course the best biographers attempt something far more difficult and subtle, revealing how a person becomes what they are. That more elaborate ambition is built, always, on the solid foundation of rigorously accumulated evidence.

So I don't know why certain biographers are so touchy about being . . . biographers! In the bibliography of *But Beautiful*, my book about jazz, I cited Brian Priestley's 'thorough' biography of Charles Mingus. Priestley reviewed my book and noted, caustically, that by 'thorough' I presumably meant 'boring'. No, by 'thorough' I meant 'thorough' which, ah, um, is why I wrote 'thorough'.

Victoria Glendinning

Victoria Glendinning is a biographer, novelist and journalist. Her most recent books are *Leonard Woolf* and *Love's Civil War: Elizabeth Bowen and Charles Ritchie, Letters and Diaries*. She is working on a book about Stamford Raffles.

Recently I underwent an exercise which taught me a lot about biography. The British Library is making a collection of 'National Life Stories' for their oral history sound archive, with interviewers recording each person for fifteen hours, in sessions of about three hours each. The collection includes people from different professions and walks of life, including writers. I agreed to do this.

Afterwards, I realised with a bit of a shock how entirely arbitrary my account of my life had been. A question posed by the interviewer rarely had one simple answer. I had to choose what to say, thereby aborting all the other answers I could have given. In talking about family members, friends, lovers, etc, I could not possibly convey either the complexity of their natures or of my relationships with them. It had to be broad brush strokes, with much left unsaid, and with the perpetual choice of depicting people either as their 'best selves' or as their 'worst selves'. Even more disturbing was my discovery of the impossibility of telling a story without imposing on it a particular tone or colour; someone else telling the same story, or myself in a different mood, would have cast quite another light upon it. And although I have experienced at least the standard amount of real unhappiness, I don't have what is called 'the tragic sense of life', and tend to turn accounts of what actually were traumatic episodes to comedy.

I feel, as a result, as if the first thing we have to acknowledge about writing biography is that it is, if not actually impossible, a very partial art. We can research the trajectory of a life and its social and historical context until we are blue in the face. But material facts, though they are the backbone of responsible biography, must be interpreted and given meaning if they are to have any more significance than a railway timetable. That's the addictive fascination of writing biography – trying to get under someone's else's skin.

But even the most attentive biographer can never do that. Jacques Derrida, the largely impenetrable French philosopher, wrote one short and perfectly accessible book called *Archive Fever* (in French, *Mal d'archive*) which is worth reading. It is partly about the limitations of the paper archive – a love-letter preserved, for example, tells posterity nothing about unrecorded tensions and rows. He writes too about the 'psychic archive' – the layers and layers of memories and associations in a person's mind, which psychoanalysis seeks to excavate. Normally we have only limited access even to our own psychic archives, so biographers can obviously only scratch the surface of their subjects'. We need what Keats called 'negative capability' – the capability 'of being in uncertainties, mysteries, doubts, without any irritable reaching after fact and reason'. Beware, therefore, dogmatic summings-up. I am haunted by the thought of my subjects turning in their graves and complaining (to quote T.S.Eliot):

> That is not it at all,
> That is not what I meant, at all.

Lyndall Gordon

Lyndall Gordon is the author of six biographies, including *Vindication: A Life of Mary Wollstonecraft*, and most recently *Lives Like Loaded Guns: Emily Dickinson and Her Family's Feuds*. She has also written a memoir, *Shared Lives*, about women's friendship in her native South Africa. She is a Senior Research Fellow at St Hilda's College, Oxford.

To write Lives is a little like the practice of friendship. We can't choose our family, but we can our friends and subjects. A memoirist or biographer chooses a companion in the past and lives with this person for a number of years. It can be closer than relations with the living, as it was for Tennyson who clung to the dead Arthur Hallam while memorialising the formative impact of this friend:

> I felt and feel, though left alone,
> His being working in my own,
> The footsteps of his life in mine.

Friendship can be routine but it can also be creative. So too with Lives; they can be compendia of fact, but they are potentially the material of art.

For George Eliot, there was no artificial distinction between the imagination of the novelist, intent on character, and that of an ordinary social being. The secret of characterisation, she said, lies in deep human sympathy. Her novels show imaginative sympathy to be a trait anyone – even the miserly recluse Silas Marner – can learn to cultivate.

The longer I lived with Charlotte Brontë and Mary Wollstonecraft, as I wrote about them, the more I admired their flair for friendship – their efforts to see, hear, and draw out others (Brontë, the discerning Scottish acumen in her light-hearted publisher George Smith; Wollstonecraft, the domestic affections lurking in the frosty philosopher Godwin, who didn't care for women's rights).

But unlike friendship, biography can be a one-sided affair. It can happen that the companion from the past does not welcome the relationship, as Henry James imagines in his tale 'The Real, Right Thing' where the dead subject – who had been, in fact, a friend – bars his biographer's way. Yet, for the most part, friendship and biography converge to professional advantage, as when Virginia Woolf invites insight from fellow-writer Vita Sackville-West: 'What I am, I want you to tell me.' Then she dares a step further: 'If you make me up, I'll make you.'

If we could 'tell' who we are, or if a friend could 'make us up', we would create one another. In writing Shared Lives, a memoir of three friends who died young, one motive was to celebrate a flair for friendship as a form of creativity – beyond anything I have since encountered – in the provincial backwater Cape Town was in the 1950s. It was the gift of a girl with cropped red hair called Flora Gevint, whom I met on the first day of high school. The daughter of Jewish refugees whom she protected and also alarmed (finding they had given birth to a disruptive alien), she bounced up, aged eleven, and perched on her desk, demanded of twenty-three girls in succession to know who we were. The more unpromising we were, the more resourceful she became – she liked the hopeless ones best. Since I was plain and freckled, she gave me a charge of confidence and when Phillippa's sister died, Flora drew out her friend's humour, her quick way with words, so that, as they lay in bed, they laughed with defiant incongruity while the funeral took place. Later, when Ellie, a psychologist, drank, despairing of the partner who sapped her strength, Flora restored her discerning clarity. All of us she urged to play our parts in character. Flora's skill was to shape people, not works, and this flair may lurk in many unwritten lives that are attuned to what *Middlemarch* calls 'that roar which lies on the other side of silence'.

Peter Hayter

Peter Hayter has been the Chief Cricket Correspondent for *The Mail on Sunday* since 1989 and has ghost-written the best-selling autobiographies of Ian Botham, Phil Tufnell and Marcus Trescothick. The last of these, *Coming Back To Me*, won the William Hill Sports Book Of the Year 2008. His latest book, *England's Ashes*, was written with the entire England team who won the 2009 Ashes.

Ghost writer. Sounds dreadful, doesn't it? Like you're dead and writing stuff from beyond the grave. Spooky. In fact, for a scribbler like me – I've been cricket correspondent for *The Mail On Sunday* for twenty years – it has been a way of sharing the extraordinary experiences of those whom readers actually do want to know more about.

Most people who write autobiographies produce, on average, one per lifetime. They may add to it, update it, or – should they live long enough – bring out a second volume. But by the definition of the Collins dictionary an autobiography is 'an account of a person's life written or otherwise recorded by that person'. Person, singular. I, on the other hand, have written a handful of autobiographies, including the life-stories of some of the best and most interesting cricketers of their generation: for Ian Botham before he became a Sir, for Phil Tufnell before he became a celebrity, and for Marcus Trescothick before, during and after depressive illness forced him to retire from international cricket at the moment he was about to confirm his status as the best batsman on the planet.

I have also ghost-written for the entire England team, on two occasions; first, when they won the Ashes in 2005, and recently when they did so again in 2009. And at various times I have also written columns for the newspaper on behalf of some of the greatest players of all time, including Sir Viv Richards, Graham Gooch, Brian Lara, Dennis Lillee, Graham Thorpe, Glenn McGrath and Steve Harmison. And, every once in while, it has been possible to imagine myself not just writing for them but being them.

I must admit that, just occasionally, it has pained me to donate some of my best lines to others, and there's no doubt this ghostly existence can be a lonely one. If you write a cracker the subject tends to get all the credit. If you come up with a stinker it's the ghost what gets the blame.

Even so, by and large the relationships I've struck with the people whose voices I have attempted to capture have lasted. And, for me, the voice is the key in this caper. Unless you are incredibly lucky, merely transcribing a series of lengthy interviews just won't do the job. Assuming that the subject has enough interesting things to tell you to make a book (or in the case of Sir Ian, that he can actually remember any of them), if you can get the voice – the sound of how and what your subject thinks, as well as what he says – you are more than half-way there.

What else? It goes without saying you must gain the confidence of your subject that he or she can tell you everything, knowing that not everything will make the page. And – easy to say, but sometimes surprisingly difficult to adhere to – you must never, ever betray a confidence, knowingly or otherwise. Accidents can happen, of course. But second chances don't.

One last thing I've always done my best to remember: the name on the cover of the book. That's the person they want to read about, not you.

Richard Holmes

Richard Holmes, the author of *Footsteps: Adventures of a Romantic Biographer* and *Dr Johnson and Mr Savage*, is a Fellow of the British Academy. He designed the new Biography MA at the University of East Anglia and taught it from 2001–6. His biographies of

Shelley and Coleridge were multiple prize-winners and are already classics. His latest, *The Age of Wonder*, a group biography of scientists of the Romantic age, won the Royal Society Science Book Prize for 2009.

People often suggest that the future of biography lies in a radical change of form – in the development of fractured or post-modern narrative modes. But this has been going on for quite a time. Peter Ackroyd's original version of *Dickens* (1989) with its flamboyant insertions of fictional interludes, is a famous example. In Australia (typically daring in biographical innovation) Brian Matthews's experimental and prize-winning biography *Louisa* (1987) was even more startling. It used multiple biographic voices (both a male and female narrator), and dramatised self-questionings on the biographer's art. Julian Barnes's *Flaubert's Parrot* (1984) even created a completely fictional biographer – Geoffrey Braithwaite – to explore factual, or counterfactual, questions about Flaubert (eg, what colour were Emma Bovary's eyes?).

My own book *Footsteps: Adventures of a Romantic Biographer* (1985) in which the biographer continually steps in and out of four different romantic 'frame' narratives (the lives of Stevenson, Wollstonecraft, Shelley and Nerval), might claim to be a fourth. It is said this invented a new biographical 'method' of footstepping, and a dangerous new doctrine of 'empathy'. Perhaps; or perhaps not. But it is interesting to me that all these experimental works appeared in the 1980s. It seemed to be a period when we all wanted to 'shake the cage' of conventional biographic form and chronologies, and see what would happen. Now we are living with the consequences.

Yet I believe that the traditional art of story-telling still remains central to biography, its power and endless fascination. What we may need is more a modernising of subjects, or development in our ideas of the kind of materials that biography can deal with. The 'monolithic' single Life is certainly giving way to biographies of groups, of friendships, of love-affairs, of 'spots of time' (microbiographies), of geographical places, 'after-life' reputations, or of collective movements in art or science. It is such new biographical *subjects* which will redefine the narrative form, not vice-versa.

Even if it is not presented chronologically, biography always takes the form of a human story, a narrative action, an *agon*. This has been so since the earliest *Parallel Lives* of Plutarch (c. 120 AD). Plutarch launched the great narrative melodramas of biography: Alexander's self-destruction, Julius Caesar's assassination, or Anthony and Cleopatra's fatal love affair. We can still learn so much from these. In his Prologue to his *Life of Alexander* Plutarch summarised his approach: he would tell 'not history, but lives'. He would look for the inside story, the intimate gesture, 'an expression or a jest', that revealed true character. He would narrate 'the souls of men'. (As his Elizabethan translator Sir Thomas North wryly observed, Plutarch was interested 'not only in how many battles Alexander won, but how often he was drunk').

And there always remains a vital uncertainty, the unknowable human heart, at the centre of the biographical enterprise. For me this is well represented by Samuel Johnson's experience. The greatest of all early eighteenth century biographies is probably Johnson's *Life of Richard Savage* (1744), which ends in a dramatic moment of profound moral ambiguity. Throughout Johnson argues that Savage's entire disreputable and unhappy career (including murder, blackmail and a stint as 'Volunteer' Poet Laureate) can be explained and forgiven by the fact that he was, as he always claimed, the illegitimate, unrecognised and persecuted son of two aristocrats, Lord Rivers and Lady Macclesfield. But on his deathbed, and almost the last page of Johnson's brilliant biography, the possibility that Savage was simply an impostor is raised.

As Savage lies dying in a debtors' prison, he seems about to confess this to his jailer. 'Savage, seeing him at his bedside, said with uncommon earnestness, "I have something to say to you, Sir", but after a pause, moved his hand in a melancholy manner; and finding himself unable to recollect what he was going to communicate, said, "'Tis gone!"'. It is one of the great biographical cliff-hangers. Years later James Boswell meticulously re-examined all the evidence while writing his own *Life of Johnson* (1792), and concluded that the ambiguity of Savage's ending must stand. In a wonderfully evocative phrase, Boswell pronounced: 'The world must vibrate in a state of uncertainty as to what was the truth'.

One can say that *vibrating in uncertainty* is part of the human power of biography.

Michael Holroyd

Michael Holroyd has written biographies of Lytton Strachey, Augustus John and Bernard Shaw as well as two volumes of memoirs, *Basil Street Blues* and *Mosaic*. He is a past President of English PEN, and was until recently President of the Royal Society of Literature. In 2007 he was knighted for services to literature. His most recent book is *A Strange Eventful History: The Dramatic Lives of Ellen Terry, Henry Irving and Their Remarkable Families*.

I become two people when I write a biography: a researcher and a writer. Although they have been working together for many years, they do not seem to be on very intimate terms. The researcher is a considerable traveller. He pursues his subject relentlessly – even on occasions to places where she never went (places, for example, which shelter her archives). Settling down rather feverishly, he examines letters, journals, drafts of her books and looks up from time to time exclaiming pathetically, rhetorically: 'What do you make of this? Will you need it?' He is addressing his *alter ego*, the writer, who seldom gives him much help.

The writer is an invisible presence – you seldom catch sight of him except perhaps as a spectre haunting the subtext or, of course, as a youthful and misleading image on the inside back cover of the book. He is vexed by these naïve questions from the researcher. How can any writer know at this preliminary stage what he will need to bring the dead to life upon the page? It is the researcher's job to bring back from his travels what is meaningful and what is magical: in short, what will enable the writer to perform this miraculous resurrection. It is a delicate operation. The researcher must not bring back too much material because biography is not simply an exercise in information retrieval.

To the researcher, visiting houses, interviewing people, studying the landscape, examining manuscripts, it is difficult to know what will inspire that solitary writer in his room. How could anyone guess, for example, that Bernard Shaw's typewriter and bicycle were essential components of his identity? The truth is that the writer only discovers what is vital to the pattern of his narrative during the actual process of writing. He is exasperated sometimes by the blindness of the researcher to the significance of trivial items. In some ways he envies him: he is an explorer, detective, adventurer who gathers problems and opportunities. It is an exciting way of life. Once the writer begins his work, however, the researcher lags superfluous, his occupation gone.

It surprises some people to be told that, like fiction, poetry and drama, good biographies are largely works of the imagination. Of course they are not 'creative works' in the sense of being invented, but 're-creative works' in the sense that they recreate the past – forget that ugly and inaccurate term 'non-fiction' (the fictions we tell are part of the lives we lead). At the end of a good day's writing, I am sometimes surprised by where the narrative has led me. Unsuspected connections suddenly reveal themselves and new ideas arise from these connections. I rely on instinct as well as factual evidence to separate the truth from what is false – and then to understand the value of falsity and how subtly it springs from the irregular habits of memory. All writers know the happiness of such discoveries.

Kathryn Hughes

Kathryn Hughes is the author of three biographies, most recently *The Short Life and Long Times of Mrs Beeton*. She is Professor of Life Writing at the University of East Anglia.

People often ask me, as a biographer, whether it's necessary to 'like' the person you are writing about. 'It's complicated,' is my usual answer. If pushed a bit further, I'd say it's rather like your feelings towards your best friend – up and down, but mostly up, until that terrible moment comes when you wonder what on earth you ever saw in her in the first place.

The first time you meet your subject, usually on the page but sometimes in a photograph, the chances are you don't take much notice. She (or he) is just sort of there, buried in a much longer cast of characters who inhabit your inner world. Gradually, though, your subject starts to emerge from the crowd and settle in the centre of your brain and it's now that you fall slightly in love. Suddenly everything she does seems wildly interesting. Her letters are extraordinary, her recorded witticisms an absolute hoot. Every house she lived in seems to take on a numinous glow. Honestly, you can't remember what life was like without her.

It's at about two years into the relationship that you can't help noticing a few annoying habits. There's that way your subject always bitches about her sister, and the fact that she always favours her sons over her daughters. And the hypochondria! If you have to read another letter in which she bangs on about her cough you'll scream (or, more likely, skip the letter altogether). And as for that casual but persistent anti-semitism which inflects everything she says and does ... well, honestly, you feel like giving her a bloody good shake.

Four years down the line and the project is drawing to an end. Mostly you're feeling really pleased. That lingering cough has turned into the consumption that will kill your subject, which means that you're now only one chapter from the end. And then, almost before you know it, she's gone, lying with her hands neatly folded on her chest while her family sobs discreetly. And, you know what, you're actually pretty sad too. In fact, you wonder now whether you shouldn't have been a bit more charitable while she was still alive. The cough was hardly her fault and, after all, lots of people bitch about their sisters. As for the anti-semitism, well many people at that time were much, much worse. And now, before you know it, you're crying too, sobbing not so much for someone who died a hundred and fifty years ago but for a relationship which has been pretty much the only thing that has kept you nourished and stimulated over the past five years.

Diane Johnson

Diane Johnson is a novelist (*Le mariage*, *Le divorce*) and critic, and author of two biographies: *Dashiell Hammett: A Life*, and *The True History of the First Mrs Meredith and other Lesser Lives*.

From 'OBSESSED', *Afterword to* Dashiell Hammett: A Life, 1983.

'OBSESSED' recounts Diane Johnson's problems with Lillian Hellman, Hammett's last lover, who wanted her to see Hammett's life as she, Hellman did – a story culminating in their ideal and happy love. Johnson does not see it that way, and things become more and more strained between them.

She next announced that the book could not possibly be finished, could not possibly be accurate, because I had not gone to Ottawa – this in midwinter, thousands of miles from where I live, for (it seemed to me) very little reason. She wanted me to talk to Nancy Hughes, a woman who had been Hammett's secretary in the early forties, had known Hammett before he went to the Aleutians, and corresponded with him while he was away, refilling his eyeglass prescription, ordering his pipe tobacco. I had spoken to Mrs Hughes on the phone, and we had corresponded. She remembered a nice older man around the place, barbecuing, and she remembered that Hammett was near-sighted – something Hellman had not been able to remember. Otherwise her memories, though helpful, were rather general, the work of a paragraph.

'Certainly no book about Hammett would be complete without her,' Lillian insisted more strongly. I must go to Ottawa or the book would never be published. I had the sense, almost, that she was depending on my refusal to go to Ottawa. And indeed I did refuse to go to Ottawa. The word began to resonate with significance in our conversations, and in Lillian's with Jason Epstein, and in mine with him. Ottawa. Heart of darkness for me, for Hellman, temple and repository of testimonials of happiness. Epstein took us to dinner, to resolve the matter, proposed that the three of us should go to Ottawa together, and, it appeared, seriously resigned himself to this cold and boring trip. He sat wretchedly between us as a rather noisy public quarrel developed.

The abrupt resolution of the scene illustrates, I think, Hellman's sudden moods of generosity and objectivity. It had grown increasingly difficult for her to feed herself, as she could hardly see her plate, but she was not yet at the stage where she would consent to be fed, and one was apt to forget her poor eyesight because of her completely normal and undiminished moral vigour. Suddenly she spilled her fish in her lap. We were all embarrassed, mopped, assisted, muttered about the carelessness of restaurants that don't push the table up properly. Although she had been berating me in strong terms, she now paused, reflected, said, 'You are polite', and abandoned the subject of Ottawa, not, I am sure, in appreciation of our solicitude, which in any case had been reflex. But perhaps an accident of mischance or frailty can remind that there is no ideal happiness, no Ottawa, nothing that can be communicated. Mrs Hughes would have her Hammett, I mine, Lillian hers, each landed with our plate of fish in our lap to deal with as we could.

Hermione Lee

Hermione Lee is a biographer, teacher and critic. She is the author of biographies of Virginia Woolf and Edith Wharton, and of books on Elizabeth Bowen, Philip Roth and Willa Cather. She has written two books about life writing, a collection of essays, *Body Parts*, and an Oxford University Press *Very Short Introduction to Biography* (2009). She is the President of Wolfson College, Oxford.

There are as many ways to start as there are subjects. You can begin with a birth date or a death-bed, with a family history or a statement of intent, with social context or meditations on writing biography. There are no rules. But the minute the first sentence hits the page, the biographer's approach is apparent, the tone of the biography is set.

What happens, though, before the beginnings? How did the biographer find the subject, what decisions and choices were made before that first sentence gets written? The version of biographical genesis we prefer is the romantic one – the powerful magnetism of the subject, the life's devotion to the task. More opportunist or pragmatic motives can be just as telling. Some biographies are the product of publishers' suggestions, some begin with a bargain struck between a still-living subject and a prospective Boswell, or with an approach from the subject's family: all dangerous, seductive transactions. Some biographies are written to set the record straight, or to do justice to a misunderstood figure, or resurrect an underdog.

Special pleading and defensiveness are the perils here. Some, perhaps, are born of more cynical attractions – lots of exotic locations, a particularly gruesome death, a lurid scandal. But naturally I've never met a biographer who would admit to starting work for such motives.

How biographers feel their way into a new subject is usually written about retrospectively. At the time, it feels too much of a hostage to fortune to say much about the first stages. There is an exhilaration at being in that free zone of possibilities and unknowns, before the dogged work of turning research into narrative has begun. But there is fear and uncertainty too. I was afraid of Virginia Woolf when I started, afraid of her mighty archive, her myths, her status, her genius, her much-told story. Richard Holmes (though he won't remember this) once helped me, by telling me that you sit down at the desk, where those malevolent voices are waiting for you, squatting at the side, muttering, 'She can't do it! She doesn't know what she's doing!' And you sweep them off with one bold movement of your arm, and start your day's work.

Above all – in my case – beginnings are about finding a shape. I take my cue from my subjects. Willa Cather's insistence that all you need to know about a writer is in their work, her love of a bare room, of simple classical shapes, influenced my book on her. Writing about Woolf, I had in mind her critique of conventional biography, and her attempt to dig out deep caves of thought and memory below the everyday lives of her characters in *Mrs Dalloway*. I wanted *Edith Wharton*, true to her interests, to be like a series of richly, thickly furnished, interconnecting rooms. These first thoughts, the beginnings before the beginning, do matter, however tentative, and should not be discarded or abandoned by the biographer as the work gathers momentum. Long after my biography of Woolf was published I found my first 'starter' notebook, full of anxious questions and head-scratching difficulties. On one page in caps I had written, 'THIS IS ALL ABOUT STRUCTURE!' And so it proved.

Andrew Lownie

Andrew Lownie is the founder of The Biographers' Club, the author of a *Life of John Buchan* and since 1988 has run his own literary agency.

We are often told we live in a golden age of biography. It is certainly true that fine biographies continue to be published, but as a literary agent in biography for twenty-five years, my own experience is that biography is in decline, and we should really be talking about a golden age of memoir.

Ten years ago I could easily sell all kinds of biography – royal, historical, political – but no longer. These are now the province of websites, magazines, academic or small publishers, or not commissioned at all.

It's true that readers want to learn about other people's lives, but they want to hear about them from the people themselves. At the time of writing, of the nine books on the Amazon biography list, eight are memoirs – and the last, Kate Summerscale's best-selling *The Suspicions of Mr Whicher*, isn't a standard biography either.

The market is not for worthy and well-crafted portraits, but for something more immediate and personal. It's bite-sized, Wikipedia gossip which interests us more than a view of the whole life. We still want to learn about the lives of some politicians, but through their diaries. We are still interested in military history, but in the stories of the soldiers more than the generals. We are less interested in how great people shape events than in how those events affect ordinary people.

I suspect we are also less respectful of members of the royal family, politicians, writers et al; and maybe they are also more boring. Perhaps that's why we seem to be more interested in the autobiography of a chimp, *Me Cheeta*, or in the whole industry of dog books, such as *Marley and Me*, than in biographies of people.

I think we can draw lessons from television, where the didactic approach of being told something by experts has been replaced by celebrities taking the viewer on a personal journey, as in the genealogy programme *Who Do You Think You Are?* Celebrity and the personal hook seem to be the key in publishing now too. This may explain the success of *The Suspicions of Mr Whicher*, and of Frances Osborne's book on her great-grandmother, *The*

Bolter. They work because they draw on a popular genre – crime writing – or else involve a quest or personal element.

There are economic factors too. Newspapers are paying less for serial rights – they can sell more copies of the paper with a free DVD. And the foreign rights market is less lucrative. We've all become more parochial, and countries are now producing their own books on their own subjects.

However, the opportunities for biographers are actually greater than ever before. With technological advances it's much easier to self-publish, and potentially make more money than trade publication. There are more festivals and prizes, and better distribution – Amazon has brought the bookshop into every home with a computer. And biographies are still a staple of the media for news and features.

The real problem is not that there are not enough good biographies, but that there are not enough people who are aware of them. The challenge for biographers is to demonstrate the range and quality of life writing today. If we can do that, together with publishers, the Arts Council and British Council, festival organisers, booksellers and libraries, the Golden Age of Biography will return.

Janet Malcolm

Janet Malcolm's books include *In the Freud Archives*, *The Journalist and the Murderer* and *The Silent Woman: Sylvia Plath and Ted Hughes*, 1993. Her two most recent are *Reading Chekhov* and *Two Lives: Gertrude and Alice*.

From The Silent Woman: Sylvia Plath and Ted Hughes.

Biography is the medium through which the remaining secrets of the famous dead are taken from them and dumped out in full view of the world. The biographer at work, indeed, is like the professional burglar, breaking into a house, rifling through certain drawers that he has good reason to think contain the jewelry and money, and triumphantly bearing his loot away. The voyeurism and busybodyism that impel writers and readers of biography alike are obscured by an apparatus of scholarship designed to give the enterprise an appearance of banklike blandness and solidity. The biographer is portrayed almost as a kind of benefactor. He is seen as sacrificing years of life to his task, tirelessly sitting in archives and libraries and patiently conducting interviews with witnesses. There is no length he will not go to, and the more his book reflects his industry the more the reader believes that he is having an elevating literary experience, rather than simply listening to backstairs gossip and reading other people's mail. The transgressive nature of biography is rarely acknowledged, but it is the only explanation for biography's status as a popular genre. The reader's amazing tolerance (which he would extend to no novel written half as badly as most biographies) makes sense only when seen as a kind of collusion between him and the biographer in an excitingly forbidden undertaking: tiptoeing down the corridor together, to stand in front of the bedroom door and try to peep through the keyhole.

Every now and then, a biography comes along that strangely displeases the public. Something causes the reader to back away from the writer and refuse to accompany him down the corridor. What the reader has usually heard in the text – what has alerted him to danger – is the sound of doubt, the sound of a crack opening in the wall of the biographer's self-assurance. As a burglar should not pause to discuss with his accomplice the rights and wrongs of burglary while he is jimmying a lock, so a biographer ought not to introduce doubts about the legitimacy of the biographical enterprise. The biography-loving public does not want to hear that biography is a flawed genre. It prefers to believe that certain biographers are bad guys.

This is what happened to Anne Stevenson, the author of a biography of Sylvia Plath called *Bitter Fame,* which is by far the most intelligent and the only aesthetically satisfying of the five biographies of Plath written to date . . . The misdeed for which Stevenson could not be forgiven was to hesitate before the keyhole. 'Any biography of Sylvia Plath written during the lifetimes of her family and friends must take their vulnerability into consideration, even if completeness suffers from it,' she wrote in her preface. This is a most remarkable – in fact, a thoroughly subversive – statement for a biographer to make. To take vulnerability into consideration! To show compunction! To spare feelings! Not to push as far as one can! What is the woman thinking of? The biographer's business, like the journalist's, is to satisfy the reader's curiosity, not to place limits on it.

Alexander Masters

Alexander Masters was born in New York in 1965. At university he studied physics and mathematics. Not good enough at the sums, he drove vans and co-wrote diet and sex manuals with the biographer Dido Davies, under the pseudonym Rachel Swift. *Stuart: a life backwards* won the Guardian First Book Award and the Hawthornden Prize. His next book, *Monstrous Moonshine*, is due out in 2011.

Biographies expose life – but they've yet to exploit a fraction of their power. They still limp along, blandly focusing on the famous, pounding through facts from grandma to the grave, missing the point. Biographies should expose not just somebody else's life, but also our own. The excitement, the place where new writers and fresh voices and clever techniques need to rush in, is with biographies of the unknown.

When I published *Stuart: A Life Backwards*, a book about a homeless man in Cambridge, my introductory chapter puffed: 'So here it is, the story of Stuart Shorter, thief, hostage taker, psycho and sociopathic street raconteur – my spy on how the British chaotic underclass spend their troubled days at the beginning of the twenty-first century: a man with an important life'. I realise now I got it wrong. The importance of Stuart's life was not that he lived on the street (for most of the time I knew him, he had a flat – even if he did destroy it several times in one of his bursts of 'rageousness'), but that he revealed something about the way everyone, from the Queen to the rat catcher, would behave if they had to endure the same emotional and physical conditions that engulfed Stuart. He was a spy not just on the chaotic homeless, but on a character that nests inside the most settled of us.

Any subject that is good for fiction is good for biography. Where do you discover such people? I found Stuart on the pavement. My current subject, Simon, was lurking under my floor. He's an 'independent' mathematician who lived in the basement of my old house. Often dressed in rags, he has heard the Voice of God and is a world expert on a mathematical object so complex and shocking that it's known as 'The Monster'. He isn't keen on talking, hates anecdotes, can't remember his childhood, and often runs away when I approach. But that's half the point. Biography is about finding a way to chase an interesting person onto the page. Any technique that's fair in fiction or gutter journalism is fair in biography: drawings, cartoons, photographs, theft, breaking and entering, hypnotism, bullying, cheating, misinformation, fraud, wails of frustration, threats to kick your subject out of the book altogether and bill him for four years of rage and stress if he isn't more cooperative. A good biography of the unknown should have the inventiveness of fiction with the depth of truth.

After Simon, my next subject will be a woman I fished out of a skip. Fifty-four volumes of her diaries were tossed onto the rubble outside a house that had been knocked down, a few streets away from Simon's house. I don't even know her name.

Biographies of unknown people also have enormous potential as campaign tools. Interesting lives that might have been our own – not just on the streets, but in prisons, refugee camps, old people's homes, behind the closed curtains of the house at the end of the road – are forced onto the attention of readers who know nothing about them except clichés and taxes.

There are seven billion people in the world. Even if only 0.1 percent of them are worth a book, that's still seventy million explorations of life and self waiting outside the door of every new writer.

Nancy Milford

Nancy Milford is the Executive Director of the Leon Levy Center for Biography at the Graduate Center of CUNY. She is the author of *Zelda: A Biography* and *Savage Beauty: The Life of Edna St Vincent Millay*, and is now writing a biography of Rose Fitzgerald Kennedy.

To be a biographer is a peculiar endeavor. It seems to me it requires not only the tact, patience, and thoroughness of a scholar but the stamina of a horse. Virginia Woolf called it 'donkeywork' – for who but a domesticated ass would harness herself to whatever is recoverable of the past and call it A Life? Isn't there something curious, not to say questionable, about this appetite for other people's mail, called Letters? What does it mean to be mulish in pursuit of someone else's life, to be charmed, beguiled even, by the past, if not held fast to it? For it isn't true that it provides insulation from the present. On the contrary, it impinges upon it, for while it is from the terrain of my own life that I work and mine hers, biography is the true story of someone else's life, and not my own.

Blake Morrison

Blake Morrison's books include two collections of poems, three novels, a study of the Bulger case, and two family memoirs, *And When Did You Last See Your Father?* and *Things My Mother Never Told Me*.

'It's always Judas who writes the biography,' Oscar Wilde said, and there's an English (or Western, or bourgeois) obsession with privacy that deems *any* non-fictional account of real people a hostile act – as though the writer's only motive is to insult, expose or humiliate. As someone who has (weirdly) written books about both of my parents, I've sometimes encountered this prejudice: it's suggested that I have automatically dishonoured my parents by putting them on the page. 'Attention all Morrisons,' wrote a columnist in *The Guardian*. 'If you value your privacy, don't even think of dying before Blake.' My sister was once approached by the *Daily Mail*, who thought she might like to put 'her side of the story', the assumption being that she must hate my books or have a hostile counter-version of the events described. Luckily for me she doesn't. And if she's quaking in her boots at the prospect of becoming Volume 3 in a family trilogy, she hasn't admitted as much.

Doubtless my reasons for commemorating my family are murkier than I like to think. But surely there's a value in documenting and celebrating 'ordinary' lives – people who would otherwise have no memorial but (to quote Ecclesiasticus) 'become as though they had never been born'. The Mass Observation experiment of the 1930s was one such effort to capture ordinary life, in the words of the people themselves. But the spirit of that endeavour seems to have gone, and the documentary movement has been replaced by Reality TV, that misnomer for a contrived scenario featuring wannabe celebrities. If no one commemorates ordinary people any more, because that's deemed intrusive or exploitative, then we're condemned to focus only on the famous, or infamous, and life as most of us experience it will go unrecorded, except in novels. Even novels might not be exempt: I can imagine a world where any realist work of fiction would be publishable only if the alleged 'real-life models' for the characters had given their written consent.

When students tell me they're desperate to write about their family but afraid what the reaction will be, I adapt the Nike slogan: 'Just do it (and worry later)'. The feelings of the living have to be respected, of course. But when you're writing a first draft, you can't have a family censor peering over your shoulder. Besides, you never know how people will respond. One person whose name I changed in *And When Did You Last See Your Father?*, in order (I thought) to save her embarrassment, told me off for having bothered; she'd rather have been her.

Yes, Life Writing does and must have scruples. But we shouldn't be bullied into feeling guilty just because we write – nor made to feel ignoble for commemorating the unfamous. As Horace put it: 'Many brave men lived before Agammenon's time; but they are all unmourned and unknown, covered by the long night, because they lack their sacred poet'. If you're that poet, however un-sacred, however iconoclastic and irreverent, you're doing a worthwhile job.

Andrew Morton

Andrew Morton is one of the world's best known celebrity biographers, author of number one bestsellers on the late Diana, Princess of Wales, Madonna, Monica Lewinsky and Tom Cruise. He is currently profiling Angelina Jolie.

On the day I was asked to contribute to this volume, my American editor sent me an intriguing newspaper story. It was about legal attempts by a Christian civil rights group in Wisconsin to win the right to burn a book which offended them. Cue references to Ray Bradbury's *Fahrenheit 451;* and cue the chance for smug Brits to sneer that it would never happen here.

But a peculiarly British variety of censorship – that is to say, a smooth, subtle and evasive self-censorship – is already in place. It has far-reaching repercussions for biography, a form of writing that originated in Britain in the work of Dr Johnson, but looks likely to die here.

Britain's notorious libel laws, the interpretation of the European human rights legislation in favour of privacy rather than freedom of expression, and the sheer cost for a publisher to navigate these expensive shoals without a high-priced lawyer as pilot, has severely curtailed the practice of life writing. These days most British publishers treat independent biographers like a bad smell – best avoided.

Let my own salutary tale serve as witness. In June 1992 my biography of the late Diana, Princess of Wales, was published to much sound and fury. I was invited to spend the rest of my days in the Tower of London, and the book was banned by reputable booksellers like Hatchards and James Thynne, as well as by the supermarket chain Tesco. Even though, as everyone now knows, the book was written with Diana's cooperation and approval, it was arguably the most banned book of the 1990s.

In 2008 my biography of the actor and infamous Scientologist Tom Cruise went to number one in America, Germany and France, but was not published in this country, as the publisher, MacMillan, feared they could end up with a long and expensive legal battle with a man and an organisation notorious for aggressive litigation. Serbians and Vietnamese got to read my efforts, but not the Brits. My current biography of Angelina

Jolie, self-confessed drug-user, self-harmer and bisexual, has had no takers in Britain to date. One publisher turned it down, saying that they had 'heard' that Ms Jolie 'might' be thinking about taking legal action.

Who can blame publishers for staying clear of independent biographies? A look at the bestseller list in Britain tells you all you need to know about the rapidly changing commercial and editorial landscape. Like the red squirrel chased out by the grey, it is now dominated by autobiographies by the likes of Jordan, Cliff Richard, Roger Moore and Barack Obama. They sell, and, as far as publishers are concerned, they don't bite back. Do they give a complete and challenging portrait of the individual concerned, or are they merely a series of self-serving platitudes served up for the salivating public? Quite frankly, does anyone care?

Soon independent biographers will go the way of thatchers and dry-stone-wallers in Britain, their sophisticated skills forgotten and dismissed – and all without burning a single book.

Clare Mulley

Clare Mulley is a biographer and a social historian. Her first biography, *The Woman Who Saved the Children: A Biography of Eglantyne Jebb*, won the Daily Mail Biographers' Club Prize. She lives with her husband and three daughters in Essex, where she is currently working on a new biography, about a controversial nineteenth century celebrity.

I first came across Eglantyne Jebb when working as a fundraiser at Save the Children. Somewhat struggling, I found my faith in human nature restored by a reassuring line Eglantyne once wrote: 'The world is not ungenerous, but unimaginative and very busy'. I was immediately intrigued by this woman, but it was only when I left the fund to have my first child – thereby showing far less commitment to the cause than Eglantyne, who never had children – that I had time to find out more.

Eglantyne not only founded Save the Children, thereby saving the lives of many millions of children, she also wrote the pioneering statement of children's human rights which has since evolved into the UN Convention on the Rights of the Child – the most widely accepted human rights instrument in history. But, for me, what makes hers such a wonderful story is that she seems such an unlikely children's champion. 'I don't care for children,' she wrote as a miserable schoolteacher in 1900, later calling them 'the little wretches'. I love this apparent paradox, showing just how complex people can be.

Soon I was hooked on the joys of researching a forgotten life. Two of Eglantyne's great-nephews and their families invited me to stay in their houses, opened up their boxes and bureaus and cooked me dinners. The granddaughter of her girlfriend also shared her memories along with her folders of photos and letters, and there were many cups of tea with other people connected to her story. Sometimes coincidences seemed to lead to uncanny new opportunities to learn something about Eglantyne. How amazing to leaf though her love letters, to sleep in her childhood nursery, and eat from her plates. Having held a curl of her auburn baby hair, and bought my own copy of her signature on eBay, I once described my research as 'psycho-stalking'. It is easy to get a bit too obsessive.

It took me seven years to write the book, although I did other things too, including an invaluable MA in social and cultural history, and having my three daughters . . . The irony of sneaking away from my own childcare responsibilities to research the life of this champion of children's welfare was not lost on me. And of course it wasn't all fun. Discovering I had a rival biographer one day was not ideal, and the nervous wait for a publisher was equally stressful. But now I am very happy to leave Eglantyne on the shelf, a little better known, I hope, while I get on with the next one . . .

Jenni Murray

Jenni Murray is a writer and journalist, probably best known for presenting Radio 4's Woman's Hour. Her most recent publication is *Memoirs of a Not So Dutiful Daughter*.

It was the American screenwriter, Nora Ephron, who first coined for me the mantra, 'Life is copy'. Her parents were writers and had made quite clear to their daughters that the family earned its bread by the pen and they must simply accept that nothing was sacred. The two girls went on to same profession and held to the motto. Nora's novel and film *Heartburn* were based on the breakdown of her marriage to the Watergate journalist, Carl Bernstein.

It's a philosophy I find slightly harsh; and though I know I am as guilty as the next scribe, I have tried to spare my children the worst excesses of my compulsion to draw humour and lessons from my family life and pass them on to a reading public. The boys have, on the whole, been compliant, exacting their fair share of advances or fees for books and articles in which they've been writ large.

My mother was not so content. She spat out her fury when I wrote in detail about the terrible time she had had – shaved, enema'd and legs held up in stirrups – during the forty-eight hour birth that nearly finished us both off. I was using our experience to make the point that attitudes to birth needed to change; she, perhaps rightly, berated me for parading her private life in public. I became more circumspect where she was concerned, and could not have written the book I was desperate to write – *Memoirs of a Not So Dutiful Daughter* – until after her death.

Nevertheless, even though I knew she would have hated the description of a difficult relationship between a mother and daughter – full of petty resentments and guilt, but showing the possibility of love and reconciliation – I had to do it. I try to reassure myself that I write to pass on experience and wisdom gained, to comfort others with the knowledge that they are not alone in their troubles, but I can't really explain it as anything but a compulsion. I guess I would write whether it were published or not, and I acknowledge it cannot be easy for those close to me to know they may well be under constant scrutiny as potential subject matter.

Only once has it really caused trouble with the children. In a book called *That's My Boy* in which I tried to show what joy there is in bringing up sons, I told a story which made the subject of the tale furious, because I had laid him open to teasing by his friends. *I* thought I was making an important point about the assumptions that are made about gender.

He was five and we had gone to the Clarks shop where they carefully measured little growing feet, to buy new school shoes. The man in the shop knew us well and offered a range of tough trainers. 'No,' said Ed, 'I don't want any of those. I'd like to try those please.' He was pointing at a pair of 'Princess' shoes which were heavily advertised at the time as suitable for running, jumping and flashing the 'diamond' that was fixed on the front. They were red and had a small heel.

The man in the shop was horrified. 'But, you can't have those – those are girls' shoes.' And my little five-year-old drew himself up to his full height and piped, 'Now, if I were a girl and wanted the trainers you wouldn't tell her they were boys' shoes, would you? And that's not fair.' I was so proud, I bought him the shoes. He wore them for a week or so, declared them uncomfortable and went back to trainers, thus learning that girls and women are forced into discomfort for their femininity and that it is worth making a principled stand. And, oh dear, I've just told it again . . .

Nicholas Murray

Nicholas Murray is the author of several literary biographies, including ones on Matthew Arnold, Aldous Huxley, Andrew Marvell, Bruce Chatwin and Kafka. He has also published two novels and a collection of poems. He is currently writing a book about the British poets of the First World War to be published by Little, Brown.

A few years ago a fellow dinner party guest rounded on me and asked, indignantly, how I dared to write a biography of someone I had never met. In this case it was a short biographical and critical introduction to a recently dead writer whom I conceivably *could* have met – but many of the subjects one tackles are in the category of the illustrious dead where such an option is not open to the biographer. Another common dinner party query takes the form of: 'Is it an *authorised* biography?' I have never undertaken such a thing and I am rather suspicious of the idea. We don't read 'authorised' history (a concept that has an unsettling Stalinist ring to it) and, apart from the obvious advantage of having the support of the literary Estate and the willing co-operation of surviving friends and family when commissioned to write the first life of a recently deceased author, I am not sure that authorisation is a Good Thing for the reader, for scholarship, or for the onward march of knowledge.

In short, I think that biographers should be free to write independently with no constraints and no fear of upsetting anyone. But I also believe that they should start from a decent ethical standpoint. It may sound old-fashioned but I think biographers should try to tell the truth in a rounded, balanced way. They shouldn't use their biography to belittle greater talents than their own, to settle old scores, to show off, to sneer, or simply to make a splash with sensational findings that may well be true (and I am not calling for censorship or even self-censorship) but which end up by obscuring the true nature of the writer's life and work. Accounts like these leave an afterglow ('Well, I don't like the sound of that character') which can interpose between the writer's books (the justification for the biography in the first place) and the potential public. A relative of mine once told me that she would not read Philip Larkin's poems because she had read a review of his letters which made him sound rather unpleasant. Some writers *are* unpleasant. Some may merely seem so. A good biography can take us through the evidence, helping us to make up our own minds. If the disagreeable facts (which must be there) ultimately put some readers off, they are at least facts (or one hopes they are).

Personally, I have never written a 'demolition job', setting out to expose the nastiness or hollowness of a particular writer. I would not want to do so. What a waste of several years of your life – and writing literary biography is a long, arduous, poorly-rewarded, yet fascinating business – if all the time you believed your subject was a worthless individual. That doesn't mean you have to be sycophantic or credulous or a sort of cheerleader for your subject. But when there is a fine balance of sympathy between biographer and subject the gains are immeasurable. You know what to look for, you know what adds up, you understand the context, where the writer is coming from, what he or she has been trying to say. If you get this right then your enthusiasm will kindle the 'facts' into life and communicate itself to the reader. The biography sings.

And a biography of a writer must sing. It must *never* be dull.

Kristina Olsson

Kristina Olsson is an Australian writer. Her third book, the novel *The China Garden*, was published in 2009. She has written a biography, *Kilroy Was Here*, and recently published a family memoir, *Boy, Lost* (2013.) This was the book she was working on when she attended a writing course in England, led by Carole and Sally. Her memoir *Boy, Lost* was published by UQP in 2013.

Writing this piece, I came to Sally and Carole's course with the same uncertainties I bring to every new piece of writing. With questions. With doubts and excitement and possibilities swirling around my head. My third book was about to be published at home in Australia, but still I stepped over the threshold of this new venture, approached this task as one steps onto the first rung of a steep ladder.

More than anything the first three books – both fiction and non-fiction – had taught me humility. They insisted daily that I strip away any shreds of delusion, especially about myself; that I prostrate myself before the needs of the story's characters; that I put myself second. Ego must be left at the door of the writing room – in my case, a shed in sub-tropical Brisbane. I am here as supplicant, as student, my foot hesitantly on the great learning curve.

That was how I felt when I arrived in England. But something else was at play here. This is what I found: when you approach the work of life writing – your own or others' – with genuine questions, and if you are ready, some alchemical reaction occurs that makes a joy of the very uncertainty you live with. You see that the answers are a by-product, nothing more; the learning curve is the thing, because the curve loops back to *you*.

All good writing requires honesty and courage; memoir, perhaps, most of all. At its best, I think, memoir can unlock for the writer the kind of fearlessness we all need to bring to the blank page every day, to fiction and non-fiction both. I began to sense that kind of fearlessness during that course in other writers as I listened to them talking about their work. Tentatively, I tried it out, tested it on the page.

Back in my sun-warmed shed in Brisbane, an interesting shift occurred. My memoir of my mother and a lost child *did* loop back to me, constantly; time became circular and hollow as my mother's life and mine entwined. The braver I got the truer the story became. I learned and learned. I'm still learning, of course. But, childlike, I'm in love with that, with the world revealing itself. And, like a child, I'm learning to fear it less.

Marion Elizabeth Rodgers

Marion Elizabeth Rodgers is the author of *Mencken: The American Iconoclast* (Oxford, 2005, 2007), one of *Booklist's* 'Top Ten Biographies of 2005–2006' and of the *Academic Library Journal's* 'Top Ten Books in Literature', included in *Chicago Tribune's* 'Best of 2005 Nonfiction List', and a finalist for the *Los Angeles Times* National Book Prize in Biography.

From an article that originally appeared in the April 2008 issue of Writer's Digest.

There had been twelve other biographies on the American journalist H.L. Mencken before I started mine. My challenge was to make a familiar story new.

The sheer volume of Mencken's material is overwhelming. It includes books, diaries, memoirs, as well as 100,000 letters, from the likes of such luminaries as Groucho Marx to Herbert Hoover. There are also the papers of his contemporaries, newspaper accounts, office files, and oral histories.

From this data, the biographer must suggest the sweep of a life, yet highlight the major behavior patterns that give that life its shape and meaning, striking a balance between personal and public achievements. When it comes to organizing material, I use a method Edmund Morris taught me from his work on Theodore Roosevelt. Notes are assembled chronologically, on five-by-eight-inch index cards. This approach allows you to stay in the moment. We do not merely learn the facts of Mencken's life: we see his changing phases and moods.

Yes, it is a slow process, but it can lead to illuminations of your subject's character, the very essence of biography. An interview with Mencken's goddaughter gave me a glimpse into the feelings of a public man who often shielded his privacy with a quip. During Christmas 1939, Mencken gave her a toy doctor's kit. Placing the tiny stethoscope to his heart, the worried little girl said, 'Uncle Henry, I don't hear anything!' To which Mencken replied, 'Just as I thought. I've been dead for years'.

Taken alone, this anecdote is worth nothing. But 1939 had been a pivotal year for Mencken. His popularity was low; he suffered a stroke. This is when the process becomes exciting – when your notes suddenly *click*. Without sacrificing scholarship, this method provides the delicate touches of humor, drama and pathos that can make your story powerful. And, as we all know, storytelling is the essential element of biography.

There can be no enlightening biography that does not include an account of a man's times, especially when your hero is a social critic. But biography is not history; material must be organized according to your subject's perspective. A central theme in my narrative is Mencken's battle for freedom. Mencken viewed Prohibition as a violation of individual liberties. That independent spirit was also demonstrated in Baltimore. How to convey this vividly to the reader? It is always better to *show, not tell.* I described Mencken's neighborhood. On Sunday afternoons the air on Union Square smelled of malt, as neighbors brewed home-made beer. Atmospheric detail like this can be created in fiction, but in biography it emerges only from research.

Ultimately, my goal is to make my readers feel they are *there.* One of the nicest compliments came from a reader who told me that Mencken's presence had been so vivid that when he dies at the end, she felt as if he had just left the room. To which my husband would say: Thank God! For years he has been trying to get rid of 'that other man' in the house.

Meryle Secrest

Meryle Secrest was a journalist in Britain, Canada and the US before turning to biography. In the past thirty-five years she has written nine studies of artists, art historians, an art dealer and an architect, and a biographer's memoir, *Shoot the Widow*. Her latest biography, of Modigliani, is due in 2011.

As a young reporter in Canada I was thrown in at the deep end. I was taken to a room full of strangers and told to go out and find a story. The room was full of ladies in cocktail dresses and my modest assignment was to ask them what they were wearing. Simple, unless you are still in your teens, barely out of a gymslip, blush easily and stammer.

I think of it as practical training for the work I do now as a biographer of people in the arts, rather loosely described – artists, composers, architects and even a stray art historian or two. As I learned later when I sat in on some group therapy sessions, everyone has a story though it may be difficult to get at and involve crying, pounding on mattresses and complete and utter exhaustion. This knowledge has come in handy more than once, when I have been faced with a particularly recalcitrant subject. James Lees-Milne, who knew a thing or two about interviewing, has remarked that some people are immune from the most compelling blandishments and it is hardly worth the struggle. For writing a biography of a living person really does require a good deal of skill at getting round all the defences people put up to prevent themselves from being known by anyone. An interviewer has to somehow extract in two or three hours what some people will never find out in a lifetime. There are ways to do this, most of them easy. One can throw in a really challenging question, like a hard-driving television personality. It's not my style. I prefer to disarm and it often works. The first time I found this out, I was interviewing

Katherine Anne Porter, who had just published her novel *Ship of Fools*. The interview was not going well. Then I said I was in the process of getting a divorce. To my surprise, she said something quite unexpected: she had married three times and it had always turned out to be the same man. The profound truth of that caught me by surprise, as did her pettishness in pointing it out.

The art of the interview is seldom discussed in my field. Perhaps that is because biography takes a certain kind of form. In the US it tends to be dominated by academics who are more interested in evidence, impartiality and the chronicle of a life. My father-in-law, a learned man, used to go straight to the index. This does not suit me at all and if people do that, I feel I have failed. Given my early start in looking for the theme of a life I am hopelessly driven in the direction of drama, colour, conflict and resolution. I do what novelists do, except of course I am bound by the facts, so I cannot invent or, most of the time, know what my subject is actually thinking. Within the straitjacket of what is known and what can never be known, I try to discern the dim outlines of a life and describe that trajectory as vividly as possible. That makes the search tiresome but nobody else can do it. I once wrote about the art historian Bernard Berenson, who began his career as an expert on the Italian Renaissance by buying works for Isabella Stewart Gardner, a collector *par excellence* and founder of Fenway Court, a museum in Boston. Berenson, the son of immigrant Jewish parents from Vilnius, managed to convince his patron that they had much in common, having had common Stewart (ie, Scottish) ancestors. The knowledge that he needed to hide the truth led me straight to my title, *Being Bernard Berenson*. Similarly, when I wrote about the American portraitist Romaine Brookes, whose relationship to her mother was horrific, I found my theme in a note she wrote to herself sixty years after her mother died. The note said, 'My dead mother gets between me and life'. So there was another title: *Between Me and Life*.

The route to discovery, the gradual unfolding of the theme, constitutes the challenge. You as the observer have to be guided by whatever it is you find, meaning you come to hasty conclusions at your peril. It has never been done better than A.J.A. Symons in his ground-breaking enquiry, *The*

Quest for Corvo, which is my model and constant inspiration. Embarking on the discovery of a life is always tedious, sometimes exasperating and usually unsettling, full of dead ends and empty promises. Just the same I cannot think of anything that is more fun, so rewarding that I would happily write without being paid. (Almost.)

Miranda Seymour

Miranda Seymour is a critic and biographer. Her most recent biography is *Chaplin's Girl: the Life and Loves of Virginia Cherrill*. Her memoir, *In My Father's House*, was published in 2006.

It has been a habit of mine, whenever I've been asked to give a class in life writing, to use the following exercise.

I hand out four or five photocopied pages from a journal. Ideally, the document is handwritten, and unpublished. It's important that the students are asked to interpret a document of which they have no previous knowledge, and which does not reveal the identity of its author.

Each student is given an identical sheaf of pages and invited to write a brief imaginary portrait of the author.

William Godwin's diary has proved unusually valuable for this exercise. Writing in a clear and regular hand, day after day, Godwin noted the weather; what he ate; what he read; where he went; what, and whom, he saw; and, lastly, what they discussed. Major events, both in Godwin's personal life and his public one, were noted with striking brevity. (The devastating experience – to take a memorable example – of losing his wife, Mary Wollstonecraft, was recorded only in a note of the time and date.) Minor events (such as the discovery of frost on the inside of Mr Godwin's bedroom window pane, one winter's morning) received more detailed attention.

The results of the exercise are shared and read out. The authors who emerge from the study invariably prove to be as various as the personalities of their presenters.

The point made by this exercise is a cheering one. Biographers should feel no shame about the fact that theirs is as subjective an art as that of the memoir-writer or autobiographer. Biography, I suggest, can be regarded (Richard Holmes's enthralling lives of Shelley and Coleridge exemplify this argument at its most extreme) as the dark twin of memoir: dark, because biographers rarely appear to be conscious of the degree to which they assess, intuit and judge their chosen subject from the island of their singular and individual experience.

This exercise provides one possible response to an often-asked question: should a biographer be put off by the discovery that he or she is not alone in the field? The answer I give is a resonant negative. You only need to imagine yourself reading biographies of Charlotte Brontë, let's say, by (to pluck out two names at random) Hermione Lee and Margaret Forster, to see why. It is inconceivable that the same Miss Brontë would emerge from two such different minds. The silhouette, the setting, the chronological outline, would remain in place; all else would be directed and shaded by the interests and by the discrete personalities of the authors themselves.

Should such subjectivity be cautioned against? I think not. Integrity is the life-writer's most precious possession. Integrity requires a commitment to the truth: the truth as it is perceived by the innately subjective biographer. Without truth, there's no honesty; without honesty, there's no risk; without risk, the project loses integrity. And without integrity, the biography becomes no more than a commercial venture, a soulless product of the marketplace.

Frances Spalding

Frances Spalding is a biographer and art historian. She has written lives of the artists Roger Fry, Vanessa Bell, John Minton, Duncan Grant and Gwen Raverat, as well as a centenary history of the Tate. Her most recent book is *John Piper, Myfanwy Piper: Lives in Art.*

Writing biography may be laborious, but it is also an undeniable pleasure. It lifts you out of time, licences obsessive interest in the details of others' lives and causes your own life to recede, worries and anxieties temporarily dipping out of sight. In this way, hours pass. You feel especially blessed if you have access to an archive which no previous scholar has seen. Slowly, as you disinter the contents, pulling out one document after another, facts emerge, as well as unexpected connections, useful dates, and hidden networks. In addition you begin to catch, through letters and diaries, a person's tone of voice and habits of mind. In this way the stuff of life accumulates, the contingencies and idiosyncratic detail which will eventually enliven your narrative. But in the midst of this work I recently had a small shock.

I was sitting in a tiny room lit by a large bow window. It overlooked the internal well that forms part of 50 Albemarle Street, in London's Mayfair, which then housed the publishing firm John Murray. It is a building rich in literary history, acquired in Byron's day by the Murray family, with earnings from his works. 'Mr Murray's' boasts the engraved brass plate inside the entrance. Portraits of Murray authors line the staircase which leads to a first-floor room and the fireplace where, in keeping with the poet's instruction, Byron's journals were burnt.

Ironically, in the bowels of this large house is a fireproof archive room. It provided a temporary resting-place for the John Piper archive, prior to its move to the Tate under the government's 'acceptance in lieu' scheme. The two families – the Pipers and the Murrays – had been close friends, and so, when I began my biography of the Pipers, I was not only offered use of this small office but also became the recipient of much good will, not to mention numerous cups of tea and coffee. Cocooned in quiet and contentment, I worked through the Piper archive, uncovering letters from legendary figures as well as the obscure or forgotten, all the while revelling in this opportunity to bury myself in history.

Until, that is, I suddenly pulled out a letter from myself. It was poorly typed on not very attractive paper and rather clumsily expressed. But it was certainly mine. Mine and yet not mine, for the careful signature bore scant resemblance to the one I use today, and it came from a city where

I have not lived for two decades. The uneven typing and the style of notepaper belonged to another era. It was a dead husk from the past. Surely it had nothing to do with me for, since writing this letter, every cell in my body must have changed?

My immediate desire was to deny, even destroy this letter. Sense, however, prevailed. From it, I learnt what I had forgotten. That in the mid-1980s I had written to Myfanwy Piper, in connection with my biography of the poet Stevie Smith. I had wanted to know more about the English teacher at North London Collegiate School, where Myfanwy and Stevie had overlapped.

Had she replied, I wondered? After a while, I remembered that she had; at least, I recollected that in my *Stevie Smith* is Myfanwy Piper's account of this English teacher and her classroom method. A glance at the book confirmed this fact. I then asked myself if I could have kept Myfanwy's reply? In the days before e-mails, I had filed letters, because it was a way of keeping the addresses of those who had helped with my research and whom I might need to contact again. It was simply a pragmatic decision, to avoid over-filling my address-book.

In a tin truck stuffed with files I found Myfanwy Piper's letter. To my astonishment it consisted of five A4 pages, covered with information, not just about the English teacher and NLCS but also much about herself. It told how Helen Gardner had helped her get into Oxford and other facts that far exceeded the questions I had asked. It was information, I now realised, available nowhere else. I suddenly had the curious sensation that, through this letter, Myfanwy was speaking directly to me as her future biographer. Later, I was pleased to discover that she had read my *Vanessa Bell*, which had preceded the *Stevie Smith* and a copy of which she had given to her friend Karen Lancaster.

Perhaps, therefore, I need not disown my ancient letter to Myfanwy Piper. And maybe the gulf between then and now is not quite so dire, horrible though it is, in this crisp age of e-mails, to think how many jejune documents have littered our journey to the present.

Hilary Spurling

Hilary Spurling's first book was *A Life of Ivy Compton-Burnett*, her latest *Burying the Bones: Pearl Buck in China*. Her biography of Henri Matisse won the Whitbread Book of the Year award in 2005. She was the Founder of the Royal Literary Fund's Fellowship Scheme for Writers and chaired the Fellowship committee in its first ten years. She is currently working on a life of Anthony Powell.

I was born on Christmas Day, 1940, during the first bombing raid on Manchester, and I spent the next five years in Bristol, where the docks were shelled nightly throughout the war. I remember the thrill of those air-raids with their sirens, searchlights, bangs and flashes. After the war every street had its own bomb-site. As children, we played all day in smashed and abandoned houses, still full of strange surreal signs of human habitation – shreds of curtains, dismembered chair and bed legs, once a whole crazily tilted shelf of broken crockery. We climbed up unstable ruined staircases and crawled through gutted chimneys, digging in the wreckage, always hoping to find an unexploded bomb.

Those early years gave me a strong sense of transience – of how fragile people are, and how easily anything they make or do can be destroyed – together with a passion for excavation and reconstruction. Biography answers these needs. I spent my childhood exploring the broken shells of other people's lives, and now I see that in one way or another I've been doing the same thing ever since. My first subject, Ivy Compton-Burnett, insisted that her life had been wholly uneventful, and made sure no one would ever disinter it by destroying the evidence herself, leaving no letters, journals or papers, except for a shoebox half-full of fanmail. Her early years turned out to be full of unexpected bombshells. All of them fed into novels that explore, as uncompromisingly as any of the great twentieth-century fabulists, the abuse of power within a closed totalitarian society.

Ivy trained me in the severe and sometimes ruthless disciplines of curiosity. Her definition of gossip – 'simple, candid probing into our friends' business' – still seems to me the backbone of biography. One of the many things I learned from writing her life was that human memory is a creative faculty. People who insist that they remember nothing can be a precious asset, precisely because their recollections – if only you can find a way to access them – lie pristine and authentic, not distorted, stylised or tampered with by the pressure of subsequent experience.

I also learned that lack of documentation is not necessarily a disadvantage. For my next book, a life of Paul Scott, who wrote *The Jewel in the Crown*, I interviewed his family and friends, then read right through his private papers – 12,000 documents scrupulously catalogued by an American university – only to realise that his archive was a self-erected smokescreen. I had emerged with a gaping hole at the centre of his life. So I flew to Tasmania to talk to the only living witness from the relevant period, who assured me that her memory was a blank. What I found there taught me that it is always worth backing a biographical hunch, however tenuous.

My next book was a biography of Henri Matisse. Before I began, the greatest Matisse expert in Britain assured me that the reason there had never been a biography was that the painter's life had been too dull to write about. Once again my biographical hunch kicked in, and this time I knew enough to trust it. Research in my experience always starts with the biographer groping and stumbling through piles of rubble, clinging to precarious handholds and leaping over chasms. It is the biographical bangs and flashes that keep me going, the shocks that jolt and shift perception, the sudden penetrating shafts of understanding that illuminate the mysterious dark secret underlife of another human being.

Boyd Tonkin

Boyd Tonkin is the Literary Editor of *The Independent*.

Any reader of the four gospels will know that 'biography' in the ancient world offered more than a chronicle of facts. For Classical writers such as Plutarch and Suetonius, as much as for Saints Luke or Matthew, a life mattered for its meaning, not its data. To write it called for narrative craft and colour on one hand, and on the other an ability to draw the moral, widen the angle and fit the person into a bigger picture than the linear space between a single birth and death.

A new wave of biographical literature has over the past two decades or so recaptured many qualities from the life-writing of two millennia ago. In 2009, Philip Hoare – once a conventional biographer – won the Samuel Johnson prize for non-fiction with his book *Leviathan, or The Whale*. Although it embeds a biographical study of Herman Melville and the making of his masterpiece *Moby-Dick*, Hoare's book showcases many features that mark this looser approach to past lives. It puts the storyteller centre-stage, and makes a drama out of his quest for the subject. It strays from the narrow path of a career to explore the history and ideas that meet in the individual. It disrupts our sense of what counts as central, and what as marginal, in the story of a life. Above all, perhaps, it creates a dialogue between past deeds and present needs that makes the biographer someone who seeks truth in art rather than in archives.

Philip Hoare is not alone among this new school of biographical non-fiction in saluting the role played by W.G. Sebald in opening new routes. From apparent 'fictions' such as *The Emigrants* to a 'travelogue' such as *The Rings of Saturn*, the German expatriate both summoned the real dead to haunting literary life, and showed how our efforts to know them must always lead down tangled narrative paths where genres intertwine. But no more than gospel writers or Roman historians do 'new wave' biographers all resemble one another. Some, like Richard Holmes in his group study of Romantic scientists, *The Age of Wonder*, have shifted their focus from single personalities to collaborative endeavours. Some, like Charles Nicholl, in *The Lodger: Shakespeare on Silver Street*, turn a microscopic gaze onto one chapter of a legendary life and augment their insight with storytelling that pushes speculation to the edge of fiction. Some, like Diana Souhami in *Coconut Chaos*, trip happily over that brink and leave the reader to work out where recorded fact ends and fancy begins. And some, like Kate Summerscale in her Victorian true-crime investigation *The Suspicions of Mr Whicher*, choose one intriguing episode from a secondary figure's life and use it to shed light on the secrets and passions of an entire age.

If this new biographical – or even post-biographical – literature tends to rob both writers and readers of faith in the solid, full-dress portrait, it yields many compensations in return. It feels closer in its sidelights, speculations and digressions to how we understand people we know. It treats the art of storytelling, with all its subtle tools, more seriously than the leaden chroniclers of old with their stolid cradle-to-grave march, glib hindsights and summary verdicts. It values 'minor' figures as much or more than the 'great', and recruits the reader in an imaginative quest for always-elusive truth. And if it often shatters the subject of biography into multiple fragments, pieces of a jigsaw that might never wholly fit, then it can also show us how the smallest life can illuminate not just its times but our shared condition. 'A man's life of any worth,' as John Keats wrote, 'is a continual allegory'. Or, perhaps, a gospel.

Edmund White

Edmund White is perhaps best known for his biography of the French writer Jean Genet, which won the US National Book Critics Circle Award in 1993. He is also the author of a trilogy of autobiographical novels, starting with *A Boy's Own Story*, and many other works of fiction and non-fiction. He has just published *City Boy*, a memoir about New York in the 1960s and 70s. He teaches writing at Princeton and lives in New York City.

As someone who has written both fiction and autobiography, I am interested if there is any real substantial difference between the two genres – or is the distinction merely a librarian's convenience or a mere matter of tradition and nomenclature? I've written two memoirs, three biographies and four autobiographical novels, as well as fantasy novels and historical novels.

For me the essential difference is the one between fiction and autobiography which starts out as a different implicit contract with the reader. The novel is made up and needs to seem truthful, perhaps, but is under no obligation literally to be true. Autobiography, however, is under the restraint of truth – it must be the truth and nothing but the truth. If the reader discovers that an autobiography has taken liberties with the truth or made things up altogether, the reader no longer trusts the author.

But there are many other differences as well. Fiction tends to normalize, to generalize, not in the details – which must always be sharp and specific – but in the facets of the leading characters, whereas autobiography can and should present the narrator and his parents and friends in all their quirkiness.

The novel, in other words, is representative of human experience in general – and a good objection to a novel is that it seems too weird or case-specific to be of much general interest or applicability. The same objection cannot be made to a memoir or an autobiography; there the author is expected to present his own past in all its particularity.

Of course these generalizations are dangerous. For example, I have suggested that fiction begins with story and ends with meditation, but one of the greatest novels, Proust's *A la Recherche du temps perdu*, actually began as a Platonic dialogue between the narrator and his mother about the limitations of the leading literary theorist and critic of the day, Ste-Beuve. Throughout his massive tome Proust is more essayistic than fictional, though clearly he is both.

And there are plenty of novels that have eccentric characters – most of Dickens, for example. But in fiction, I suggest, there is often a reaching after representative types. In James Joyce's *Ulysses*, Bloom is an intelligent small time businessman who is endlessly speculating about how things work in the real world and how they got to be the way they are. His wife, Molly, is lusty, egotistical and highly artistic. Stephen Dedalus is a trained intellectual haunted by his own endlessly proliferating thoughts and rather obviously a stand-in for the younger author himself. These three main characters are too rounded, too psychologically subtle to be called 'types', but Joyce was all the same careful to find three quite distinct and representative Irish characters of the beginning of the twentieth century. Yes, his characters are quirky – but they are above all representative and typical. Fiction deals in types; autobiography deals in the truth, no matter how far-fetched or bizarre it might seem. The reader of novels objects to strange byways of experience; the reader of autobiography treasures the author's past in all its queerness.

Part 3:
Write on

Planning

Important general points for all life writers

* Whichever genre you want to write in – read, read, read!

* Learn from good writers.

* Learn what to avoid from bad writers.

* Fiction can be about ordinary people, but life writing is about extraordinary individuals (or ordinary individuals in a special time or place.)

> **TOP TIP**
>
> *Writing autobiography, biography and memoir is by definition dramatic and special because:*
>
> * *in* **biography** *it is easier to write about special people or those to whom something interesting happened than it is to write about people who lead ordinary mundane lives*
> * *in* **autobiography and memoir** *special events (sometimes disturbing, sometimes joyous) are often the triggers for writing*

There have been many fascinating debates about life writing among critics and among life writers themselves. We have tried to sum up some of them in Part One.

The main issues and challenges discussed in Part One are:

* Is biography history or literature, art or craft?

* What are the ethical and legal problems of writing about real people, including your own family?

* Can life writing be true? Objective? Adequate to life? Possible at all?

* The problems of memory and myth-making in life writing.

* Should there always be a story and an interpretation, or just a record of facts?
* The role of the life writer.

IMPORTANT NOTE

Some of the points in this part will be the same for biography, autobiography and memoir. Some will be different. Where they are different we signal them under appropriate headings.

---

1. Planning a biography

When planning a biography you will need to focus on how to choose a subject, on the type of biography you wish to write, on problems of cost and availability of funding, on how to write proposals and get commissioned, and on what help is available, including journals, courses and mentoring schemes.

Most important: you will have to plan the *structure* of your book itself.

How to choose a subject

When choosing your subject – or if you already have someone you long to write about – think how these points will impact on your work.

Should your subject be:

* alive or dead? There are terrible problems attached to writing about living subjects. They, their family and friends may interfere at the research stage; there may be attempts to control/censor your work; or you may be tempted to self-censor, out of sympathy, obligation, or plain fear.

* group or single? The classic single subject biography is perhaps the hardest to sell today, but good ones still do sell. If that is the book you want to write, you will find a way.

* famous/already done or unknown/new? If famous/already done, have you a new angle? If unknown/new, what original slant do you have to interest publishers and readers?

Question: Do you have to like your subject?

* Biographers from a journalism background, who are used to making money from writing, may be willing to take on anyone.

* Freelancers used to penury, or biographers with a well-paid day job, may be able to choose only subjects they love. We have both been lucky enough to choose our subjects for love (usually for the first reason).

* Neither method is a predictor of quality. Brenda Maddox once told the Biographers' Club she would take on anyone she was hired to do, but her biographies of Rosamund Franklin and Ernest Jones betray sympathy and dedication.

* Sometimes you may start with a modest interest in your subject, even a mild antipathy, but you will always be curious about them, or you wouldn't want to spend several years in their company. As your book develops and you grow to know your subject, you may find that with a deeper understanding comes genuine affection.

Question: What happens if you dislike your subject?

* No biographer (we hope!) can like Hitler or Stalin, but there are countless biographies of them.

* Some biographers may start positively but end up loathing their subject. Mark Schorer finally disliked Sinclair Lewis. More recently, J.D.F. Jones deplored Laurens van der Post and Roger Lewis ended up hating Anthony Burgess. The result may be as off-putting to the reader as it was to the writer. Why read about someone whom even their biographer saw no point in?

* On the other hand, if the writer is so in love with the subject that he/she can see no flaw, readers may soon lose interest in the subject and faith in the biographer's judgement.

TOP TIP 1

There are only two things you really need: curiosity and respect. If you lose these, you are in trouble.

TOP TIP 2

The solution is not in what you feel, but how you write.

The key is to keep a balance in your writing, whatever you feel. (See Balancing empathy and detachment, *in* Writing, *below.)*

Checking out

When you first decide on a subject, it is a good idea to check whether anyone has written a previous biography. There is no reason why you should not offer a new treatment, but it is wise to see what has been said before, by whom, and how long ago. If it was twenty years ago, it is time for a new biography. If it was two years ago, you may have to think again.

You can check out the competition in several ways:

* Search internet book-selling sites, eg, www.amazon.co.uk or the US counterpart www.amazon.com

* Search second-hand book sites such as www.abebooks.com or use the excellent meta-sites (those which search through all the others for you) such as www.bookfinder.com

* Browse the bookshops and second-hand bookshops near you. They should also have a copy of *Books in Print*, which you can ask to consult.

* Consult the copyright libraries or their online catalogues, eg, the British Library http://blpc.bl.uk or the US Library of Congress http://catalog.loc. gov

* *British National Bibliography* lists books published since 1950.

* *Biographical Books,* published by R.R. Bowker, New York, is a guide to biographical writing up to 1980.
* Check the bibliographies in books with similar subjects.
* Consult *The Bookseller's* major lists of up-coming new titles (usually in the February and July issues).

INTERESTING FACT

Biographer Michael Holroyd tried to set up a register of the biographies people were planning. The scheme failed because writers did not want to divulge their good ideas before securing a contract!

Level of work

Before you begin to structure your book, decide on its level.

* Is it for a main-stream audience?
* Is it for an academic audience?

Extra skills you may need to acquire

Before you make a final decision, find out if you need special skills to do justice to the subject.

* Do you need to become familiar with contemporary theatre?
* Do you need to take a course in Russian culture?
* Should you learn about the history of fourteenth century China?
* If you want to write about a non-English speaker, will you have to learn a foreign language to a very high level to conduct interviews and read source materials?

FASCINATING FACTS

For her biography of Primo Levi, Carole had to learn to speak and read Italian fluently. Hilary Spurling (for her biography of Matisse) and Carole Seymour-Jones (for her biography of Simone de Beauvoir and Jean-Paul Sartre) both perfected their French. Judith Thurman even managed to learn Danish to write *Isak Dinesen*.

TOP TIP

If you have to learn to speak a language fluently, it will add at least a year to your preparation.

Types of biography
Advantages and disadvantages

1   Commissioned or uncommissioned

If you are **commissioned** by a publisher to write a biography, you will usually get one third, or even two thirds, of your advance on signing your contract. This is paid to you ahead of any research you undertake, and is very helpful in funding it. Research can be costly, especially if archives and contacts for your subject are abroad.

Uncommissioned biographies are almost impossible, because of the time and money costs involved; but labours of love are always possible.

If your biography is not commissioned, your main problem will be how to fund it. (See Funding, below.)

2   Non-authorised or authorised

The advantage of **non-authorised biographies** is freedom. But if the estate and/or the subject's family do not wish to help you, this is a serious disadvantage. Apart from withholding their own help, they can, for example, prevent other relatives and friends from speaking to you.

The advantage of an **authorised biography** is that you will have unique access to any private materials. People will also feel more relaxed about answering your queries and being interviewed. The disadvantage is that someone may peer over your shoulder and interfere with your work.

CONTRIBUTOR'S TIP

A graphic example of the perils of being authorised comes from our American contributor Diane Johnson, who describes how Lillian Hellman controlled and restricted her every move as she wrote the authorised biography of Dashiell Hammett.

3   Chosen by you or suggested by someone else

* For example, by an agent or publisher.
* This is not as rare as you might think. Arranged marriages *can* work!

SALLY CLINE'S TIP

Although I had written several non-fiction books, I had never attempted a biography. But I had always wanted to write one. One day I was washing up a load of dishes when the phone rang. It was a Commissioning Editor from the publishers John Murray whom I had never met. She said pleasantly: 'Hi, we wondered whether you would like to write a biography for us? If you would, come to our offices the day after tomorrow, with two or three suggestions you are passionate about'.

I left the washing up and wrote down three names: Radclyffe Hall, Diane Arbus, Zelda Fitzgerald.

I arrived at the publishers, shared my passions and some wonderfully steaming coffee, and they commissioned first the Hall, then when that was over, the Fitzgerald. It happened to me, and I bet it happens to one of you. By the way, I never did finish those dishes!

Practical issues, especially cost

* Are there legal risks you should keep in mind?
* Don't forget you will have to clear copyright for all quotations beyond short phrases.

161

* You will have to pay permissions, often for quotations, always for illustrations.
* Most publishers make you pay for your index (usually out of your advance). Indexes can be long and therefore costly in a serious biography.
* For a more detailed discussion of these points, see Research below.

TOP TIP

Don't choose a famous painter unless you're rich! Museums and private owners can charge high prices. The only free photographs are snapshots from family albums.

Consider the implications of each practical issue for your choice of subject.

* American subjects can be expensive, because the permissions system is best organised there.
* Subjects out of copyright (dead for more than seventy years, if European or American) are cheapest and easiest in terms of permissions.

COST WARNING FOR BIOGRAPHERS

There are big financial constraints on writing biographies because of the amount of research and travel, often abroad, that is needed. If you are fortunate enough to have your biography commissioned, it is important to explain to the publishers exactly the kind of cost involved so that this can be reflected in your advance. If you are starting to research before you are commissioned, ensure you have budgeted enough money or know how to access funds. You don't want your fascinating project to run aground because you can't afford to finish your research!

Our advice is: either choose a reasonably commercial subject, so your book has a chance of earning back what you've put into it. Or else be prepared to finance it out of your own income, or grants. (See Funding, below.)

2. Planning a memoir

* Memoirs can feature special places (eg, Miranda France's prize-winning *Bad Times in Buenos Aires*); special events, eg, a war, or a sporting success; a special time in your life, or someone else's life, or the life of a group.

* Ask yourself: which period or event in your life do you want to write about? What is interesting about it?

* As in autobiography, you need to research the period, as well as evoke your memories of it. Although memoir is your impression, it is your impression of other people, places or times. If you get some crucial fact wrong – the date of a battle, or the name of an illness, for example – your readers will lose faith in you.

> **TOP TIP**
>
> *As in autobiography, you should speak to the other people involved – but do not give them a veto. You need to be in full editorial control!*

* Because everyone knows and accepts that memoir is by nature partial and thematic, you can begin and end where you like, and leave out what you like – though you cannot add or invent what you like! (Remember Frey, Wilkomirski, see Part One above.)

* You can expand a conversation of which you recall the drift but not the detail.

* But you cannot give someone a medal she or he did not win, or kill off someone still alive.

> Memoir is the most subjective genre and has the least duty to reality; but it still has some. If this remaining restriction is still too much for you – if you'd like to add and invent important things – then you should be writing fiction instead.

Point to remember: The trade-off is that your story will lose the appeal of the real. Its success will depend not only largely but entirely on the quality of your writing. With memoir, as with autobiography, the connection to reality often helps your book to sell. In fiction (except for biographical fiction) you cannot get this help.

Cost of writing memoirs

Memoir tends to be the least costly in time and money of the three genres, as well as the freest. As in autobiography, the research is limited, because you already have the main memories and documents – your own. Unlike autobiography, memoir doesn't have to cover your whole life to date; so again less time and money are probably needed.

Nevertheless, you will still need a budget, for example if you want to revisit places you are writing about. There may also be costs of interviews (you might want to take small presents), travel to interviews or archives, tape recorders, stationery, inkjet cassettes, laser refills, equipment costs (updating computers, scanners, printers), etc. There can be expenditure on courses and mentoring. And there are likely to be costs for permissions (both quotations and illustrations.)

TOP TIP FOR MEMOIRISTS

Make sure it is a memoir you wish to write, not an autobiographical novel. Memoirs have a greater loyalty to reality and 'the truth'.

3. Planning an autobiography

Decide whether you want to write about the whole of your life to this point, or perhaps rather take themes that have interested you. Ask yourself:

* why do I want to write this now?
* what role does 'truth' play in my autobiography?
* what is my special angle of interest that will capture the attention of an agent or publisher?

True, everybody has a story to tell, but if it is to interest the general reader, not just your friends and family, it must have some distinctive quality. (The distinctive quality *can* be brilliant writing, but it is a bit risky to rely on that.)

There are very few autobiographies about absolutely ordinary, non-famous people, not distinguished in any way.

If they *are* ordinary, perhaps they are disabled, or adopted, or the child of a famous person (eg, Christopher Robin), or they have taken part in dramatic events. Or though ordinary, they have come from a time or place that is nostalgic or exotic to readers: someone who grew up in a Welsh mining town, or an Inuit village, or a Turkish harem, for example.

> **TOP TIP ON PLANNING AUTOBIOGRAPHY**
>
> *If you do have a special story to tell – are you sure you want to tell it this way? Are you sure it wouldn't be better as a memoir, confined to one main period or incident? Only if the whole story up to the present is required for what you want to show/say, is autobiography the right form for you.*

Cost of writing an autobiography

* The legal risks, copyright for quotes, permissions for any quotes and pictures, and costs (time and money) for these, are all similar to those for biography.
* But a shorter time is involved in research.
* Autobiographers also save time by not needing long end notes.

* They save money by not needing the long place and subject index, compiled by a professional indexer, that biographers need.
* They can save still more money by compiling a short name index themselves.

However:

* Unless you're already famous, say Wayne Rooney or Madonna, don't expect a commission and advance. You will have to write the book first, and look for a publisher after. Finding a publisher will depend entirely on how well written it is – no help from your subject, as in biography.
* Even if you're already known as a novelist, dramatist or short story writer, publishers may be reluctant to let you change genre – unless of course you are very well known, in which case they've probably been trying to get you to write an autobiography for a long time!

4. When you have decided on your biography, memoir or autobiography

* How should you approach an agent or publisher?
* How do you write a proposal for an agent or publisher?

Before you approach an agent:

* Have the proposal for your book ready.
* Give your book a compelling title. (See Choosing titles, below.)
* Find out about the competition, so that you can tell the agent how your book is different in content, area or themes covered, or in the slant you intend to take.
* If there is no competition, you need to show why this subject is worth publishing a book on.
* You must convince the agent that *this* book needs to be written *now*, and by *you*.

To look for a suitable agent, use either or both the *Writers' and Artists' Yearbook*, published by A & C Black or *The Writer's Handbook*, edited by Barry Turner and published by Macmillan. The former has several useful articles on finding an agent, the latter a good section on the same subject.

Make sure you get the most up-to-date edition.

Some agents provide editorial and creative support. Some help on long-term career planning. Some are subject specialists. Some are more involved in marketing and promotion. All of them handle finance, contracts and business with publishers. Work out what your needs are. Check which agents handle life writing.

* Only approach an appropriate agent who handles the category of book you are writing.
* Make your approach professional.
* Check how agents want their submissions.
* Only submit neat typed work on single-sided A4 paper.
* Send a short covering letter with your proposal and/or manuscript.
* If your book is finished, don't send the whole thing. Usually a synopsis and three chapters.
* Your letter should summarise briefly what your book is, why you wrote it, who is the intended audience, and any other important information.
* Always say why you are uniquely placed/qualified to write this particular book.
* If it is an autobiography, explain why it is of public interest and/or why your experiences set you apart.
* Provide a CV. Neat, typed, up-to-date and relevant.
* Provide a large stamped addressed envelope for the return of your material.

Think of your approach to an agent as an application for a job. Be thorough, make it relevant, and be as brief as you can.

Planning proposals for biography, autobiography and memoir

Note: your proposal will almost certainly go to your agent first. Once they have approved it, it will be sent to a publisher.

The following headings are a good way to structure your proposal for a **biography**:

* Introduction to your biography.
* Why a publisher would want to commission this subject.
* Timeliness of your book.
* Critical intentions (where relevant).
* The subject's work (where relevant).
* The subject's life. Include timeline.
* Limitations of previous biographies.
* Research programme and travel.
* Likely costs.
* Preliminary research completed and contacts already established.
* Relevance of the author's previous works or interests.
* Competition with other works in the same area.
* An outline of the book, including proposed Part and Chapter divisions. (It often feels too early for this, but it can help to structure your ideas).

Proposals for autobiographies and memoirs are easier to write than those for biographies, but pointless at this stage. As we've pointed out earlier, unless you are a celebrity or a well-established writer or have a *very* special story to tell, you are unlikely to find a publisher in advance for an autobiography or memoir.

However, you will need an outline of your book to apply to an agent, for a grant, life writing course or mentor. You can use most of the suggestions in Biography proposals as a guide, omitting the ones that don't apply (eg, Critical intentions or Competition with other works in same area).

The most important point is to show why this book is needed, why now, and why by you.

The next important point is to choose a good title.

Choosing titles for biography, autobiography and memoir

* Titles are key selling points. They are also influential in whether your book will be remembered in the future.

* Jean Rhys almost gave *Wide Sargasso Sea* the title *The Wild Sea of Wrecks Where I Was Wrecked*. Scott Fitzgerald wanted to call *The Great Gatsby*, *Trimalchio in West Egg*. Thank goodness they didn't!

* There are no copyrights on titles, so you *could* call your memoir *Crime and Punishment*. But you would probably be better off inventing something fresh.

* Good titles in autobiography and memoir are standard – and very important.

* Fine examples are:

  The Year of Magical Thinking

  A Room of One's Own

  Bad Blood

  Lucky

  This Is Not About Me

  Stuart: A Life Backwards

  A Heart-breaking Tale of Staggering Genius

These titles make you want to pick up the books immediately. Good titles are less important in a classic single subject biography, but only if the subject is famous and needs no help to draw readers. Today even single-subject biographies usually have a title.

Titles should do several jobs:

* They must attract readers' attention.

* They must be brief enough to be memorable (or in some cases long enough, eg *A Heart-breaking Tale* above).

* They should give readers a hint of the content (as in *A Room of One's Own, Bad Blood, Stuart*) or intrigue them as to what it is (as in the others.)

In biography the name of your subject(s) should appear somewhere in the title, either in the main part or in the sub-title. This makes for immediate recognition. It also helps people using computerised catalogues to access it quickly.

TOP TIPS FOR TITLES

Sally Cline used the subject's name first, Zelda Fitzgerald, *then added an intriguing sub-title,* Her Voice in Paradise, *to evoke echoes of Scott Fitzgerald's* This Side of Paradise.

Carole Angier did the opposite, starting with one of her subject's own titles, The Double Bond, *then putting his name in the sub-title,* A Life of Primo Levi.

Claire Tomalin used her well-known subjects' names first in Samuel Pepys: The Unequalled Self *and* Thomas Hardy: The Time-Torn Man. *But for forgotten Nelly Ternan she used the other method: the thematic title* The Invisible Woman, *followed by the sub-title* The Story of Nelly Ternan and Charles Dickens.

Hilary Spurling has also used both ways. In her biography of Matisse, Volume 1 is entitled The Unknown Matisse, *followed by the sub-title* A Life of Henri Matisse. *For her less famous subject she reversed the procedure.* The Girl From the Fiction Department *is the appealing title, followed by the explanatory sub-title* A Portrait of Sonia Orwell.

Grants and other sources of funding for biography, autobiography and memoir

Try websites and e-mail addresses for information on these useful institutions:

* Arts Council of England: www.artscouncil.org.uk
* British Academy: www.britac.ac.uk
* New Writing North: www.newwritingnorth.com
* New Writing South: www.newwritingsouth.com
* Leverhulme Research Fellowships: www.leverhulme.ac.uk/grants_awards

* Biographers' Club: offers prizes to new writers wishing to write biographies. www.biographersclub.co.uk

* The Royal Society of Literature, Jerwood Awards: gives grants to unpublished writers. Has included life writers in the past; watch for a repeat. www.jerwoodcharitablefoundation.org

* Winston Churchill Memorial Trust: offers Travel Fellowships. They too have featured biography as a category in the past and may do so again. www.wcmt.org.uk

TOP TIP 1

Think of other possible grant areas your subject could fit. There are special interest funds for sport, social benefit, music, etc. There are EU grants, if your subject is continental, or had a continental connection, eg, Anglo-French relations, Holocaust studies, etc. And there are many American grants, mostly for American citizens, but some may be open to British applicants as well.

TOP TIP 2

At most public libraries there are two huge books containing grants and funding information: the annual Grants Register, *published by Palgrave Macmillan, and the* Directory of Grant Making Trusts, *published by Directory of Social Change. Put some time aside to browse through them. You could be eligible for a surprising number.*

Other helpful information at the general planning stage

Mentoring

It isn't easy for writers to break through into the publishing world on their own. Everyone, however talented, can use guidance through this process. Mentoring is an increasingly popular solution.

* Several mentoring organisations now exist in the UK. The best known is Gold Dust, directed by the novelist Jill Dawson, one of our distinguished guests; Sally is one of its mentors. In 2013, Carole and several other writers founded a new one, The Writer's Project. Both agencies offer one-to-one mentoring by well-known writers in their specialist areas. Contacts: www.gold-dust.org.uk; www.writersproject.co.uk

* The Jerwood Foundation organises some mentoring and writing schemes. E-mail: info@jerwood.org

Literary consultancies

A number of professional organisations offer critiques of your work for a fee. The best known is the Literary Consultancy, directed by Rebecca Swift. It has a good reputation, uses qualified writers and critics, and offers detailed feedback in a reasonably short time. E-mail: info@literaryconsultancy.co.uk. Other reputable literary consultancies can be found in the *Writers' and Artists' Yearbook*.

Courses

* Many universities now offer a Creative Writing MA, either full- or part-time. These are most useful if they allow you plenty of time to write, and if their tutors are both published writers and good mentors.

* Today there are also on-line MA courses. In place of personal contact, these offer communication with many fellow writers from different backgrounds and disciplines.

* Undergraduate creative writing degrees or diplomas. Universities and colleges are now starting to offer creative writing courses for those who do not already have a degree. They are generally three-year full-time courses for a degree (diplomas will be shorter), and may offer creative writing either on its own or in conjunction with English, Film Studies, Media Studies etc.

* Creative writing classes. Most local authorities used to run Community Education creative writing classes. Many have now cut back, but it is worth trying to track down those still run by enlightened councils. Contact your local Literature Development Officer or library, and check Community College listings in local newspapers. For writers over

fifty who are not in full-time employment, many branches of the University of the Third Age run very successful writing classes. Worth investigating!

* Writing circles or associations. These have begun to develop instead of, or as well as, classes. Writers bring their own work, read other people's, and exchange constructive criticism. Groups are run in libraries, at bookshops, or in private homes, like book clubs. They can have a friendly, encouraging atmosphere and may be most supportive to new writers.

Journals

There are too many magazines and journals devoted to writing to list them. If you Google 'writers' magazines' you will find a huge selection. Two of the best are: *Mslexia Magazine* (for women writers), e-mail: postbag@mslexia.co.uk and *Writers Journal* (for all writers), www. writersjournal.com.

There is a new online magazine devoted to biography alone: *The Biographers' Craft*, edited by James McGrath, and subtitled 'A monthly newsletter for writers and readers of biography'. It is based in the US, but has a strong British connection, and is packed with information, analysis and the latest news about biography. And it's free! You can subscribe on the website: www.thebiographerscraft.com

Organisations

* Arvon is the oldest creative writing foundation in the UK, offering week-long residential courses with two professional writers in one of four historic houses. We both work regularly for Arvon, and believe that the Arvon experience is among the most creative an emerging (or experienced) writer could have. Website: www.arvon foundation.org

* The Leon Levy Centre for Biography. An important new centre for the study and support of biography. Founded in 2008 as part of the Graduate Center at the City University of New York (CUNY). It offers paid residencies to three biographers a year, an annual conference, the Leon

Levy Biography lecture, workshops, forums and public presentations. Its executive director from 2009 is our guest, Nancy Milford. Website: www.leonlevycentreforbiography.org

* The International Auto/biography Association, IABA, founded at the University of Peking in 1999. It has held six conferences so far, in China, Canada, Hong Kong, Australia, Germany and the USA. The next is planned for 2010 and will be held in Britain, at the University of Sussex, in association with the Centre for Life History and Life Writing (see following entry). Website: www.iaba.org.cn. The archive of the IABA is available through the University of Hawaii: https://listserv.hawaii.edu/archives/iaba-1.html

* The Centre for Life History and Life Writing Research, University of Sussex, established 1999, houses the Mass Observation archive. This contains the original Mass Observation papers (1937–1950s) on the daily life of Britain and a continuing Mass Observation project from 1981. Website: www.sussex.ac.uk/clwlhr

* The Centre for Editing Lives and Letters (CELL) at Queen Mary's College, London. The research centre was established in 2002 for projects in the period 1500–1800. Its director is the biographer Professor Lisa Jardine. CELL offers seminars, events, and a post-graduate programme. It also offers an annual HarperCollins History Lecture, whose speakers so far have included Amanda Foreman, Simon Schama, Amanda Vickery and in 2009 Stephen Fry. Website: www.livesandletters.ac.uk

* Biographers International Organization, to be established in 2010. Its first conference, to be held in May 2010 at the University of Massachusetts, Boston, will focus on the practical aspects of writing biography. E-mail: info@biographersinternational.org

* The Center for Biographical Research at the University of Hawaii at Manoa, the first centre for biographical studies in the US (or anywhere), founded in 1976. Publishes *Biography, an Interdisciplinary Quarterly*. Website: www.hawaii.edu/biograph

Planning your writing – all genres

1. Referential matter

This is all the material that goes before and after the main text:

* The preliminaries go before – table of contents, list of illustrations, family tree, preface and prologue or introduction.

* The concluding material after – end notes, bibliography, list of works, index.

* The dedication comes at the start.

* Acknowledgements (to people and organisations who have helped, supported or funded you) and permissions can go either before or after the text.

For autobiography and memoir you usually do not have a subject index (though you may want a name index), and probably not a bibliography. End notes are optional.

The preliminaries, up to and often including the preface, are paginated separately, in lower case Roman numerals, to show where the text proper begins. Nonetheless most readers will start with the preface, so this is in fact where your book begins.

2. Use of preface and prologue for biographies, memoirs and autobiographies

Preface

* Introduces your book.

* Distils scope, content, aims and themes.

> **TOP TIP 1**
>
> Start with your preface, to make clear to yourself your main aims and themes when you begin. Then go back and rewrite it at the end, to sum up the final version.

> **TOP TIP 2**
>
> *Especially if your book (most likely a biography) is long, both the PR person at your publishers and the more idle reviewers will rely heavily on your summary in the preface. So make it brief, accurate and attractive.*

Prologue or introduction for biographies, autobiographies and memoirs

Prologues are not necessary but they are very useful to give readers an immediate sense of the whole book. The prologue can be an account of why you wrote it, or what you hope it will achieve. Even better, it can be a vivid introductory scene. This could be:

* a key place: for example, Hillary on the summit of Everest, or setting out to Nepal from New Zealand
* the cemetery where the subject is buried
* a key moment in your life, or in your subject's life
* the death, after which you return to the start of the subject's life
* a formative early event, a rape or a lie, for example
* a symbolic object, for example, a childhood toy (think of Citizen Kane's *Rosebud*)
* a house, a landscape, the first meeting between your parents/your subject's parents.

> **TOP TIP 1**
>
> *Whatever you choose, it should capture the atmosphere and main point of the biography or memoir.*

> **TOP TIP 2**
>
> *Whatever you choose, it must hook in the reader.*

In a thematic biography of a scientist, choose a dramatic moment in their life that is the seed of one of the themes.

Write two paragraphs that will start off the prologue.

3. Structure

The single most important thing about your book is its structure.

Biography

Length

Length is crucial and often contested.

* The standard word count for biography is somewhere between 80,000 and 130,000 words. Today the publishing world would rather have short biographies.

* Even end notes, which traditionally ran to dozens of pages, should now be kept to a minimum.

* Keeping these points in mind, make your choice. If it's a six hundred page scholarly biography with twenty pages of endnotes – go for it.

* A good and increasingly popular solution is to put end notes on a website, to which you refer readers in the book. The only problems are: will your publisher host the site? For how long? Can you do it yourself, and can you spare the time?

* Chapters are usually around five to eight thousand words, but there are no absolute rules. A short chapter between two long ones can add variety and pace to a book.

* Some biographers use 'factual asides' or even brief fictional scenes to punctuate lengthy factual chapters. These can expand the themes without interrupting the narrative flow. (But be aware that some readers and critics will be disturbed by such 'experimental' devices. See Part One above.)

BIOGRAPHERS' TOP TIPS

In her biography of Primo Levi, Carole Angier used a two-level structure. Most chapters narrate traditionally 'true', evidenced events, while shorter chapters between them use Levi's suppressed experiences and the biographer's own encounters to reach hidden truths.

Kathryn Hughes' biography of Mrs Beeton interlaces topics related to food – such as whether Mrs B ruined British cooking – between the main narrative chapters. The flow of the book in each case is enhanced rather than interrupted.

Cradle to grave structure

* This is the classic form for single subject biography.

* It would also be used for a family history.

* Typically it starts with the subject's birth and continues chronologically until her/his death.

* Advantage: the story line is easy to follow, and if you write it sufficiently dramatically it can keep readers wondering what will come next.

* Disadvantage: its length means that it can seem weighty, even stodgy. Keep it tight. Also, it isn't trendy, so may not catch reviewers' eyes.

* Danger: the most exciting events in your subject's life may come at the beginning, but nothing much may happen after middle age (or vice versa).

TOP TIP

Choose people who die young, or be original with the process. Sally Cline chose Zelda and Scott Fitzgerald, who died at 44 and 48 years old. Alexander Masters reversed chronology in Stuart: A Life Backwards and told the story back to front. Or choose people with rich inner lives. The outer life of Carole's subject Primo Levi had a terrible shape: one world-historical year in Auschwitz, with long periods of uneventful bourgeois existence either side. But what went on inside was dramatic throughout.

In How To Write Memoir and Biographies *Midge Gillies suggests you condense the dull parts and lengthen the tempestuous ones. But be warned that your structure may look slightly unbalanced.*

Thematic structure

* Dominating themes in the subject's life and work can structure the book, rather than chronology. Or you can mix the two.

* Pick out such themes and give a chapter to each. You might choose 'Keats and illness' or 'Keats and his friends', for example.

* It is easier to use the thematic approach when the subject and their history are already well known, as in the case of Keats, or Virginia Woolf.

BIOGRAPHERS' TOP TIPS

Hermione Lee uses a variety of themes to structure her biography of Woolf, including first love, siblings, women's friendship, madness, Bloomsbury, childhood sexual abuse and marriage.

Louise De Salvo uses a single important theme – the impact of child sexual abuse on Woolf's life and work – to structure hers.

Partial and particular themes structure

This method focuses on a particular theme or time in the subject's life, for example, Lyndall Gordon's *Private Life of Henry James*, which focuses on James' relationship with two important women in his life; or Claire Tomalin's *Katherine Mansfield: A Secret Life*, which explores the thesis that Mansfield had gonorrhoea. Hilary Spurling's *Burying the Bones: Pearl Buck in China* looks only at Buck's youth and her formation as a writer. Diane Middlebrook's *Young Ovid* does the same for Ovid. This time-limited technique is often known as 'A-Year-in-the-Life' structure.

Quest biography structure

* This is a classic alternative to chronological structure, pioneered by A.J.A. Symons in his famous *Quest for Corvo* over seventy-five years ago. It is generally used when not enough information exists on the subject, but the little the biographer has found is intriguing.

* Instead of a standard third-person 'objective' account, we follow the biographer's first-person quest – which may be just as interesting when it fails.

* After *Corvo*, the best-known modern quest biography is Ian Hamilton's *J.D. Salinger*, though opinions have differed about its success. Other examples are Will Wyatt's *The Man Who Was B. Traven* and Rachel Lichtenstein and Iain Sinclair's *Rodinsky's Room*.

* Chapters in quest biography will break down naturally into the successive stages of the quest, each pursuing a part of the subject's life (but see Chapter breakdown below).

TOP TIP FOR QUEST BIOGRAPHY

Though the biographer is part of the narrative, you must be careful how often you enter the story. If you appear too often, the book will become about you instead of your subject. Tone is crucial. Do not sound too smug, paranoid or despairing, though you may feel all of these and more.

EXERCISES FOR QUEST BIOGRAPHY

You are writing the quest biography of the secret lover of a well-known politician. Both are recently dead. You learn that the secret lover, your subject, left their letters with his/her sister. You interview the sister, hoping to persuade her to give you the letters.

i. You succeed. Write two paragraphs (max. 200 words) about this event, as they will be in your biography.

ii. You fail. Write the same paragraphs.

Borrowed structure for biography

An exciting new approach is to use the structure of another genre for your biography. Both Patrick Marnham and Kate Summerscale have used the structure of a crime thriller, eg, Marnham in his biography of Lord Lucan, *Trail of Havoc*, and Summerscale in her best-selling *The Suspicions of Mr Whicher*, the story of the first detective told through his main case.

As Boyd Tonkin argues in Part Two, the German writer W.G. Sebald led the way in introducing new structures into life writing. Sebald's work rolls biography, autobiography, memoir, literary criticism, scholarship, architectural, historical and travel writing into one unique and compelling form. Following his example, life writing has started to borrow structures from many different genres. Philip Hoare's book of the whale, *Leviathan*, which won the 2009 Samuel Johnson Prize for non-fiction, combines childhood memoir, cetacean biology, literary criticism, zoology, history and travel as well as biography.

It is not yet clear whether many writers will, like Hoare, follow Sebald on his protean path. We hope so. The question will be decided by the writers of the future – that is, by you.

Biography and memoir

Biography and memoir don't have to focus on the classic single subject. They can also focus on

1   a pair or couple
2   a group

Group and pair biographies and memoirs

* A theme can unite a group biography, as in Sebastian Faulks' *Three Fatal Englishmen*, in which all three subjects are heroic failures.

* But a particular time is a more common way into a group biography, as in Alethea Hayter's *A Sultry Month*, Penelope Hughes-Hallett's *The Immortal Dinner*, or Richard Davenport-Hines' *A Night at the Majestic*. These all look at groups of artists who were in the same place at particular moment.

* Time might possibly be used in a single-subject book as well, eg, a biography or memoir of Sir Edmund Hillary concentrating on the day he climbed Everest.

* If your subjects are a domestic, marital or sexual couple, this can increase the interest and drama (as in Sally's pair-biography of Lillian Hellman and Dashiell Hammett). The interaction between the two will give your readers a deeper comprehension of each individual.

* If there is rivalry between your subjects, this will further heighten the drama (eg, all biographies of Sylvia Plath and Ted Hughes.)

Other group subjects might share a similar background. They could be families, like Andrew Motion's *The Lamberts* or Jeremy Lewis' *Shades of Greene*; siblings, such as James Fox's *The Langhorne Sisters* or Penelope Fitzgerald's *The Knox Brothers*; or the inhabitants of a village, as in Ronald Blythe's *Akenfield*. The connection might be a culture, as in the many books on the Bloomsbury Group, or in Jenny Uglow's *The Lunar Men* and Richard Holmes' *The Age of Wonder*. Extreme events such as war, genocide or natural disaster all make natural links for group memoirs or biographies: Paul Rusesebagina's memoir of the Rwandan genocide, *An Ordinary Man*, for example, or the anonymous *A Woman in Berlin*, an account of the mass rape of German women by the Red Army in 1945. Nell Dunn has written two books based on shared roles – *Talking to Women* and (26 years later) *Grandmothers Talking to Nell Dunn*. Caroline Moorehead has written the biography of an institution (*Dunant's Dream*, about the Red Cross) and *Human Cargo*, a memoir of some of the world's most dispossessed refugees.

This approach gives you a chance to point to differences and trace similarities. It also allows lesser known members of a group to be brought into the wider picture. And you can include letters, journals and interviews that will enliven your book with varied, authentic voices.

> **TOP TIP**
>
> *In James Fox's book one Langhorne sister takes centre stage – Nancy Astor, the first woman to sit in Parliament. If one character is dominant, you might need to assess whether a single-subject biography rather than a group biography or memoir is the best choice.*
>
> Clue: *There were already several biographies of Nancy Astor. So in this case the group focus was a clever new idea.*

> **TOP TIP ON STRUCTURE**
>
> *Whatever structure you choose may be fashionable or unfashionable at any given time. The more innovative methods – especially the partial, group and borrowed-structure ones – are currently in fashion. But they are not new. Alethea Hayter's* A Sultry Month *was published in 1965. And there will always be a call for the classic chronological life story.*

Parallel lives approach to memoir or biography

You might compare and contrast two famous or infamous figures with features in common, eg, Stalin and Hitler (though that's been done!), or two or more characters you have found fascinating.

> **TOP TIP 1**
>
> *In* How To Write Memoir and Biographies, *Midge Gillies suggests that writing about two or more people whose lives have a natural symbiosis can give readers more for less.*

183

> **TOP TIP 2**
>
> In Writing Biography and Autobiography, *Brian Osborne agrees, but warns that it isn't easy keeping the narrative thread clear when moving from figure to figure.*

Autobiography

Autobiography faces the same questions as memoir and biography. Should you simply go through your life chronologically, up to the point of writing, or should you use some other, more innovative structure? The advantages and disadvantages of the classic 'cradle to grave' (or for autobiography, cradle to the point of writing) structure are discussed on pages 178–179.

The alternative possibilities for autobiography are the same too. You could pick out the key themes of your life, and base your chapters on those (eg, 'Sisters', 'Love', 'False starts', 'My music'). But note that chronology is always the underlying principle. It would be odd, for example, to have 'Love' before 'Sisters', even if you followed your relationship with your sisters into later life – unless 'Love' didn't just mean adult romances, but started with childhood loves, for example of your parents, your best friend, a place, a pet.

Autobiography is always partial, because writers cannot tell their own deaths. It cannot tell the whole period, however long, after the end of the book. Think of Wayne Rooney, who wrote his autobiography (or had it written for him) in his twenties.

> **TOP TIP**
>
> *What distinguishes autobiography from memoir is not so much the partial/whole divide, but the central focus. Autobiography asks, What happened to me? How am I affected by it? Memoir focuses on the event, person, group or time.*

Autobiography using borrowed structures

Gore Vidal's *Palimpsest* is exactly that – a first version altered and added to a year later. Sandy Balfour's memoir, *Pretty Girl in Crimson Rose (8)*, uses his obsession with crossword puzzles not only as an organising theme but also as a model, for example in his teasing title. In Nigel Slater's best-selling *Toast* each memory starts with food, from the 'Cheese on Toast' of his childhood to the 'Salade Tiède' of his adult life as a chef. And Art Spiegelman's *Maus* famously borrows the structure of a comic strip about mice to tell the story of growing up with parents who had survived the Holocaust.

An early example of this quirky model was *The Periodic Table*, the autobiography of Carole's subject, Primo Levi, who was a chemist as well as a writer. Here each chapter takes its title from an element of Mendeleev's famous Periodic Table, and tells of an event or a person in Levi's life connected in some mysterious and metaphorical way to that element.

As all these examples show, the borrowing of a structure from a special area – a science, an art, a hobby – can add an extra, enriching level to your book.

WARNING

It has to be a genuine passion of yours, or it will show.

EXERCISE ON BORROWED STRUCTURE AUTOBIOGRAPHY

Imagine you are a shoe fetishist, a gambler, a golfer, or a forger. Write the first paragraphs of three of your chapters, with their titles. Max. 150 words.

Chapter breakdown in all genres

After the overall structure, the next most important decision you will make is the detailed structure, ie, the way you divide your chapters.

Don't forget: structure, structure, structure!

The outline of what is to be in each chapter will be useful to an agent or publisher in assessing your book. It is useful to you to help organise your material – and your thoughts.

* In the cradle-to-grave method (eg, the classic chronological biography), divide chapters by dates/periods.

* In the thematic method, divide chapters by themes or parts of themes: eg, Virginia Woolf and her family; the Bloomsbury group; her diaries; politics; mental illness, etc.

* In a group biography or memoir, chapters can be divided by dates, themes, events, or characters. For example, you can follow each character out from the uniting moment and watch the effect on him or her.

* In a partial biography or memoir, depending on the kind, divide chapters by dates, themes, events or characters.

* In a quest biography or autobiography, divide chapters by stages of the quest. But you don't have to tell the truth, since the main story is still the subject's, and the quest is just a device: so if the order of discovery is too confusing in relation to the order of the life, you can adjust.

* In a borrowed structure biography or autobiography, chapter divisions will depend on the subject and the model genre. In a biography modelled on a crime thriller, for example, chapters might go chronologically through the case, interspersed with some that look back at the history of the subject.

EXERCISE ON CHAPTERS

You are writing the cradle-to-grave biography of a contemporary British female painter. She was born a twin but was separated from her sister at the age of ten. She has not seen her since. She began to paint pairs of people at art school. Now suddenly famous at 27, she is to have her first Lost Twin exhibition. The night before the opening a fire breaks out in her studio.

i. Your first two chapters cover this period. Decide where to break them.

ii. Write the last two paragraphs of both chapters.

TOP TIP

End chapters on a dramatic or thematically important moment, and with a 'hook' to the next chapter – a hint of drama to come, so that the reader will want to read on.

Research

A. Where to go

Basic printed resources

* The DNB – the *Dictionary of National Biography*. First edition 1885, first editor Leslie Stephen, father of Virginia Woolf. The DNB is constantly kept up to date. There is a Concise DNB, and since 2004 an online edition, the *Oxford Dictionary of National Biography*: website www. oxforddnb.com. This can be accessed free with most public library cards.

* The equivalents elsewhere: *American National Biography, Allgemeine Deutsche Biographie and Neue Deutsche Biographie, Dictionnaire de Biographie Française, Dizionario Biografico degli Italiani*, etc.

* Other biographical dictionaries include Chambers' and Webster's, and biographical encyclopedias, such as the *Cambridge Biographical Encyclopedia* and the *McGraw Hill Encyclopedia of World Biography*.

* *Who's Who* for contemporary biography, and *Who Was Who* for past figures. *Who's Who in America, Who's Who in France, Who's Who in Italy, Wer ist Wer?* and *Who's Who in Germany* and many others.

* There is also an *International Who's Who* and an *International Who's Who of Women*.

* Group directories: *Debrett's Peerage and Baronetage, the Macmillan Dictionary of Women's Biography*, etc.

* Professional directories: *Who's Who of British Members of Parliament*, the *New Grove Dictionary of Music and Musicians*, the *Medical Register*, the *Army, Navy* and *Air Force Lists, Crockford's Clerical Directory*, the *Writers' Directory* and many others.

* Business directories: eg, the *International Directory of Company Histories* and *Who Owns Who*.

* Obituaries: eg, in *The Times Index* and *Obituaries from the Times*, and in *The New York Times Obituaries Index* in the US. Also in the archives sections of the online *Guardian* and other national papers, and in local papers held in the Newspaper Library in Colindale (see Libraries below.) Obits, like wills, are an excellent place to begin. Death is when people look back over a life.

National archives

* The main national UK archive is the *Public Record Office* at Kew. Its website is www.nationalarchives.gov.uk. This has links to its catalogue and guides, but a direct link to its online catalogue is at www.pro.gov.uk/catalogues/default.htm

* Addresses and further details of the PRO and other key organisations below are listed in the Address List at the back of this book.

* Scotland and Northern Ireland have their own national archives, the General Register Office for Scotland and the Public Records Office of Northern Ireland (websites www.gro-scotland.gov.uk and www.proni.gov.uk respectively).

* Birth, marriage and death records are now all kept at the Family Records Centre in Islington; detailed information on its holdings is at www.familyrecords.gov.uk/frc/default.htm and at www.pro.gov.uk/research/familyhistory.htm

* Records of wills after 1858 are now kept at the Probate Search Room in Holborn. The Search Room does not have its own website. The best website to use is the National Archives site: put National Archives into Google and click on wills. This explains wills before 1858 as well; or go to www.documentsonline.pro.gov.uk

* An up-to-date guide to will research in the UK is *Wills and Probate Records* by Karen Grannum and Nigel Taylor, published by the National Archives in 2009.

Local archives

* Most local libraries have good local history sections, the bigger city libraries, eg, London, Manchester, Liverpool, very extensive ones. Many of these have put their catalogues and much of their material online. You can search the Oxfordshire Studies local history archive at www.oxfordshire. gov.uk/wps/portal/publicsite/doitonline/finditonline/heritage, for example.

* Local authorities' records offices contain documents going back centuries on local government matters – health, welfare, education, housing, burial grounds.

Between them, these local archives will contain:

* censuses and electoral registers

* valuation rolls (property registers) and local tax records

* school, church and welfare records (eg, workhouses)

* local business and institution records

* local publications (eg, newspapers and magazines, directories and business directories, books and pamphlets)

Many schools, businesses and local newspapers (especially old-established ones) will have their own archives.

Other important records include for example:

* *Hansard: Parliamentary Debates* from 1803 onwards

* *All England Law Reports* from 1558 onwards

* Parish records of baptisms, marriages and burials from 1538

* Other denomination records (eg, Non-conformist and Catholic churches, synagogues, mosques)

* The National Sound Archive, for broadcast speeches and interviews; also Parliamentary sound recordings

* Shipping records, eg, Lloyd's Shipping Index and the P & O Company records at the National Maritime Museum. The National Archives hold passenger lists both inward-bound and outward-bound from the UK up to 1960. There is also a website called AncestorsOnBoard.com on which you can search for your fortune-seeking ancestors.

There are many tools, both printed and online, to help you navigate the vast world of archives. There are books such as *British Archives: a guide to archive resources in the United Kingdom* and *Record Repositories in Great Britain* (see Bibliography for details), and advice on the National Archives site itself. There is also the Access to Archives project, which aims to put all UK archive catalogues on the Net: see http://www.a2a.org.uk. The PRO publishes many books and leaflets to help researchers find their way through its own collections, plus *The Family Records Centre: a user's guide* by Stella Colwell.

Once we get into family research and genealogy, the field expands even further. There are countless books, websites, courses, television programmes and organisations devoted to genealogy, from the Society of Genealogists in London to websites like www.findmypast.com (the partner site of the National Archives). Among the most famous and assiduous genealogists are the Genealogical Society of the Church of Jesus Christ of the Latter Day Saints, the Mormons, who have compiled the International Genealogical Index, the IGI, containing over a billion names from birth, death and marriage records around the world. The IGI is too vast to be consistently reliable, but it is an excellent starting point. It is accessible, free of charge, at www.familysearch.org. You can also access the online catalogue directly at www.familysearch.org/Search/searchcatalog.asp

Libraries & museums

Libraries

The Copyright Libraries: the most complete, because they are entitled to a copy of every book published in the UK and the Republic of Ireland (as is the Library of Congress for the US).

* The British Library, London
* The Bodleian Library, Oxford
* Cambridge University Library, Cambridge
* The National Library of Scotland, Edinburgh
* National Library of Wales, Aberystwyth
* Trinity College Library, Dublin

The national libraries are all online. The British Library's website, for example, is www.bl.uk, and its catalogue is directly accessible at http://catalogue.bl.uk

Their catalogues are also listed online by Copac, the National, Academic and Specialist Library Catalogue. Copac contains over 34 million records from the national and main university libraries, plus many specialist libraries, such as the National Art Library at the V&A. Its website is at www.copac.ac.uk, or just put Copac into Google.

University libraries

* Most other universities, especially the larger and older ones, have excellent libraries.
* They all subscribe to the online unified catalogue Copac. Most have their own catalogues and reservation systems online: Oxford has OLIS, Cambridge has Newton and Bristol has ALEPH. These are all accessible to members online. Other universities' library catalogues are accessible to members through their own systems or websites.
* If you have a publisher, or proof that you are a bona fide scholar (often a letter from a current member will do), it is not usually difficult to obtain a membership card for a limited period.

Public libraries

* Very useful resources, as we've seen, especially for local history.
* If you have more time than transport, the Inter-Library Loan Service means that any book in the UK system can be delivered to your local library. Some will even extend the service to libraries abroad, if necessary, for a charge (currently £26.75 in the case of Oxford Central Library, so it might be cheaper to buy the book through www.abebooks.fr or www.abebooks.de etc.).

Other libraries

There are all kinds of specialist libraries including:

* Picture libraries. Of the famous old picture libraries, the Mary Evans Picture Library still exists, while the Hulton Picture Library is now a

special archive at Getty Images. All the national museums and the Birmingham and Manchester art galleries have picture libraries, as have the National Archives and the British Library, all of which can be accessed online. There are many picture libraries in specialist institutions such as English Heritage, the British Geological Survey, the Scott Polar Institute and the RSPCA. These and dozens more can all be found through the website of the British Association of Picture Libraries and Agencies, www.bapla.org.uk. Google Images and Getty Images are both well-known online sources. Don't forget that most paintings and photographs are subject to copyright and/or owners' fees.

* Manuscript libraries. The main manuscript depository in England is the Manuscript Department of the British Library. However, manuscripts are also held in many other libraries and archives. Check the ARCHON (Archive Contacts) facility of the National Archives, or with the Historical Manuscripts Commission, website www.hmc.gov.uk. This also has the UK National Register of Archives, which can be searched directly at www.nationalarchives.gov.uk/mdr/mdr.htm. There are also reference books like *British Archives*, already mentioned, or *The ASLIB Directory of Information Sources in the United Kingdom*.

* For literary manuscripts, consult the Location Register of English Literary Manuscripts and Letters at the University of Reading (www.rdg.ac.uk/ SerDepts/v/Lib/ Projects/locreg.html).

* Newspaper libraries. The main one is the British Library Newspaper Library in Colindale in North London, which holds over 50,000 newspapers, periodicals, magazines, comics, etc. All the UK daily papers since 1801 are kept, and local UK and Irish papers since the eighteenth century (though anything from before 1800 is held at the main British Library at St Pancras). Selected foreign papers are also kept. The newspaper catalogue is a subset of the main British Library catalogue and clearly signposted on the BL website.

* Subscription libraries. The London Library is the biggest and best known, with over a million books. Others include the Bath Royal Literary and Scientific Institution, the Central Catholic Library in Dublin and

the Nottingham Subscription Library. The Association of Independent Libraries lists them all (www.independentlibraries.co.uk).

* Special interest libraries. There are many specialist collections in university libraries, local Records Offices and local trade and historical associations, as well as, for example:

> The British Architectural Library of the Royal Institute of British Architects.
> The British Film Institute Library
> Companies House for company records
> Horniman Library for musical instruments and ethnography
> Lindley Library, the Royal Horticultural Society
> Poetry Library
> Royal Geographical Society Library
> Society of Genealogists Library
> Wellcome Institute Library for medical history
> Wiener Library for Jewish history
> The Women's Library for women's history and women's studies – and these are just in London.

Museums

Museums, often with their own libraries, are also a precious resource. Apart from the National Gallery, Tate Modern, Tate Britain, the city galleries of Birmingham and Manchester, etc., here are just a few:

> Ashmolean Museum, Oxford
> British Museum
> Courtauld Institute of Art Library
> Fitzwilliam Museum, Cambridge
> Imperial War Museum
> Museum of Transport
> National Army Museum
> National Maritime Museum
> National Monuments Record
> National Portrait Gallery Library and Archive
> Royal Air Force Museum

Science Museum Library
Theatre Museum
Victoria and Albert Museum Library, and hundreds of others.

Online sources

❋ Today almost all your research can be done on the internet. The British Library and the Library of Congress both have websites on which you can check their holdings (www.bl.uk and www.loc.gov). You can check the holdings of all UK university libraries on Copac, and the holdings of your local library through your local council's website. You can check the holdings of all London public libraries online through www.librarylookup.org.uk (we haven't managed the rest of the UK yet). The website based at Northwestern University in the US, www.libraryspot.com, will locate and link to the online catalogues (if available) of public and academic libraries around the world. The complete OED (*Oxford English Dictionary*) is at www.oed.com and *Encyclopedia Britannica* at www.britannica.com (though both charge for access. The famous 1911 edition is browsable free at www.1911encyclopedia.org). The *Columbia Encyclopedia* is at www.encyclopedia.com, Merriam-Webster at www.merriam-webster.com and Microsoft's Encarta encyclopedia at www.encarta.msn.com

❋ Through the many internet search engines you are connected to the biggest library in the world. Everyone knows Google and Yahoo; other main ones are AltaVista, Ask Jeeves, Excite, Hotbot and Lycos. Once you've learned how to refine your search with AND, OR and NOT, quote marks, brackets and so on, you can find anything you need. If you still haven't found the answer, you can go to www.mimas.ac.uk, a research information site maintained by the University of Manchester. Their website, www.mimas.ac.uk/portfolio/current, lists their most useful projects: for example, archiveshub.ac.uk, which locates archives; a link to www.jstor.org, which gives academics access to over 1000 journals; and zetoc.mimas.ac.uk, which gives access to the BL's electronic tables of contents of journals and links to the texts.

❋ Excellent news and newspaper sites, with archives, are www.bbc.co.uk, www.guardian.co.uk, www.telegraph.co.uk and www.independent.co.uk.

As you'll know, Google is proposing to put every book ever published on the Web, and despite some resistance from authors has already begun. Project Gutenberg has been digitising the contents of archives and libraries for nearly 40 years, and now has nearly 30,000 free e-books available on its website, www.gutenberg.org; Amazon now has the *Look Inside* facility for millions of new books. You can even get translations (though not very good ones) and quotations on the net. Google has a translation facility on its homepage and a website, Google Translate (www.translate.google.com). Yahoo has its own facility (www.babelfish.yahoo.com); and there are many other websites as well (eg, www.translation.langenberg.com). For quotations there are www.bartleby.com/quotations and www.information-britain.co.uk/famousquotes.php. We need never leave our desks again.

For US research, the list could be as long again. For a more than comprehensive guide, consult the website of the Center for Biographical Research at the University of Hawai'i at Manoa, the longest-established life writing centre: www.hawaii.edu/biograph ('biograph' is not a typo!).

> **TOP TIP 1**
>
> *Get all the public records you'll need –birth, death, marriage certificates for everyone in your story – early. It will give you confidence, and allow you to start drawing up a family tree. (See C below.)*

B. What to do

* Read all source materials, take notes. Watch for your pattern in the carpet – but be flexible. Looking out for themes is one thing; approaching your research with preconceived ideas is another.

> **TOP TIP 2**
>
> *Keep complete records of where you found everything, especially in archives, which can have complicated reference systems. And keep records of everyone who has helped you: no matter how vivid they are now, by the time you've finished your book years later, you will probably have forgotten who was who and where.*

For biography

* If your biography is of a long-dead subject, with no one left alive to remember them, your research is done. It might be anyway, as it was for George Painter, who refused to talk to anyone about Proust; or for Lytton Strachey, who worked only from published sources. So this is a method with obvious dangers – perpetuating errors, for example – but with a good pedigree.

* If your biography is of someone with relatives and friends still alive, your main task is to find and interview them. Track them down from family letters, previous contacts with them (for example, the journalist's interview which first interested you), wills.

> **TOP TIP**
>
> *Wills are very useful tools to find relatives and friends, since they often list addresses as well as relationship to the subject ('To my niece Anna James, of 28 Seafield Court, Harrogate. . .'). Even if the addresses are out of date, they can make a good starting point for inquiries.*

So far you've needed many scholarly skills. Your need of human skills begins here – even before the interviews themselves.

* Approach thoughtfully, adapting to what you know or can guess about the person (for example, the widow would require a very different approach from the employer).

* Send an account of yourself and your work, a letter from your publisher, etc. Do not hesitate to make yourself sound as respectable and well-qualified as possible – include all your degrees and don't hide any honours, grants, etc. (unless this sort of thing might put off this sort of person, the drop-out hippy cousin, for example).

* If refused, wait for a few weeks and gently try again. People often say no at first, but on reflection are intrigued, or regret the opportunity to talk to someone about their past – even to talk to someone at all, in the case of many lonely old people (and in biography most of your interviewees will be old).

C. Other things to do in the research period

Copyright research

Especially for literary biographies, but for all quotations, you will have to clear, and often pay for, all the copyright material you use. You can start the process now.

* Copyright in published material extends to 70 years after the author's death in the USA and Europe, including Britain (but not, for example in Canada, where it extends for only 50 years).

* Copyright in unpublished material is more complicated. See the Society of Authors' Quick Guides to copyright and permissions, downloadable free from www.societyofauthors.org/guides-and-articles.

* Note that though most material on the web is free to download, everything on the internet is under copyright, and you require permission to quote from it as you would from a printed book. And don't forget that letters are also subject to copyright.

* You must seek permission from the author's publisher or agent, or from the author in person, if they are is still alive and you can find them.

* If a book is out of print, and/or the author is dead, you can turn to WATCH – Writers, Artists and their Copyright Holders – an online database of literary and other creative estates run jointly by Reading University and the Harry Ransom Humanities Research Centre of the University of Texas at Austin: http://tyler.hrc.utexas.edu/. Other alternatives are the Authors Licensing and Collecting Society (www.alcs.co.uk), the Association of Authors' Agents (www.agentsassociation.co.uk), and several others. See the Society of Authors' Quick Guide to Permissions, as above.

* Keep records of all your quotations longer than a few words.

How much you can quote without permission has never been definitively settled. 'Fair use' or 'fair dealing' for critical purposes, for example in a review, article or biography, is generally accepted to be up to 800 words in total from a prose work, with a maximum of 400 words in a single extract, so long as the extract is used for comment on works and not on persons. But it is safest to ask for permission, and essential in all cases to credit the work clearly and quote accurately. Again see the Society of Authors' Quick Guide to Permissions. (The Society also provides guides to libel, indexing and other vexed questions for a small fee.)

Fees can be charged for permissions, sometimes quite high ones, and permission can be refused, perhaps because the estate doesn't want a biography. In these cases you can paraphrase, provided that you credit the source, and make it clear that this is your own summary.

Other things you can do

* Make pilgrimages to the places connected with your subject, partly for the feeling of imaginative contact and partly for practical understanding of the background and geography. Take notes and photographs.

* When you've learned enough, make a time-line, with world events, country events and local events, together with the key events, inner and outer, of your subject's life.

* When you have enough family information, draw up a family tree.

For autobiography and memoir

CAROLE ANGIER'S TIP

When I offered to help Jean Rhys with her autobiography, she declined: 'It's just what you remember, isn't it?' she said. But if anything is 'just what you remember', it's memoir, not autobiography – and even in memoir you should check anything that involves a date or place or other people, though you can still present scenes as you remember them, as long as it's clear that's what you're doing.

The claims you implicitly make about the objectivity of your story are strongest in biography and weakest in memoir. Autobiography is in between: your story, from your point of view, but as objective as you can make it. Moral: research is needed in both autobiography and memoir.

Where to go

* You may need any of the places/sources listed at the beginning of this section.

* The rest depends upon your subject. Track down all the people in your story from your records, from family members, letters, documents etc. See the TOP TIP above about wills, page 197.

What to do

* Read other autobiographies/memoirs. Read classics, for example, Edmund Gosse, *Father and Son* (1907), Vladimir Nabokov, *Speak, Memory* (1951), Primo Levi, *The Periodic Table* (1975). Read classic autobiographical novels such as James Joyce, *Portrait of the Artist as a Young Man*, Thomas Wolfe, *Look Homeward, Angel*, Jack Kerouac, *On the Road*, the whole of Proust . . . and think about the differences, if any. Perhaps you can learn some techniques from those too – but be careful, retain your respect for reality! Read great contemporary autobiographies, memoirs and autobiographical novels, and do the same: for example, Alan Bennett's *Writing Home*, Mary Karr's *The Liars' Club*, Tobias Wolff's *This Boy's Story* and Geoffrey Wolff's The *Duke of Deception*, Diana Athill's *Instead of a Letter*, Jeanette Winterson's *Oranges Are Not the Only Fruit*. (See the Bibliography for more.)

* Read autobiographies and memoirs by people different from you – of the opposite sex, from other cultures and other times, with different trainings and interests – to loosen you up and give you new ideas.

* Look back at your own letters, journals, diaries and e-mails, scrapbooks and photograph albums, school reports and yearbooks, wills, deeds and divorce papers; newspaper clippings you kept, childhood books in which you tried out different names, books of your youth in which you scribbled marginalia. If you don't have any of these, you may have a problem.

* Talk to everyone concerned – check your memories. If someone has a different version, that doesn't mean you have to give up yours, but considering/including it may add depth to your story.

* Read all your source materials, trying to remain open-minded and objective – don't get sucked back into old battles, treat your own letters like everyone else's. Pretend (for the time being) that you will be writing a group biography of these people, including yourself.

* Make notes and keep clear records. Watch for themes to coalesce, atmospheres and images to dominate.

* When you're ready, make a timeline and family tree, as for Biography above.

* Make pilgrimages to the places connected to your story, as for Biography. It may be many years since you've been back to your childhood home, to the scene of your abduction, your violent marriage, your wartime escape: whatever you find, and whatever you feel, will deepen your account.

* Keep records for, and perhaps start, all the business you may have to do for autobiography and memoir as for biography – clearing copyrights and permissions, remembering people and institutions you'll want to thank, etc.

* For memoir: when you are ready to write, make sure you know which type of memoir yours fits into. Then keep that focus. Publishers are not keen on blurred edges.

D. Interviewing for all the genres

There are three basic interview techniques:

* the hard journalistic technique, with prepared, closed questions requiring specific, limited answers

* the soft journalistic technique, with prepared but open questions, allowing the interviewee to move in different directions

* the non-journalistic, open technique, in which you know the general area of first questions, but once these have broken the ice, you let the interviewee lead wherever they want to go, even if it seems irrelevant, and hope to find things not only you but even they didn't know they knew

What to think about when interviewing

* Interviewing well is as hard as writing well. You have to find a similar balance between empathy and detachment. (See the section under that heading in Writing below.)

* You have to be sensitive to your interviewee, both for common decency and because otherwise you won't gain their trust.

* On the other hand, you have to persist when they don't want to answer. And in the end you will have to write your book as objectively as you can, not favouring the sensitivities of any interviewee. (See Ethics in all the genres, in Writing below.)

* What do you do if you know someone is lying?

  a. Don't be surprised!

  b. It depends on you and the interviewee. If you're both good at conflict, you could try direct challenge. Otherwise, pursue the point subtly; or drop it for the time being and return to it later.

* What do you do if interviewees disagree?

  a. Get as many accounts of the event/person in question as you can, and keep the residue of agreement.

  b. Don't throw the rest away: the differences show character, and identify awkward – and therefore revealing – points. They also raise interesting issues of truth, the limited nature of our experience, etc., which will enrich your understanding, and which you may decide to include in your text.

* Do you ever tell interviewees about other interviewees' evidence?

  a. No! You don't want them conferring, adjusting their memories, etc. Keep them separate, like witnesses at a trial. You do the adjusting.

  b. Yes. Showing interest, not disbelief, you could say: 'Are you sure? X seems to remember that . . .' But only do this with a thoughtful witness who is willing to query his/her memories without taking offence or being destabilised.

* What do you do if you have only one witness?

  a. You should never use information for which you have only one witness. But this happens so often that the rule is almost impossible to obey.

  b. In fact your one and only star witness can often be the best thing in your book!

  c. You should use one of the 'ugly tribe' of words (see pp. 18–19) that signal to the reader that your usual impeccable level of evidence could not be reached: 'possibly', 'probably', 'it's most likely that', etc.

* Do you show interviewees the use you've made of their evidence before you publish it?

  a. Yes. And write and thank them afterwards.

  b. It depends. If you think they may sue you or try to stop you – for example take out one of the terrifying new 'super injunctions' (see p. 12), you might not. Ask your publisher's lawyer for advice.

* Do you give them a veto?

  a. This one is easy: No. You must retain control of your book.

  b. But be sure to tell everyone this, gently but firmly, from the start, when you promise to let them see the part(s) of the story where they enter.

* Advantages and disadvantages of interviewing people in your own life.

  a. You may be more trusted than any outsider could be. Carole had a family member who like Primo Levi was an Auschwitz survivor, but who unlike Levi had never spoken. With the objective excuse of a book, Carole was able to ask her relative to talk to her about her experience; and not only did she agree, but this broke the barrier for her, and she has spoken to children in schools ever since.

b. You may be less trusted than any outsider could be. The problems of talking to people about a shared and often difficult past need no spelling out by us. We'll just add that if you're doing it to write about it, those problems will be multiplied many times over. See Ethics, in Writing below, and in Reflections 1, Part 3, pp. 9–13.

* Advantages and disadvantages of tape recorders.

a. The great advantage of recording your interviews is that you have proof of what people have said, if it comes to a dispute. If you are used to tape recorders and manage them well, they are invaluable aids.

b. If not, they can have serious disadvantages. You can make awful mistakes with them. They can frighten people or put them on their guard. And you need to process all your information through your own brain, and even more important, through your unconscious. If you allow too many artificial aids to take over, you may lose that deep knowledge of your subject that good writing needs.

c. On the other hand, taking notes is dangerous – you are selecting as you go along, so you may miss something important that doesn't fit your current interest. And just listening is the most dangerous of all – you may forget everything. But sometimes you just know that you can't take out your pen or the spell will be broken.

Hilary Spurling gives the best advice. Trust your unconscious, she says. If you've forgotten something, you don't need it; or it will come back when you do.

> **TOP TIP 1**
>
> *Go and see everyone on your list, even if they seem unimportant. You never know what may come out of it.*

TOP TIP 2

Always go back to people as often as you can: trust takes time to grow.

But don't be too trusting yourself. Remember that even with the best intentions, people's memories are faulty, and they always exaggerate their own role.

TOP TIP 3

Watch out not only for others' misrememberings and distortions, but also your own. They may be right, and you wrong!

TOP TIP 4

If you do use a tape recorder, always take more than one.

EXERCISE ON INTERVIEWS

This is a role-playing exercise for writers in groups.

The daughter of a well-known pop star was murdered four years ago. The murderer was never found. You are writing the pop star's biography, or a memoir of that year in his life. Think about the three different interview methods and decide which to use in each case.

i. Interview the widow of the pop star, ie, the mother of the murdered girl. You are trying to get at the 'truth' of what happened that night.

ii. Interview the detective in charge of the case who failed to find the perpetrator.

iii.Now switch roles – you play the interviewees, and the person who played the interviewees plays the biographer.

When you've finished, compare your methods and results.

> **TOP TIP**
>
> *Remember that interviewees don't always tell the truth!*

Other things to do in the research period.

* The same as for biography, but less onerous and time-consuming, since Jean Rhys wasn't completely wrong – you can rely on your own memory more.

E. The last thing to think about before writing

* When have you finished your research and can start writing? This is one of the hardest questions to answer in our whole trade.
* Which is worse, too much information or too little?

> **TOP TIP**
>
> *Both too much and too little information can be a problem. If gathering it has taken a great deal of passion, time and money, we may become too attached to it. But too much information will bore the reader and clog the narrative. Be ruthless.*
>
> *What can you do if you have too little information? Denys Finch Hatton left no record of himself. Ivy Compton Burnett destroyed all hers. Ovid and Pontius Pilate lived thousands of years ago. But their biographers all found solutions. Sara Wheeler researched the history of the period and the accounts of people who knew Finch Hatton, and reconstructed him from the points where they met. Hilary Spurling recreated Compton Burnett from her novels. Diane Middlebrook researched Ovid's world and reconstructed his as it must have been. Ann Wroe imagined Pilate from scraps of evidence, stripping away the myths.*

For biography

* In biography especially, there will always be more research to do, one more clue to follow up, one more letter awaited. Your work is inevitably incomplete and of its time. So you must simply decide.

* Some people start writing before they've finished the research, or even throughout the research period; but it's easy to see the problems in that (possible re-writing). The best we can say is: when new information starts to repeat old, when the pattern in the carpet – *your* carpet – is clear, then it's time to start writing.

For autobiography and memoir

* In memoir and autobiography, you probably thought you knew the shape and main points of your story before you began. But as you re-read your own diaries and letters, and talked to everyone else, these may well have changed. Once you have every document and every person in the story you can find; and once you have the new story – or the old one – you are ready to start writing.

> **WARNING**
>
> This decision is crucial, because your material dictates your story. It may even change the book you meant to write. Perhaps one main theme has emerged. Or conversely, perhaps you have enough material for a whole life now, instead of just the youth. Trust your material and change your plan.

Writing

Where to start

The beginning is the most important part of your memoir, autobiography or biography.

a. It is classic to start with the death or another end point – for example, the time of writing, in autobiography – and then go back to the beginning and trace the journey to that end point.
b. Alternatively you could start with some key or symbolic moment/place/event, and then begin the chronological story.

In all three genres your book must have a read-on 'hook' for the start.

If you have an Introduction, you may already have chosen a key moment, place or object with which to begin your story. But now Chapter 1 poses the same question: where to begin?

Because it has a limited time period, memoir may offer you clearer choices than biography or autobiography.

* In biography/autobiography, do you start with the birth of your subject/your own birth? With your subject's ancestors/your own?

* How much of that material should you put in? If it is a family history you are writing to tell your grandchildren about their origins, put in more. If it is an autobiography of a theoretical physicist who was the first in her family to go to university, put in less.

* Generally include the least background that is consistent with your aims. Include what illuminates your subject/theme. Leave out or condense the rest.

* Is your biography/autobiography chronological or does it use another organising principle? Let that principle dictate the starting point.

* The best clue is to start with the most important thing that illuminates your subject (or the most important after the one you've used in your

Introduction): for example, the place or house where she/he/you were born; the first day at school; the central trauma.

> **EXERCISE**
>
> You, or the subject of your biography, passed yourself/herself/himself off as a doctor and practised for years without qualifications. Then you/she/he were discovered and jailed for 25 years. You think this career of deception had its seed in an important death in your/her/his early life.
>
> Write the first paragraph of three different ways of starting this story. Maximum 100 words for each paragraph.

Managing time in all the genres

As we have seen, life writing can be structured thematically as well as chronologically. But a strong chronological structure underneath all stories is essential.

* Stories take place in time.
* They take time to read.
* Clearly time relations are vital to story-telling.

1. Narration in autobiography and memoir

The key time question in autobiography and memoir is whether to tell the story in the voice of the past − for example, of yourself as a child − or in the voice of the present, of the adult looking back.

* The standard method is looking back. This is usually the richest and most satisfying, because of the added element of adult reflection. It is also the truest − you *are* the adult looking back.
* If you write in the voice of your past self there is always a doubt about how much fictionalising has taken place.

* An example in which this doubt never arises is Aharon Appelfeld's Holocaust memoir, *The Story of a Life*, in which many of Appelfeld's memories are told in his childhood voice. The whole of Wilkomirski's *Fragments* is told this way (though of course the book turned out to be a fiction), as are many good and bad memoirs of childhood abuse.

* As these examples show, this technique seems to work best for traumatic experience, which it is natural to remember in flashback, as though you are still there.

* A good solution can be to use both methods, writing sometimes as the child, sometimes as the adult looking back. Xandra Bingley in *Bertie, May and Mrs Fish*, for example, does this very successfully.

EXERCISE

Think of an unforgettable event from your childhood.

1. Narrate it from the point of view of the child.

2. Narrate it from the point of view of the adult looking back.

Write 2 paragraphs for each exercise. Max. 200 words.

---

2. Narration in biography

The key time question for the biographer is: should you tell the story as the subject lived it, not knowing where they were heading, so that you see patterns only looking back, as they would have done? Or should you point ahead, picking out patterns as they form?

* The first method is truer to life.

* The second method is truer to story-telling, which happens when the life is over and can be seen as a whole.

* Examples of pointing ahead:

    'This was the first time that . . .'

    'This was the last time that . . .'

* Example of pointing back:

  'It had all started when . . .'

* Purists favour the true-to-life method, but it makes it harder to create suspense and structure your story.

TOP TIP

Some of the best editorial advice Carole ever received was from her first editor, Diana Athill. Diana said: 'Decide whether you will point ahead or back, for your central themes about the life. But not both.'

Viewpoint in biography

In biography the classic viewpoint is the third person omniscient narrator. This classical approach is being increasingly challenged, as are all classical approaches in our postmodern times. We no longer accept the voice of 'objective' authority, but increasingly require to know who is speaking, and for that person to take individual responsibility.

* Book reviews have been signed for a long time (though a few are still anonymous, eg, in *The Economist*.)

* Obituaries are now also mostly signed, a change pioneered by *The Independent*. But obituaries in *The Times*, for example, are still anonymous.

* Recently biographers, like post-modern novelists, have been entering the text, taking responsibility for it and commenting on the biographical process.

  ○ They can enter 'truthfully', as researcher (as in Janet Malcolm's *The Silent Woman*, or Carole's *Primo Levi*, for example).

  ○ This can even happen fictionally. In Peter Ackroyd's *Dickens*, Ackroyd talks to Dickens by his fireside. In *Dutch*, Edmund Morris accompanies Reagan through every step of his life.

* It is not new for the biographer to enter the text. Johnson entered *Savage* as Savage's friend, and Boswell is on practically every page of *Johnson*. (But Johnson was Savage's friend, and Boswell shadowed Johnson for 20 years; so this was not fiction in either case.)

WARNING

For all the welcome given to innovation by scholars and prizes, and despite the precedents of Johnson and Boswell, this is probably still the hardest innovation to manage successfully for the bulk of readers, and even for many reviewers. Do it – especially the 'fictional' variety – at your peril!

EXERCISE 1 ON VIEWPOINT IN BIOGRAPHY

You are writing a biography of the cross-dressing entertainer Barry Humphreys, alias Dame Edna Everage, or of Daniel Barenboim, the composer, musician and conductor.

Scenario: Your subject is on stage in the middle of a performance. Suddenly something unusual happens. You, the biographer, are in the audience.

Write two paragraphs about the event (max. 200 words):

a. in classic third person style,

b. in the first person, inserting yourself into the scene.

TOP TIP for b.

Think about your reasons for entering the scene. Is your relationship with the subject part of the story? Does it allow you some reflections, on the biographical process, for example, that you could not otherwise include? Does it make the scene more dramatic?

Use this technique to achieve one or more of these effects.

Be careful to keep the focus on your subject, not on yourself.

EXERCISE 2

You are the biographer of a sports star or a famous actor. Your subject has had a much-discussed ten-year break from their career. They are now about to return. This is the point you have reached in your biography.

• Write about this moment graphically and excitingly. Give your subject a name and make them come alive. Do this in the classic third person, keeping yourself out of the text.

• Write the moment again, inserting yourself into the text:

i. as a biographer who was not involved in the subject's life;

ii. as a biographer/memoirist who *was* involved in the life – especially the ten-year absence. You may have been a partner/wife/husband or a lover/stalker/psychiatrist. Write the scene from this point of view.

CAROLE ANGIER'S TOP TIP for i.

You, the biographer, witnessed this return. It was not only a great event in your subject's life but in your own. It was what made you want to write the biography.

SALLY CLINE'S TOP TIP for ii.

This is highly personal. The ten-year gap was very important to you as well as to the subject. But remember that as the narrator you will also need some detachment. (See Empathy and detachment *below.)*

Truth in biography

Together with authority, the notion of a single objective truth has declined since the first rumblings of post-modernism in the 1960s and 70s. In addition, biography adds a few truth problems of its own, eg:

* What can we do about inevitable gaps in the record?

* What can we do about the arbitrariness of what survives?

* How do we deal with the unreliability of memory?

* How do we stop the distortions of personal interest, both ours and other people's?

* How much trust do we place in witnesses' accounts?

* How do we overcome the difficulty of escaping the assumptions of our own culture and the impossibility of entering other minds?

Many of these questions are hard to solve, some are unanswerable, but we must be aware of them. Sally and Carole discuss them in detail in Part One.

They can be very interesting, but as practitioners we have to come up with practical solutions. The practical decisions may throw light back on the theory.

EXERCISE 2

Scenario: Three couples are having dinner. The first couple are your subject Magda, a geneticist, and her partner Tim, a gardener. The second couple are a novelist, Cassandra, and her husband Terry, a film maker. The third couple are a teacher, Janet, and her civil partner Meg, a doctor.

A row breaks out during dinner and someone stabs Magda in the hand with a steak knife.

You interview all three couples. Everyone has a different version of who was the stabber and what happened.

EXERCISE 2 *continued*

On the basis of your knowledge of the characters and the background, you decide which version is true (or work out your own). You write the scene. But before your book goes to press, a piece of new evidence comes to light that shows the version you have written cannot be true.

a. Write the account you first settled on, and give your reasons in an end note.

b. Though the new evidence shows that your first version can't be right, it doesn't prove which version *is* right. Decide what probably happened, and write a new account with a new end note. Or admit it cannot be known what happened at this stage, and include your reflections as the biographer on the problem.

c. Compare your decisions in b. with other people's decisions and discuss the results.

TOP TIP

Falsification is possible. But is complete verification ever possible?

Truth in autobiography and memoir

Truth is even more elusive in autobiography and memoir than in biography, because your memory is involved as well. And your memory may be as faulty as other people's. (Sally has a vivid example of this in Part One.) This creates special problems in autobiography and memoir.

EXERCISE

Scenario: One of your clearest memories is of taking your next door neighbour's toddler Sam for a buggy ride. You are ten, Sam is three. You run too fast with the buggy and Sam flies out onto the ground. You are terrified, but a grown-up picks Sam up and puts him back in the buggy, and he's fine. You remain friends with him until he and his family move away.

Twenty-three years later, researching for your autobiography, you track Sam down. He is not fine now. He is an alcoholic and walks with a stick. You tell him what you remember. He says: 'I had no idea it was you! But everything you have just told me is a lie. I crashed into a lamp-post and injured my head so badly that I had to have operations for years. I was left with seizures and one paralysed leg. What's more we certainly did not remain friends. I was never allowed to talk to you again!'

a. Write the episode as you recall it.

b. Write Sam's version, having decided that that is the true account.

c. Write Sam's version as above, but add reflections on your own long denial and adjustment of the truth.

d. Write the episode, having decided that it is not clear which version is true. Include your reasons, and some reflections on the problem of truth.

CAROLE ANGIER'S TOP TIP for d.

Don't forget that everyone can be wrong. Sam's situation is sad and moving. But he is an alcoholic, and your memory is clear.

Ethics in all the genres

The major problem in life writing is that our subjects are or were real people. Many have families, who in autobiography and memoir will include our own.

* If our subjects are alive, they can feel hurt or harmed. And they may try to stop us, or sue us for libel.

* You cannot libel the dead. But subjects' families can feel hurt or harmed as well, or can claim that we have harmed the subject's reputation.

* British libel law so favoured the protection of reputation over free speech that by 2009 London was known as the 'libel capital' of the world. After a campaign led by English PEN, this was finally ended by the Defamation Bill, passed by Parliament in 2013.

The safest book, both for your conscience and your purse, is a biography of a long-dead historical character with no living descendants. Contemporary biography and all autobiography and memoir (both by definition close to contemporary) are more dangerous.

Even when you tell your own story, you cannot keep other people out, and they may mind a great deal what is said about them. We cannot blame them. The printed word is powerful. Their lives are literally in our hands. We have a responsibility to them as well as to truth and history.

This is the life writer's dilemma.

WARNING

Remember the **'magic of print'** syndrome. Even when someone gives you permission to tell their story, when they see it in print they are often horrified and furious. Somehow on the printed page it looks different.

SCENARIO: You are writing a memoir of your youth. You remember, or discover now, that a teacher, Mr Taylor, seduced your best friend Maria when she was fourteen. Then she was the most beautiful girl in the school. Today, ten years later, she is a famous model.

TOP TIP

When deciding how (or whether) to include delicate material, there are three choices:

i. Leave it out.

ii. Include it boldly, and risk hurting some people and being sued by others.

iii. Include it subtly, keeping ethical and legal considerations in mind.

EXERCISE 1

Write the incident truthfully and boldly in 200 words.

TOP TIP 1

Your plan should depend on how crucial the incident is to your story. If it is not crucial it is wise to leave it out.

EXERCISE 2

Write a subtle account, using suggestions and clues, and keeping ethical and legal considerations in mind. 200 words.

TOP TIP 2

Changing names can avoid legal problems. Ethical ones are not so easily dealt with.

SALLY CLINE'S EXAMPLE OF WRITING IT BOLDLY

Maria and I, who had just celebrated our 30th birthdays, were having our weekly supper before our book club evening. This week we were reading a novel we had first read in Mr Taylor's French class when we were both fourteen.

At the time I hadn't noticed, but looking back I realised that often, when he talked to Maria, he used the 'tu' form of the verb rather than the 'vous' which he used with the rest of us. After class he frequently asked her to stay behind and help clear the room.

'Do you think old Taylor had designs on you?' I asked her.

'He wasn't old,' she said and looked uncomfortable. 'Well, not that old.'

She changed the subject a shade too fast.

'Maria, did he ever make a pass at you?'

'I don't want to discuss it.' She got up; began to clear the dining room table. 'It's over, I'm 30. None of it matters.'

She looked as though it mattered a great deal.

'Tell me.'

'He seduced me on my fourteenth birthday.'

'Seduced? ' I asked.

Maria was silent, trying not to cry.

'No. No. Raped.'

CAROLE ANGIER'S EXAMPLE OF WRITING IT SUBTLY

That Saturday I went as usual to Maria's. I tugged and tugged at
the mermaid bell-pull, but no one answered. I let myself in. The
house was empty. I ran up to the top floor as fast as I could, but
it felt slow. When I got to Maria's room, she was curled up on
her bed, sobbing.

'Mar,' I said, kneeling down beside her. 'What's wrong?'

It took a very long time, and she never told me everything,
I know. It was that teacher – the handsome, careless one, like
Robert Stephens in *The Prime of Miss Jean Brodie*, with his
hair over his eyes and a spoiled look, as though he drank too
much and it was beginning to show. He – well, she didn't tell
me everything, as I said. But she, who has been paid absurd
sums for her beauty since the age of eighteen, has never felt any
good since then. She thinks she's trash. She thinks everything is
her fault. Despite all the famous photographers, all the famous
designers, all the famous men who want only her. That's what you
did to my friend, Mr Jean Brodie. You spoiled her. You made her
the same as you.

QUESTION FOR MEMOIRISTS AND AUTOBIOGRAPHERS

Which was your choice: to tell the story as your 14-year-old self,
as the adult looking back, or some combination of the two? Why
did that seem right? Now try it another way.

How to manage balance

1. Balancing empathy and detachment

* After structure, probably the most important thing to get right is your
  book's *tone*.

* If you are too close to your subject, and/or too uncritical of them (especially when your subject is yourself!), readers will lose faith in your judgement, and start criticising you/her/him themselves.

* If you are too cool, distant and critical, they will lose interest, or (in autobiography and memoir) will think you are secretly fishing for compliments. Either way you will have lost them.

* Keep checking your balance, and remember that humour helps.

(See Irony and humour below.)

EXERCISE on EMPATHY and DETACHMENT FOR BIOGRAPHERS

Something terrible has happened to your subject. Write three paragraphs (max. 150 words) describing this moment. Aim for maximum effect on your readers.

EXERCISE on EMPATHY and DETACHMENT FOR MEMOIRISTS and AUTOBIOGRAPHERS

You have just reached a triumphant high point in your career. Write three paragraphs (max. 150 words) describing this moment. Aim for maximum effect on your readers.

TOP TIP

Keep cool. The worst thing is to show readers how you want them to feel, by word or sign. (So we have just removed the exclamation mark after 'Keep cool'.) Make readers feel it merely by what you describe and how you describe it.

2. Balancing accuracy and elegance

This is probably the most pervasive problem in life writing, which it shares with other forms of creative non-fiction, especially history and science writing: how to integrate research and narrative; how to transform facts into a readable, gripping story. The problem is even worse in history and science writing, with their vaster or more esoteric subjects: at least we are talking about a life.

* What do you do with all the detail you know about your or your subject's ancestors, or school career, or work in engineering?

* What do you do if you have spent half your life in prison for a crime you didn't commit, and have amassed one hundred pages of highly technical evidence that proves your innocence?

* What do you do with gaps in the record, for example the seven years of your subject's disappearance in the Hindu Kush, about which no information has ever emerged?

* What do you do with the awkward shapes we discussed under Structure: for example, the fact that all your or her poetry, and all three of your or her marriages, were packed into your/her forties, and before and after that you/she seemed to do nothing at all?

To summarise: *how do you balance accuracy and truth to the facts with well-paced, elegant and apparently easy writing?*

The answers to these questions are theoretically simple. You boil the facts down to their essence, like refining a sauce. You don't leave your research showing, like lumps in the sauce, but stir it smoothly into the narrative, without distorting or simplifying.

How you do this is more difficult. It is a matter of practice – but however long we practice, we sometimes fail. The important thing is to be aware of the problem, and to keep trying.

EXERCISE on ACCURACY and ELEGANCE

You or your subject win(s) a complex, rather dry legal case, which you must now describe. Pick a case from a recent *Times Law Report*, as complex and/or dry as you can find.

Use three quotations from the *Times* report. Each quotation must be at least six words. Write two paragraphs (max. 200 words) to make the issues clear. Make your victory, or your subject's, as exciting as possible.

How to manage fictional techniques

Life writing can use the whole panoply of techniques available to fiction, adapted to your specific genre. Dialogue is more problematic in biography than in memoir and autobiography, as we will see. That apart, biography can use all fictional devices as well. What follows applies to all three genres.

Description

* sets scenes and provides background
* helps readers to visualise characters
* helps to evoke character traits and themes
* reflects atmosphere and mood

EXERCISE in DESCRIPTION

Describe an important place (indoors or outdoors) in your childhood or that of your subject. Use concrete details and colourful imagery.

Three paragraphs. 150 words max.

TOP TIP

Keep in mind your main traits or your subject's, and/or the main themes about her/him/you, that you will be emphasising, and – while not distorting the facts – make your description evoke them.

Dialogue

Dialogue brings your story to life. However, dialogue is more problematic in biography than it is in the other genres.

For biography

* Unlike in memoir and autobiography, you were not there to hear exchanges between your characters – unless you are writing the biography of a friend, as Boswell did of Johnson.

* The only remembered dialogue you can include is that which you took part in or heard: conversations among your contemporaries, as in the Boswell case, or exchanges between you and your interviewees.

* The only time you can use dialogue you didn't hear is when it is recorded, eg, in a radio or television discussion or interview (and then you must have the owner's permission to use it).

* Otherwise you can only use substitutes for dialogue: exchanges in letters, e-mails, text messages, etc. You can arrange these exchanges as much like normal dialogue as they allow, but must identify them as letters, emails, etc.

* All these sources must be identified in detail in your end notes.

For memoir and autobiography

* In memoir and autobiography you were there, so you can use remembered speech. You can use it exactly as you would in fiction. The only limitations are length and the time elapsed since it occurred.

* If it is a short exchange, it is credible that you can recall it accurately, even if it took place long ago.

* If it is long and detailed, you will need to build in a reference to a source (eg, a diary or a letter), even if it was quite recent. Otherwise readers will start to doubt its accuracy.

* In sum, the longer an exchange was and the longer ago it happened, the less credible it is that you remember it accurately, and the more likely it is to need a source.

* The exception is something very important or traumatic: the uniformed man telling your mother that your father is dead, or your older sister telling you she is really your mother, are likely to be remembered word for word even if they happened many decades ago.

In life writing, as in all writing, you are trying to catch your characters' voices.

TOP TIP FOR DIALOGUE

Write dialogue as if for a radio play.

After the first line, identify the speaker with 'said Pauline', for example.

Thereafter write each person's speech on a separate line and use 'he said' and 'she said' as sparingly as possible.

Avoid adverbs, as in 'She said kindly'. Show the kindness in the dialogue.

DIALOGUE EXERCISE FOR BIOGRAPHY

Your subject, a psychiatrist, had an important exchange with a suicidal patient. This exchange was in the form of:

- texts
- phone messages
- notes
- or emails

Set this exchange as 'dialogue' in a short prose narrative of no more than one paragraph on either side.

Also write the source note to this page of your biography.

DIALOGUE EXERCISE FOR AUTOBIOGRAPHY & MEMOIR

One day when you were 12 years old, walking to school with a friend, you met a flasher. In your autobiography or memoir, write six lines of remembered dialogue between all or any of the three characters.

Set the dialogue in a short prose narrative of the event, no more than one paragraph on either side.

Suspense

* As in fiction, suspense helps to keep readers reading.

* It keeps them wondering what will happen next.

* A good suspense device is to point forward mysteriously at key moments, for example at the end of a chapter you might write: 'He couldn't put it off much longer' or 'She didn't ask his name. But he told her anyway'.

* Suspense in life writing (unlike in crime fiction) does not have to keep readers guessing about the denouement.

* In biography, readers know from the start that the end will be the subject's death. Indeed you may decide to start with it. Nonetheless, you can heighten the suspense so that readers will still wish it not to happen. They want the subject to live. Not to be burnt in that fire, not to wade out and drown, not to die gruellingly of cancer, not to die of TB at 25 if the subject is Keats, or at only 18 if the subject is Chatterton.

* The greatest suspense occurs around bad stuff, evil deeds, horrors.

* Readers become addicted to fearing (and yet loving) the next dreadful thing around the corner.

TOP TIP

Writers always know what will happen next. Characters never know.
Sometimes readers know, sometimes they don't.
Both methods can work to create suspense.

EXERCISE ON SUSPENSE: WHEN READERS KNOW

You show readers a suicide bomber approaching the market place. Now four key characters of your autobiography, memoir or biography approach the market place from a different direction.

Write the next three paragraphs. 150 words.

You, or the subject of your biography, is a star of a profession: a famous singer, athlete or business leader. You have arrived at a turning point of the story. It is the moment of realisation that this is what you/they wanted to do; or the first step of the career; or the first big starring event.

You/they didn't know at the time that this would be the turning point, and you have not told the readers. Write the three paragraphs leading up to that moment. Max. 150 words.

Pace and narrative drive

* Keep your story moving. Don't clog your prose with too many adjectives or adverbs.
* Watch for any addiction to the 'ing' form: it slows up the action. Use it only for slow and static states.
* Use active verbs instead to add pace.
* Too many words make your writing verbose. Be sparing, cut, edit, all the time.

EXERCISE

An ageing woman in your autobiography, memoir or biography is in a care home. She and another woman friend have had a sad conversation: neither of them has any surviving family. There will be no one to attend their funerals.

Suddenly the door to the sitting room bursts open. In hurtles a young person in wild orange silk with an emerald feather hat.

'Mother!!', the young person screams.

Write the next three paragraphs (max. 200 words), keeping up the pace.

Rhythm and variation

In writing, as in music, it's important to vary quick passages with slow, action with reflection, landscapes with inwardness, long paragraphs with short, etc. If you *always* write in short action paragraphs, your work will be staccato and journalistic; but if you go on reflecting on an event for too long, eg, the reader will stop caring about the characters, and the story will lose narrative drive. You need balance and variation.

EXERCISE

You or your subject fail(s) an exam at a crucial point in your/her/his career. Write two paragraphs (max. 200 words) describing the dramatic moment of learning the news. Include reflections on the significance for your/her/his future, but don't lose the focus on the moment.

Conflict

* Conflict is the essence of a riveting story. 'No trouble, no story,' as we've said before.

* There are three main types of conflict:

1. Between the subject and another person or people

2. Between the subject and the environment

3. Between the subject and him- or herself

EXERCISE ON CONFLICT

Two climbers have reached the peak of a mountain. One of them is you or your subject. The other falls and breaks their leg.

Write the event and its consequences three times, using each form of conflict (max. 100 words each):

a. Between the two climbers.

b. Between the climbers and the bad weather.

c. Between you or your subject and your/her/his conscience. Should you/she/he leave the other climber and save your-/her-/himself?

Characterisation

* Your real-life subjects, whether in biography, autobiography or memoir, must be as colourfully characterised as they would be in fiction.

* There are many ways to bring out character:

    1. By physical and mental description: people's appearance, clothes, manners, attitudes, opinions.

    2. By their actions.

    3. In dialogue between them and other characters.

    4. In monologue or reported thoughts.

    5. In comments by other characters.

    6. By authorial comment of the third person narrator in biography, or the first person narrator in memoir and autobiography.

    7. By association. Use their room décor, golf clubs, music certificates or walking boots to point up people's tastes, hobbies or interests.

Autobiography and memoir can use all of these.

Biography can use all of them as well, as long as you remember the reservations and adaptations mentioned for dialogue.

EXERCISE on CHARACTERISATION 1

Write two/three paragraphs, max. 250 words, about yourself or your subject, using as many tools of characterisation as you can.

EXERCISE on CHARACTERISATION 2

Do the exercise again about a subsidiary character in your biography, autobiography or memoir.

Imagery and symbolism

* Images are the ultimate device to *show, not tell* in writing.

* You can pick up (though not invent) any recurring motifs in your life or your subject's. (See TOP TIP 1 below).

* Even if no images naturally arise for your characters, they may do so for themes and places: emphasise the fog and calling seabirds of a melancholy seafarer's tale, for example, or the sun and clarity of a fearless explorer's.

* The general use of imagery in simile and metaphor enlivens your prose and kick-starts readers' own imaginations.

TOP TIP 1

Images and symbols that attach to and evoke a character – for example a colour, a song, an animal associated with that character – can be as successfully used in non-fiction as in fiction. Unlike in fiction, you can't invent them, but you can watch for recurring motifs in letters and interviews. Carole found that the image of dancing recurred in accounts of Primo Levi, as a symbol of the joys of life he felt were barred to him. And Sally found that the image of fire recurred in Zelda Fitzgerald's life, until her death by fire, locked into her room in a nursing home.

Coleridge: Early Visions ends with Coleridge on a ferry for France, his future 'tragically, comically before him' (p. 364). Richard Holmes hesitated over how to end it, until he found a letter describing Coleridge sitting on deck on a duck-crate, gazing up at the stars, the ducks quacking behind his legs.

Keep alert for such 'fertile facts', as Virginia Woolf called them, and use them.

TOP TIP 2

Images and symbols may arise for themes as well as characters. In Hilary Mantel's memoir Giving Up the Ghost a main theme is secrets. Some were secrets kept from her as a child. Others were her own secrets, which she wanted to keep from the grown-ups.

She describes something real, yet symbolic of this second part of the theme: her favourite toy, a magic slate. Children can write on this, then lift the plastic cover from the slate below, and the writing disappears.

Write two paragraphs (max. 300 words) of a biography,
autobiography or memoir, describing an important
person, place or event. Use simile, metaphor, imagery
and symbolism as effectively as you can.

Irony and humour

* There wasn't a glimmer of humour in all three volumes of Victorian
Lives – which is why in *Eminent Victorians* Lytton Strachey introduced
irony into modern English biography.

* Strachey loathed the public school system. He especially loathed
Thomas Arnold, the founder of Rugby, where older boys were made to
flog younger boys, in order to develop 'responsibility' in the older ones
and obedience (unnamed) in the young.

* Strachey's irony exposed both the cruelty and the humbug of the
system: 'The younger children, scourged both by Dr Arnold and by the
elder children, were given every opportunity of acquiring the simplicity,
sobriety and humbleness of mind, which are the best ornaments of
youth.' (*Eminent Victorians*, p. 152 in the Oxford Classics edition.)

* Michael Holroyd, Strachey's biographer, is often wry about Strachey,
Augustus John and Shaw. But his memoirs offer him the best subjects
for humour: himself and his family.

HOW A MEMOIRIST USES IRONY AND HUMOUR

*This is Holroyd's paean to the financial acumen of his grandfather,
Fraser, who had fallen in love with Lalique glass in the late
1920s, and determined to sell it in England:* 'He looked about
him – there were hunger marches, miners' strikes, lengthening
dole queues and street demonstrations protesting against
unemployment throughout Britain; there was the Wall Street
crash in the United States, civil disobedience in India, the

Japanese invasion of Manchuria, revolution in Argentina, revolt in Peru, the rise of Hitler in Germany and Mussolini in Italy, and throughout the world an economic crisis – Fraser looked and saw, reflected in his glass, that all was well. The omens were good, he decided, for further business expansion.' (*Basil Street Blues*, p. 60.)

TOP TIP

Note how, apart from irony, this passage whips lumpy historical facts (like Arnold's little boys) to fit into the tone and point of the prose.

EXERCISE

Write two paragraphs (max. 200 words) of a biography, autobiography or memoir, describing an event or character in it, using irony, satire or humour as effectively as you can.

QUESTION

Compare your results with other people's. What sorts of events or characters did you choose? Is humour ever out of place?

Playing with order

* Playing with order – starting at the end, moving back and forth in time – can be just as useful in life writing as in fiction.
* Moving between the past and the present can add variety and illuminate your story.
* Flashbacks can be vivid and exciting.
* But keep the chronology clear.

* Don't confuse readers. This is even more important in non-fiction than in fiction, as our obligation is not only to readers but also to other real people, and to reality itself.

> **TOP TIP**
>
> *You can make stylistic alterations to avoid confusion.*
>
> *In her biography of Lillian Hellman and Dashiell Hammett, Sally kept the Hammett chapters in normal chronological order, but moved some of the Hellman chapters back into Hellman's childhood. To avoid confusion, she used different tenses and different fonts. The Hammett chapters are Roman and past tense, as are the ordinary chronological Hellman chapters. The Hellman flashback chapters are in italics and in the present tense.*

EXERCISE

Write three paragraphs of a biography, autobiography or memoir, making the middle paragraph a flashback. Max. 300 words.

QUESTION

Compare your results with other people's. Did many people pick biography? Is it harder to do flashbacks in biography than in the first-person varieties of life writing? If so, why?

Playing with tense

Can you ever use the present tense in life writing? Yes. Varying tenses is a stylistic device that adds immediacy and drama to every kind of writing.

The present tense can be used successfully in autobiography and memoir because these are your own stories, and readers will find it natural that some episodes are close and present to you, the writer.

A memoir could even be told entirely in the present, in the child's voice, as in the Holocaust memoir *Fragments*, though that turned out to be fiction.

What about in biography? Can we ever use the present tense there? Life writers differ.

Carole: Only if the subject is still alive, and you are recounting genuinely present events. Telling any part of someone else's past in the present tense is too close to fiction.

Sally: I've used it successfully myself (see TOP TIP above). If is it is managed carefully and sparingly it can enhance your biography.

Example: Frances Wilson's *The Ballad of Dorothy Wordsworth* starts strikingly, 'She can stand it no longer' and continues in the present for several paragraphs.

Clue: Wilson was working from Dorothy's diaries.

EXERCISE 1

Write three paragraphs (max. 300 words) of an autobiography or memoir. Write the first paragraph in the present tense.

EXERCISE 2

Do the exercise again, this time for a biography.

QUESTION

Discuss the results with other people. Did you feel there were differences? If so, what were they? Did you agree more with Carole's rather austere old-fashioned view, or Sally's more open experimental one?

Good openings

The function of a good opening is:

* to hook the reader

* to set the tone

* to establish the atmosphere

* to begin to create characters

* to start the plot

* to signal the theme(s)

Some famous opening lines do many of these jobs on their own. For example,

* 'The two women were alone in the London flat.' Doris Lessing, *The Golden Notebook.*

* 'Someone must have slandered Joseph K, for one morning, without having done anything truly wrong, he was arrested.' Kafka, *The Trial.*

* 'Mrs Dalloway said she would buy the flowers herself.' Virginia Woolf, *Mrs Dalloway.*

Good openings of life writing books are not as easy to write as in novels, because the novelist must only write a good beginning, whereas the life writer must draw that good beginning from reality. But here are some examples:

* 'Amongst his earliest memories were dreams.' Grevel Lindop, *The Opium Eater: A Life of Thomas de Quincey.*

* 'Grandfather's skirts would flap in the wind along the churchyard path and I would hang on.' Lorna Sage, *Bad Blood.*

* 'The room in which I am sitting is white.' Joan Bakewell, *The Centre of the Bed.*

* 'Oxford was losing its young men.' Carole Seymour-Jones, *Painted Shadow: A Life of Vivienne Eliot.*

* '"My name is Evelyn Waugh I go to Heath Mount school I am in the Vth Form, Our Form Master is Mr Stebbing."' Paula Byrne, *Mad World: Evelyn Waugh and the Secrets of Brideshead.*

* And perhaps the greatest opening line of all, from one of the greatest autobiographies: 'The cradle rocks above an abyss, and common sense tells us that our existence is but a brief crack of light between two eternities of darkness.' Vladimir Nabokov, *Speak, Memory*.

Satisfying endings

* Endings do not need to be happy in order to satisfy readers.
* The best endings may be ironic or ambivalent. You can leave several possibilities open. Leave room for readers to use their imagination.
* Pick up a key theme or feeling and leave it richly in readers' minds.

Examples of famous novel endings

* 'He loved Big Brother.'

  George Orwell, *1984*.

* 'So we beat on, boats against the current, borne back ceaselessly into the past.'

  Scott Fitzgerald, *The Great Gatsby*.

* 'Now at last I know why I was brought here and what I have to do. There must have been a draught for the flame flickered and I thought it was out. But I shielded it with my hand and it burned up again to light me along the dark passage.'

  Jean Rhys, *Wide Sargasso Sea*.

Examples of good life writing endings

* 'Edna St. Vincent Millay had survived her beloved cavalier by one year, one month, and twenty days.' Nancy Milford, *Savage Beauty: The Life of Edna St Vincent Millay*.

* 'You must not forget anything.'

  Philip Roth, *Patrimony*.

* 'It was a case of "Everything or Nothing"; and thus desperately challenged, the young man's conscience threw off once for all the yoke of his "dedication", and, as respectfully as he could, without

parade or remonstrance, he took a human being's privilege to fashion his inner life for himself.'

Edmund Gosse, *Father and Son.*

* And the original last line of the first modern biography, Johnson's *Life of Savage:*

'Those are no proper Judges of his Conduct who have slumber'd away their Time on the Down of Plenty, nor will a wise Man easily presume to say, "Had I been in Savage's condition, I should have lived, or written, better than Savage."'

Beginnings and endings are above all what readers remember.

EXERCISE 1

Write down what each of the opening lines above tell you about the plot, style, characters, themes or atmospheres of their books.

Write down what the closing lines above do in relation to the points in Satisfying endings above (or anything else you'd like to say about either.)

Discuss your results with others.

EXERCISE 2

Write a good opening line for a biography, autobiography or memoir.

Write the whole first paragraph but keep it short. Max. six lines.

Discuss your results with others.

EXERCISE 3

Repeat Exercise 2 for ending lines and endings.

> **TOP TIP**
>
> *Mystery is always good, vagueness is always bad.*

What to avoid in all writing

> **TOP TIP**
>
> *Avoid clichés, for example, 'heart beating' or 'pounding', 'all her eggs in one basket', 'green as grass', etc. Clichés are useful to point out the general area you wish to write about, but then you must delete the cliché and use your own fresh phrase.*

Good writing!

Acknowledgments

Carole and Sally would like to thank:

David Avital, our editor, for his enthusiasm, patience and hard work in support of this book and the whole series.

Rachel Calder, our imaginative agent, for her unflagging help and support, and for never leaving us waiting for a reply.

Jenny Ridout, our first editor, for commissioning the series and supporting us throughout the writing of this first book.

The Arvon Foundation for their initial backing for the series, and for hosting our course at Lumb Bank since 2006.

Glenn Jobson, our computer wizard who made superb sense of our Luddite materials.

Our 32 guest contributors who have made our Guest Section one of the best things we have read.

Carole's acknowledgments.
First of all, I want to thank Sally for being such an unfailing, hard-working and generous co-writer and co-tutor.

I also want to thank Michael Holroyd, for writing the Foreword, and for always making me laugh. My own computer wizard, my cousin Zac Manasseh. Hilary Spurling, for her unerring advice over the years, and for our shared friendship with Diane. Finally, Diane Middlebrook, biographer and friend, for her thoughtfulness and generosity to me even in the last stages of her illness.

Sally's acknowledgments.
My most important thanks go to my co-writer Carole Angier who has been flexible, tolerant, generous, and funny. She has also kindly corrected my hasty grammar!

My appreciation goes to my recently bereaved daughter Marmoset Adler who despite many tragic months has offered me steady encouragement, and to Vic Smith who has never once failed to urge me on.

The Royal Literary Fund has again granted me an Advisory Fellowship and much practical assistance which has allowed me to write with a measure of security. I thank especially Steve Cook and Eileen Gunn.

I am indebted to Tracy and Richard Baker for time and space, twice, to write at beautiful Atlantic Lodge, Sennen Cove, and to Frances (Frankie) Borzello for the peace to write in her white attic.

For time to write through her typing, editing and many other practical kindnesses I thank Rachel Senior. For generously reading and revising the Preface, Introduction and much of my section of Part 1 I thank Chris Carling.

For special support during the writing, I thank Kathy Bowles, Jonathan and Joan Harris, Colette Paul, Sally Lawrence, Michelle Spring, Paul Flynn and the other valued family, friends and colleagues. You will know who you are.

Three women have made my part of this book possible: my close friend Jill Dawson (Ruby) has been, as ever, my inspiration and source of writerly strength. Angie North has managed my house while I was away and listened to endless drafts and ideas when at home. Finally, I thank Ba Sheppard whose optimistic realism and faith in the words has encouraged me for 32 years. For this book her wise understanding helped me through the hardest challenges.

Permissions

The authors and publisher would like to thank the following for their kind permission to reproduce quotations.

Quotation from *Basil Street Blues* by Michael Holroyd, Little Brown, London, 1999, by permission of the author.

Quotation from 'OBSESSED', *Afterword* to *Dashiell Hammett: A Life* by Diane Johnson, Random House, New York, 1983, by permission of the author.

Quotations from Janet Malcolm, *The Silent Woman: Sylvia Plath and Ted Hughes,* Knopf, New York, 1993, are published with permission of Knopf Imprint, Random House Inc, New York.

Quotation from 'Writing Another Life' by Marion Elizabeth Rodgers in *Writer's Digest,* USA, April 2008, by permission of the author.

Address list

ALCS (Authors' Licensing and Collecting Society): The Writers' House, 13 Haydon Street, London EC3N 1DB

Arts Council of England: 14 Great Peter Street, London SW1P 3NQ

Association of Authors' Agents: www.agentsassoc.co.uk

BIO (Biographers International Organization): www.biographersinternational.org

The Biographers' Club: 79 Marsham Street, Suite 6.17, London SW1P 4SB

The Biographers' Craft: PO Box 864, Tesuque NM 87574, USA

The Bodleian Library: Broad Street, Oxford OX1 3BG

British Academy: 10 Carlton House Terrace, London, SW1Y 5AH

The British Library: 96 Euston Road, London NW1 2DB

British Library Newspapers Colindale: Colindale Avenue, London NW9 5HE

Cambridge University Library: West Road, Cambridge CB3 9DR

CELL (Centre for Editing Lives and Letters): Arts Research Centre, Queen Mary, University of London, Mile End Road, London E1 4NS

The Centre for Biographical Research: University of Hawaii at Manoa, 2500 Campus Road, Honolulu, HI 96822, USA

The Centre for Life History and Life Writing: University of Sussex, Sussex House, Brighton BN1 9RH

Family Records Centre: 1 Myddelton Street, Islington, London EC1R

Gold Dust: PO Box 247, Ely CB7 9BX

IABA (International Auto/biography Association): www.iaba.org.cn

The Leon Levy Center for Biography: The Graduate Center, CUNY, 365 Fifth Avenue, Room 5103.03, New York, NY 10016

Leverhulme Research Fellowships: The Leverhulme Trust, 1 Pemberton Row, London EC4A 3BG

The Literary Consultancy: Free Word Centre, 60 Farringdon Road, London EC1R 3GA

Location Register of 20th Century English Literary Manuscripts: The University of Reading, Whiteknights, PO Box 217, Reading, Berkshire RG6 6AH

The London Library: 14 St James' Square, London SW1Y 4LG

Mslexia: PO Box 656, Newcastle upon Tyne NE99 1PZ

The National Library of Ireland: Kildare Street, Dublin 2, Eire

The National Library of Scotland: 57 George IV Bridge, Edinburgh EH1 1EW

The National Library of Wales: Aberystwyth, Ceredigion, SY23 3BU

National Maritime Museum: Romney Road, Greenwich SE10 8XJ

National Sound Archives: British Library, 96 Euston Road, London NW1 2DB

New Writing North: Culture Lab, Grand Assembly Rooms, Newcastle University, Newcastle upon Tyne NE1 7RU

New Writing South: 9 Jew Street, Brighton, East Sussex BN1 1UT

Probate Search Room: 42–49 High Holborn, London WC1V 6NP

Public Records Office: The National Archives, Kew, Richmond, Surrey TW9 4DU

Public Records Office Northern Ireland: 66–70 Balmoral Avenue, Belfast BT9 6NY

Public Records Office Scotland: General Register Office for Scotland, New Register House, 3 West Register Street, Edinburgh, EH1 3YT

The Royal Society of Literature, Jerwood Awards: Somerset House, Strand, London WC2R 1LA

The Society of Authors: 84 Drayton Gardens, London SW10 9SB

Society of Genealogists: 14 Charterhouse Buildings, London EC1M 7BA

Trinity College Dublin Library: College Green, Dublin 2, Eire

Winston Churchill Memorial Trust: 15 Queen's Gate Terrace, London SW7 5PR

Writer's Journal: PO Box 394, Perham MN 56573, USA

Bibliography

Note: where a book has appeared in more than one section, it has been listed only in the first.

Part 1
Reflections 1 by Carole Angier
Select Bibliography
Ackroyd, Peter, *Dickens*, Sinclair Stevenson, London, 1990.

Bayley, John, *Iris*, Abacus, London, 1999.

Batchelor, John, ed., *The Art of Literary Biography*, Oxford University Press, Oxford, 1995.

Beer, Thomas, *Stephen Crane*, Knopf, New York, 1923

Burnside, John, *A Lie About My Father*, Vintage, London, 2007.

Clubbe, John ed., *Froude's Life of Carlyle*, John Murray, London, 1979.

France, Peter and St Clair, William, eds., *Mapping Lives*, Oxford University Press, Oxford, 2002.

Hamilton, Ian, *In Search of J.D. Salinger*, Random House, New York, 1988.

Hamilton, Nigel, *Biography: A Brief History*, Harvard University Press, Cambridge MA, 2007.

Holmes, Richard, *Shelley: The Pursuit*, Harper Perennial, London, 2005. *Footsteps: Adventures of a Romantic Biographer*, Vintage, London, 1996. *Johnson on Savage*, Harper Perennial, London, 2005.

Holroyd, Michael, *Lytton Strachey – The New Biography*, W.W. Norton, New York, 2005. *Works on Paper*, Little Brown, London, 2002.

Homberger, Eric and Charmley, John, *The Troubled Face of Biography*, Macmillan, London, 1988.

Lee, Hermione, *Virginia Woolf*, Vintage, London, 1999.

Malcolm, Janet, *The Silent Woman: Sylvia Plath and Ted Hughes*, Picador, London, 1994.

Meyers, Jeffrey, ed., *The Biographer's Art*, Macmillan, London, 1989.

Morris, Edmund, *Dutch: A Memoir of Ronald Reagan*, HarperCollins, London, 2000.

Summerscale, Kate, *The Suspicions of Mr Whicher*, Bloomsbury, London, 2009.

Symons, A.J.A., *The Quest for Corvo*, Penguin, London, 1966.

Woolf, Virginia, *Collected Essays*, Vol. IV, Hogarth Press, London, 1967.

Reflections 2 by Sally Cline
Memory and Myths

Biographies of Jane Austen: Henry Austen, 'Biographical Notice', 1818.

Anna Lefroy, *Recollections of Aunt Jane*, 1864.

Caroline Austen, *My Aunt Jane Austen*, 1867 (not pub. till 1952), Jane Austen Society, 1991.

James Edward Austen-Leigh, *A Memoir of Jane Austen*, 1870, Oxford World's Classics, Oxford.

Fanny Lefroy, *Family History*, from the 1880s.

Bradford, William, *Of Plymouth Plantation*, Johns Hopkins University Press, Baltimore 2002.

Cline, Sally, *Zelda Fitzgerald: Her Voice in Paradise*, Faber Finds, London, 2010. *Lillian Hellman and Dashiell Hammett: Memories or Myths* (forthcoming).

Fiedler, Leslie, *Cross the Border, Close the Gap*, Stein & Day, New York, 1971.

Gaskell, Elizabeth, *The Life of Charlotte Bronte*, Oxford World's Classics, Oxford, 2009.

Lee, Hermione, *A Very Short Introduction to Biography*, Oxford University Press, Oxford, 2009.

Smith, Captain John, *The General History of Virginia, New England and the Summer Isles, 1624*.

Role of the Life Writer

Cline, Sally, *Lifting the Taboo: Women, Death and Dying*, Abacus, London, 1996. *Women, Passion and Celibacy*, Carol Southern Books, New York, 1993. *Radclyffe Hall: A Woman Called John*, Faber Finds, London, 2010.

Dillon, Millicent, *A Little Original Sin, The Life and Work of Jane Bowles*, Virago, London, 1988.

Dunn, Jane, *Antonia White, A Life*, Jonathan Cape, London, 1998.

Hall, Radclyffe, *The Well of Loneliness*, Virago, London, 2008.

Mellow, James R., *Invented Lives: F. Scott and Zelda Fitzgerald*, Houghton Mifflin, Boston MA, 1984.

Peters, Margot, *May Sarton: A Biography*, Knopf, New York, 1997.

Secrest, Meryle, *Between Me and Life: A Biography of Romaine Brooks*, Macdonald and Jane's, London 1976.

Seymour-Jones, Carole, *Painted Shadow: A Life of Vivienne Eliot*, Constable, London, 2001.

Tomalin, Claire, *The Invisible Woman: The Story of Nelly Ternan and Charles Dickens*, Viking, London, 1990.

Telling Stories, Telling Facts

Bruccoli, Matthew, *Some Sort of Epic Grandeur: The Life of F. Scott Fitzgerald*, Cardinal Harcourt Brace Jovanovitch, New York, 1981.

Dillon, Millicent, *You Are Not I: A Portrait of Paul Bowles*, University of California Press, Berkeley, 1998.

Haslam, Sara and Neale, Derek, *Life Writing*, Routledge, London, 2009.

Hillier, Bevis, *John Betjeman: The Biography*, John Murray, London, 2007.

Masters, Alexander, *Stuart: A Life Backwards*, Fourth Estate, London, 2005.

Wilson, A.N., *Betjeman*, Arrow Books, London, 2007.

Woolf, Virginia, 'The Art of Biography', *Selected Essays*, Oxford World's Classics, Oxford, 2008. *Orlando: A Biography*, Oxford World's Classics, Oxford, 2008. *Flush: A Biography*, Vintage, London, 2002.

Truth

Bruccoli, Matthew, ed., *The Notebook of F. Scott Fitzgerald*, Harcourt Brace Jovanovitch/Bruccoli Clark 1978.

Karr, Mary, *The Liars' Club*, Picador, London, 2001.

Spurling, Hilary, *The Life of Ivy Compton Burnett*, Metro Books, London, 1996.

Tradition
Biography by Carole Angier
(Select bibliography, in chronological order)
The Epic of Gilgamesh, Penguin Classics, London, 2003.
Theophrastus, *Characters,* Cambridge Classical Texts, Cambridge, 2007.
Suetonius, *The Twelve Caesars,* Penguin Classics, London, 2003.
Plutarch's Lives, Modern Library, London, 2001.
Vasari, Giorgio, *Lives of the Artists,* Oxford World's Classics, Oxford, 2008.
Cavendish, George, *The Life of Cardinal Wolsey,* Forgotten Books, 2009.
Walton, Izaak, *Lives of Donne, Wotton, Hooker, Herbert,* BiblioBazaar, 2007.
Pepys, Samuel, *The Diaries of Samuel Pepys: A Selection,* Penguin Classics, London, 2003.
Aubrey, John, *Brief Lives,* Boydell Press, Woodbridge, 2009.
Johnson, Samuel, *Selected Writings,* Penguin Classics, London, 1986.
Boswell, James, *The Life of Samuel Johnson,* Wordsworth Classics, 2008.
Lockhart, James Gibson, *The Life of Sir Walter Scott* (abridged), Kessinger Publishing, Whitefish MT, 2009.
Smiles, Stanley, *Self-Help,* Oxford World's Classics, Oxford, 2002.
Gosse, Edmund, *Father and Son,* Oxford World's Classics, Oxford, 2009.
Strachey, Lytton, *Eminent Victorians,* Oxford World's Classics, Oxford, 2003.
Nicolson, Harold, *The Development of English Biography,* The Hogarth Press, London, 1927.
Scott, Geoffrey, *Scott on Zelide,* ed. Richard Holmes, Harper Perennial, London, 2004.
Edel, Leon, *The Life of Henry James,* 2 Vols., Penguin, London, 1977.
Ellmann, Richard, *James Joyce,* Oxford University Press, Oxford, 1983.
Painter, George, *Marcel Proust: A Biography,* Peregrine Books, 1983.
Holroyd, Michael, *Augustus John,* Vintage, London, 1997. *George Bernard Shaw,* Vintage, London, 1998. *A Strange Eventful History,* Vintage, London, 2009.
Johnson, Diane, *Lesser Lives,* Plume, New York, 1999.
Rose, Phyllis, *Parallel Lives: Five Victorian Marriages,* Vintage, London, 2001.
Dyer, Geoff, *Out of Sheer Rage,* Abacus, London, 2003.
Blackburn, Julia, *Old Man Goya,* Vintage, London, 2003.

Holmes, Richard, *Sidetracks*, HarperCollins, London, 2000.

Hoare, Philip, *Leviathan*, Fourth Estate, London, 2009.

Gordon, Lyndall, *Lives Like Loaded Guns: Emily Dickinson and her Family's Feuds*, Virago Press, London, 2010.

Spurling, Hilary, *Burying the Bones: Pearl Buck in China*, Simon & Schuster, London, 2010.

Biography in Fiction by Carole Angier

Bainbridge, Beryl, *According to Queeney*, Abacus, London, 2002.

Barnes, Julian, *The Porcupine*, Picador, London, 1992.

Arthur and George, Vintage, London, 2006.

Brown, Dan, *The Da Vinci Code*, Corgi, London, 2004.

Byatt, A.S., *Possession*, Vintage Classics, London, 2007.

Carey, Peter, *True History of the Kelly Gang*, Faber & Faber, London, 2004.

Chevalier, Tracy, *The Girl with the Pearl Earring*, HarperCollins, London, 2006.

Duffy, Bruce, *The World as I Found It*, Mariner Books, Boston MA, 1995.

Fitzgerald, Penelope, *The Blue Flower*, Flamingo, London, 1996.

Graves, Robert, *I Claudius*, Penguin Classics, London, 2006.

Harris, Robert, *Imperium*, Arrow Books, London, 2007.

James, Henry, *The Aspern Papers and Other Stories*, Oxford World's Classics, Oxford, 2009.

Lodge, David, *Author! Author!* Penguin, London, 2005.

Lurie, Alison, *The Truth About Lorin Jones*, Abacus, London, 1993.

Malamud, Bernard, *Dubin's Lives*, Vintage Classics, London, 1999.

Maugham, Somerset, *The Moon and Sixpence*, Penguin Classics, London, 2005. *Cakes and Ale*, Vintage Classics, London, 2000.

Nabokov, Vladimir, *The Real Life of Sebastian Knight*, Penguin Modern Classics, London, 2001.

Renault, Mary, *The King Must Die*, Arrow Books, London, 2004.

Stead, C.K., *Mansfield*, Vintage, London, 2004.

Toibin, Colm, *The Master*, Picador, London, 2005.

Toynton, Evelyn, *Modern Art*, Delphinium Books, Encino CA, 2000.

Yourcenar, Marguerite, *Memoirs of Hadrian*, Penguin Modern Classics, London, 2000.

Autobiography by Sally Cline
Angelou, Maya, *I Know Why the Caged Bird Sings*, Virago, London, 1984.
Bakewell, Joan, *The Centre of the Bed: An Autobiography*, Sceptre, London, 2003.
Dillard, Annie, *An American Childhood*, Harper Perennial, London, 1988.
Cole, Natalie, *Angel On My Shoulder*, Times Warner International, London, 2000.
Franklin, Benjamin, *Autobiography*, Digireads, 2005.
Griffith, Mattie, *Autobiography of a Female Slave*, University Press Mississippi, Jackson MS, 1998.
Kollontai, Alexandra, *The Autobiography of a Sexually Emancipated Communist Woman*, Herder and Herder, New York, 1971.
McClellan, Barr, *Blood Money and Power: How LBJ killed JFK*, Hannover House, Fayetteville AR, 2004.
Malcolm X, Alex Haley and Paul Gilroy, *The Autobiography of Malcolm X*, Penguin Modern Classics, London, 2001.
Merton, Thomas, *The Seven Storey Mountain*, Harcourt Brace Jovanovitch, New York, 1948.
St Augustine of Hippo, *Confessions* (4th century AD).
White, Mel, *Stranger at the Gate:To Be Gay and Christian in America*, Plume, New York, 1995.
Whitehorn, Katharine, *Selective Memory, An Autobiography*, Virago, London, 2007.

Autobiography in Other Genres by Sally Cline
Autobiographical novels
Gaines, Ernest J., *The Autobiography of Miss Jane Pittman*, Bantam, London, 1982.
Johnson, James Weldon, *The Autobiography of An Ex-Colored Man*, Sherman French & Co., New York, 1912.
Stein, Gertrude, *The Autobiography of Alice B. Toklas*, Vintage, London, 1990.

Vidal, Gore, *Two Sisters: A Memoir in the Form of a Novel*, Ballantyne
    Books, New York, 1987.

Autobiography in creative non-fiction
Auster, Paul, *New York Trilogy*, Faber & Faber, London, 2004. *Leviathan*,
    Faber & Faber, London, 2001. *Oracle Night*, Faber & Faber, London, 2005.
Burroughs, William, *Naked Lunch,* 1959
Cooper, James Fenimore, *The Last of the Mohicans,* Penguin, London, 2007.
Dawson, Jill *The Great Lover*, Hodder & Stoughton, London, 2009.
Gold, Herbert: *Fathers: A Novel in the Form of a Memoir*, Random House,
    New York, 1966.
Grisham, John, *A Painted House*, Doubleday, New York, 2001.
Hawthorne, Nathaniel, *The Scarlet Letter*, Bantam Classics, New York, 1981.
Hustvedt, Siri, *The Sorrows of an American*, Henry Holt, New York, 2008.
Kerouac, Jack, *On the Road,* Penguin, London, 2007.
Lessing, Doris, *Alfred and Emily*, Fourth Estate, London, 2008.
Plath, Sylvia, *The Bell Jar*, Harper Perennial Modern Classics, London, 2000.
Roth, Philip, *My Life as a Man*, Vintage, London, 2005. *The Facts: A
    Novelist's Autobiography*, Vintage, London, 2007. *I Married a Communist*,
    Vintage, London, 2005. *Portnoy's Complaint*, Vintage, London, 1998. *The
    Counterlife*, Vintage, London, 2005. *Deception*, Vintage, London, 1998.
    Operation Shylock: A Confession, Vintage, London, 1998. *The Plot Against
    America*, Vintage, London, 2005.
Seymour, Miranda, *The Telling*, John Murray, London, 1998.
Theroux, Paul, *My Other Life*, Mariner Books , Boston MA, 1997.
Winterson, Jeanette, *Oranges Are Not the Only Fruit*, Vintage, London, 1991.
Wolfe, Thomas, *Look Homeward Angel*, Scribner Paperback, London, 1995.

Autobiographical poetry
Alvarez, Al, ed., *The New Poetry*, Penguin, London, 1966.
Berryman, John, *77 Dream Songs*, Faber & Faber, London, 2001. *Love and
    Fame*, Faber & Faber, London, 1971.
Ginsberg, Allen, *Howl, Kaddish and Other Poems*, Penguin Modern Classics,
    London, 2009.

Hughes, Ted, *Crow*, Faber & Faber, London, 2001. *The Birthday Letters*, Faber & Faber, London, 1999.

Lowell, Robert, *The Dolphin*, Faber & Faber, London, 1973. *For the Union Dead*, Faber & Faber, London, 1985. *Life Studies*, Faber & Faber, London, 2001.

Plath, Sylvia, *Ariel*, Faber & Faber, London, 1968.

Sexton, Anne, *The Complete Poems*, Houghton Mifflin, Boston MA, 1999.

Snodgrass, William, *Heart's Needle*, Marvell, 1961.

Memoir 1 by Carole Angier

Anonymous, *A Woman in Berlin*, Virago, London, 2005.

Appelfeld, Aharon, *The Story of a Life*, Hamish Hamilton, London, 2005.

Barnes, Julian, *Flaubert's Parrot*, Vintage Classics, London, 2009.

Borowski, Tadeusz, *This Way for the Gas, Ladies and Gentlemen*, Penguin Twentieth Century Classics, London, 1992.

Botton, Alain de, *Kiss and Tell*, Picador, London, 1996.

Bourdain, Anthony, *Kitchen Confidential*, Bloomsbury, London, 2001.

Boyd, William, *Nat Tate*, 21 Publishing, 1998. *Any Human Heart*, Penguin, London, 2009.

Bunyan, John, *The Pilgrim's Progress*, Wordsworth Classics, 1996.

Cherry-Garrard, Apsley, *The Worst Adventure in the World*, Pimlico, London, 2003.

Dante, *The Divine Comedy*, Oxford World's Classics, Oxford, 2008.

Frey, James, *A Million Little Pieces*, John Murray, London, 2004.

Graves, Robert, *Goodbye to All That*, Penguin Modern Classics, London, 2000.

Holden, Edith, *The Country Diary of an Edwardian Lady*, Top That! Publishing, Woodbridge, 2006.

Homer, *The Odyssey*, Penguin Classics, London, 2003.

Juska, Jane, *A Round-heeled Woman: My Late-Life Adventures in Sex and Romance*, Vintage, London, 2004.

Kelly, Kath, *How I Lived on Just a Pound a Day*, Redcliffe Press paperback 2008.

Kertész, Imre, *Fatelessness*, (now titled *Fateless*), Vintage, London, 2006.

Levi, Primo, *If This Is a Man*, Abacus, London, 1991. *Moments of Reprieve*, Penguin Modern Classics, London, 2002.

Maitland, Sara, *The Book of Silence*, Granta Books, London, 2009.

Mayle, Peter, *A Year in Provence*, Penguin, London, 2000.

Orwell, George, *Down and Out in Paris and London*, Penguin Modern Classics, London, 2001.

Polo, Marco, *The Travels*, Penguin Classics, London, 2004.

Sebald, W.G.S., *Vertigo*, Vintage, London, 2002. *The Rings of Saturn*, Vintage, London, 2002. *The Emigrants*, Vintage, London, 2002. *Austerlitz*, Penguin, London, 2002.

Simpson, Joe, *Touching the Void*, Vintage, London, 1997.

Van der Post, Laurens, *The Lost World of the Kalahari*, Vintage Classics, London, 2002.

West, Rebecca, *Black Lamb and Grey Falcon*, Penguin, London, 2007.

Whymper, Edward, *Scrambles Amongst the Alps*, National Geographic Books, 2002.

Wiesel, Elie, *Night*, Penguin, London, 2008.

Zsolt, Béla, *Nine Suitcases*, Pimlico, London, 2005.

Memoir 2 by Sally Cline

Adler, Larry, *It Ain't Necessarily So*, Fontana Collins, London, 1984.

Bakewell, Joan, *The View from Here: Life at Seventy*, Atlantic Books, London, 2006.

Bauby, Jean-Dominique, *The Butterfly and the Diving Bell*, Harper Perennial, London, 2008.

Blackburn, Julia, *The Three of Us*, Vintage, London, 2009.

Bloom, Claire, *Leaving a Doll's House*, Virago, London, 1997.

Bogarde, Dirk, *A Particular Friendship*, Penguin, London, 1990.

Chang, Jung, *Wild Swans*, Harper Perennial, London, 2004.

De Beauvoir, Simone, *The Second Sex*, Vintage Classics, London, 1997.

Diamond, John, *C: Because Cowards Get Cancer Too*, Vermillion, London, 1999.

Hanff, Helene, *84 Charing Cross Road*, Futura Macdonald, London, 1976.

Hellman, Lillian, *An Unfinished Woman: A Memoir,* Penguin, London, 1972. *Maybe: A Story,* Quartet Books, London, 1981. *Pentimento,* Back Bay Books, London, 2000. *Scoundrel Time,* Little Brown, London, 2000.

McCarthy, Mary, *Memories of a Catholic Girlhood,* Harcourt Brace, New York, 1957.

McCourt, Frank, *Angela's Ashes,* Harper Perennial, London, 2004.

Motion, Andrew, *In the Blood,* Faber & Faber, London, 2006.

Murray, Jenni, *Memoirs of a Not So Dutiful Daughter,* Bantam Press, London, 2008.

Pelzer, Dave, *My Story: A Child Called 'It'/The Lost Boy/A Man Named Dave,* Orion, London, 2004.

Rieff, David, *Swimming in a Sea of Death: A Son's Memoir,* Granta, London, 2008.

Seymour, Miranda, *In My Father's House: Elegy for an Obsessive Love,* Simon and Schuster, London, 2007.

Sonnenberg, Susanna, *Her Last Death: A Memoir,* Scribner, London, 2008.

Welty, Eudora, *One Writer's Beginnings,* Harvard University Press, Cambridge MA, 1995.

Letters

Bishop, Elizabeth, *One Art: Letters,* selected and edited by Robert Giroux, Farrar Strauss Giroux, New York, 1994.

Thompson, Tierl, ed., *Dear Girl: The Diaries and Letters of Two Working Women 1897–1917,* The Women's Press, London, 1987.

Travisano, Thomas and Hamilton, Saskia, eds., *Words in Air: The Complete Correspondence between Elizabeth Bishop and Robert Lowell,* 2008.

Diaries, Blogs, Twitter

Aciman, Alexander and Rensin, Emmett, *Twitterature,* Penguin, London, 2009.

Part 3
Planning

Angier, Carole, *Jean Rhys: Life & Work,* Faber Finds, London, 2010. *The Double Bond: A Life of Primo Levi,* Faber Finds, London, 2010.

Balfour, Sandy, *Pretty Girl in Crimson Rose (8)*, Atlantic Books, London, 2004.

Bowker, R.R., *Biographical Books*, Bowker, East Grinstead, 1988.

Blythe, Ronald, *Akenfield*, Penguin Classics, London, 2005.

Davenport-Hines, Richard, *A Night at the Majestic*, Faber & Faber, London, 2006.

De Salvo, Louise, *Virginia Woolf: The Impact of Childhood Sexual Abuse on Her Life and Work*, The Women's Press, London, 1989.

Didion, Joan, *The Year of Magical Thinking*, Harper Perennial, London, 2006.

Dunn, Nell, *Talking to Women*, Pan, London, 1966. *Grandmothers Talking to Nell Dunn*, Chatto & Windus, London, 1994.

Eggers, Dave, *A Heart-breaking Work of Staggering Genius*, Picador, London, 2000.

Faulks, Sebastian, *The Fatal Englishman: Three Short Lives*, Vintage, London, 1997.

Fitzgerald, Penelope, *The Knox Brothers*, Flamingo, London, 2002.

Fox, James, *The Langhorne Sisters*, Granta Books, London, 1999.

France, Miranda, *Bad Times in Buenos Aires*, Phoenix, London, 1999.

Galloway, Janice, *This Is Not About Me*, Granta Books, London, 2009.

Gillies, Midge, *How to Write Memoir and Biographies*, The Guardian and The Observer, 2009.

Gordon, Lyndall, *A Private Life of Henry James*, Vintage 1999.

Hayter, Alethea, *A Sultry Month*, Faber Finds, London, 2009.

Holmes, Richard, *The Age of Wonder*, HarperPress, London, 2009.

Hughes, Kathryn, *The Short Life and Long Times of Mrs Beeton*, Harper Perennial, London, 2006.

Hughes-Hallett, Penelope, *The Immortal Dinner*, Viking, London, 2000.

Johnson, Diane, *Dashiell Hammett: A Life*, Random House, New York, 1983.

Jones, J.D.F, *Storyteller: The Many Lives of Laurens van der Post*, Simon & Schuster, London, 2002.

Levi, Primo, *The Periodic Table*, Oxford Modern Classics, London, 2000.

Lewis, Jeremy, *Shades of Greene: One Generation of an English Family*, Jonathan Cape, London, 2010.

Lewis, Roger, *Anthony Burgess*, Faber & Faber, London, 2003.

Lichtenstein, Rachel and Sinclair, Ian, *Rodinsky's Room*, Granta Books, London, 2000.

Maddox, Brenda, *Rosalind Franklin: The Dark Lady of DNA*, HarperCollins, London, 2003. *Freud's Wizard: The Enigma of Ernest Jones*, John Murray, London, 2007.

Marnham, Patrick, *Trail of Havoc*, Penguin, London, 1988.

Middlebrook, Diane, *Young Ovid* (forthcoming).

Moorehead, Caroline, *Dunant's Dream*, HarperCollins, London, 1999. *Human Cargo*, Vintage, London, 2006.

Motion, Andrew, *The Lamberts*, The Hogarth Press, London, 1987.

Osborne, Brian D., *Writing Biography and Autobiography*, A&C Black, London, 2004.

Rusesebagina, Paul, *An Ordinary Man*, Bloomsbury, London, 2007.

Schorer, Mark, *Sinclair Lewis*, McGraw Hill, 1961.

Sage, Lorna, *Bad Blood*, Fourth Estate, London, 2001.

Sebold, Alice, *Lucky*, Picador, London, 1999.

Seymour-Jones, Carole, *A Dangerous Liaison*, Arrow Books, London, 2009.

Slater, Nigel, *Toast*, Harper Perennial, London, 2007.

Spiegelman, Art, *The Complete Maus*, Penguin, London, 2003.

Spurling, Hilary, *Matisse*, Vols. 1 & 2, Penguin, London, 2006. *Matisse: The Life* (one-volume edition), Penguin, London, 2009. *The Girl from the Fiction Department: A Portrait of Sonia Orwell*, Hamish Hamilton, London, 2002.

The Writers' and Artists' Yearbook, A&C Black, London, 2009.

Thurman, Judith, *Isak Dinesen: The Life of a Storyteller*, St Martins Press, New York, 1982.

Tomalin, Claire, *Katherine Mansfield: A Secret Life*, Penguin, London, 1988. *Samuel Pepys: The Unequalled Self*, Penguin, London, 2003. *Thomas Hardy: The Time-Torn Man*, Penguin, London, 2007.

Turner, Barry, ed., *The Writers' Handbook*, Macmillan, London, 2009.

Uglow, Jenny, *Lunar Men: The Friends Who Made the Future*, Faber & Faber, London, 2003.

Vidal, Gore, *Palimpsest*, Abacus, London, 1996.
Woolf, Virginia, *A Room With a View*, Penguin Modern Classics, London, 2002.
Wyatt, Will, *The Treasure of the Sierra Madre: The Man Who Was B. Traven*, Harcourt Publishers, Boston MA, 1985.

Research
We found the following books helpful in putting together the first part of this section:
Research for Writers by Ann Hoffmann, A&C Black, London, 2003.
Writing Biography & Autobiography by Brian D. Osborne, A&C Black, London, 2004.
The Internet for Writers by John Ralph, Teach Yourself Books, London, 2003.

Note: standard reference works are not listed. They can be found in the reference sections of any library, and online addresses are given in the text.

Athill, Diana, *Instead of a Letter*, Granta Books, London, 2001.
Bennett, Alan, *Writing Home*, Faber & Faber, London, 2006.
British Archives: A Guide to Archive Resources in the United Kingdon, Macmillian, London, 2000.
Colwell, Stella, *The Family Records Centre: A User's Guide*, PRO Publications, London, 2002.
Grannum, Karen and Taylor, Nigel, *Wills and Probate Records*, The National Archives, London, 2009.
Joyce, James, *Portrait of the Artist as a Young Man*, Oxford World's Classics, Oxford, 2008.
Nabokov, Vladimir, *Speak, Memory*, Penguin, London, 2009.
Proust, Marcel, *In Search of Lost Time*, six-volume paperback box set, Modern Library, London, 2003.
Record Repositories in Great Britain, Stationery Office Books, London, 1991.
Wheeler, Sara, *Too Close to the Sun: The Life and Times of Denys Finch Hatton*, Vintage, London, 2007.
Wolff, Geoffrey, *The Duke of Deception*, Vintage, London, 1990.

Wolff, Tobias, *This Boy's Story*, Bloomsbury, London, 1999.

Wroe, Anne, *Pilate: The Biography of an Invented Man*, Vintage, London, 2000.

Writing

Bingley, Xandra, *Bertie, May and Mrs Fish*, Harper Perennial, London, 2006.

Byrne, Paula, *Mad World: Evelyn Waugh and the Secrets of Brideshead*, HarperPress, London, 2009.

Holmes, Richard, *Coleridge: Early Visions*, Harper Perennial, London, 2005.

Holroyd, Michael, *Basil Street Blues*, Abacus, London, 2000.

Lindop, Grevel, *The Opium Eater: A Life of Thomas de Quincey*, Weidenfeld & Nicolson, London, 1993.

Mantel, Hilary, *Giving Up the Ghost*, Fourth Estate, London, 2004.

May, Steve, *Doing Creative Writing*, Routledge, London, 2007.

Milford, Nancy, *Savage Beauty: The Life of Edna St Vincent Millay*, Random House, New York, 2001.

Roth, Philip, *Patrimony*, Vintage, London, 1992.

Wilson, Frances, *The Ballad of Dorothy Wordsworth*, Faber & Faber, London, 2009.

Index

Printed in Great Britain
by Amazon